WITH

AMERICAN

D1386267

This book is to be returned on or
the last date stamped below

7-DAY

28 JUN 91

20 SEP 99

5 A

DA

LIVERPOOL POLYTECHNIC LIBRARY

3 1111 004 17 6192

Gatlin, R
American women since 1945
H M 301.412097 1987

The Contemporary United States

Series Editors: CHRISTOPHER BROOKEMAN AND WILLIAM ISSEL

PUBLISHED TITLES

FORTHCOMING TITLES

AMERICAN WOMEN SINCE 1945

Rochelle Gatlin

MACMILLAN
EDUCATION

© Rochelle Gatlin 1987

All rights reserved. No reproduction, copy or transmission
of this publication may be made without written permission.

No paragraph of this publication may be reproduced, copied
or transmitted save with written permission or in accordance
with the provisions of the Copyright Act 1956 (as amended).

Any person who does any unauthorised act in relation to
this publication may be liable to criminal prosecution and
civil claims for damages.

First published 1987

Published by
MACMILLAN EDUCATION LTD
Houndmills, Basingstoke, Hampshire RG21 2XS
and London
Companies and representatives
throughout the world

Typeset by Wessex Typesetters
(Division of The Eastern Press Ltd)
Frome, Somerset

Printed in Hong Kong

British Library Cataloguing in Publication Data
Gatlin, Rochelle
American women since 1945.—(The
Contemporary United States)
1. Women—United States—Social
conditions
I. Title   II. Series
305.4′2′0973   HQ1420
ISBN 0–333–31181–7
ISBN 0–333–31182–5 Pbk

Series Standing Order

If you would like to receive future titles in this series as they are
published, you can make use of our standing order facility. To place a
standing order please contact your bookseller or, in case of difficulty,
write to us at the address below with your name and address and the
name of the series. Please state with which title you wish to begin your
standing order. (If you live outside the United Kingdom we may not
have the rights for your area, in which case we will forward your order
to the publisher concerned.)

Customer Services Department, Macmillan Distribution Ltd
Houndmills, Basingstoke, Hampshire, RG21 2XS, England.

Contents

PART III: CURRENT ISSUES AND FUTURE PROSPECTS

*With love
to my parents
Selma and Gabriel Baumgarten
and to my best friend
Ward*

Editors' Preface

Mention the United States and few people respond with feelings of neutrality. Discussions about the role of the United States in the contemporary world typically evoke a sense of admiration or a shudder of dislike. Pundits and politicians alike make sweeping references to attributes of modern society deemed 'characteristically American'. Yet qualifications are in order, especially regarding the distinctiveness of American society and the uniqueness of American culture. True, American society has been shaped by the size of the country, the migratory habits of the people and the federal system of government. Certainly, American culture cannot be understood apart from its multi-cultural character, its irreverence for tradition and its worship of technological imagery. It is equally true, however, that life in the United States has been profoundly shaped by the dynamics of American capitalism and by the penetration of capitalist market imperatives into all aspects of daily life.

The series is designed to take advantage of the growth of specialised research about post-war America in order to foster understanding of the period as a whole as well as to offer a critical assessment of the leading developments of the post-war years. Coming to terms with the United States since 1945 requires a willingness to accept complexity and ambiguity, for the history encompasses conflict as well as consensus, hope as well as despair, progress as well as stagnation. Each book in the series offers an interpretation designed to spark discussion rather than a definite account intended to close debate. The series as a whole is meant to offer students, teachers and the general public fresh perspectives and new insights about the contemporary United States.

CHRISTOPHER BROOKEMAN
WILLIAM ISSEL

Preface

As an adolescent in the late 1950s, I briefly exchanged my parents'
liberal Jewish politics and trade union values for the prevailing
ideology of Cold War anti-communism. In a much-applauded high
school speech, I claimed that American democracy was like a
sturdy tree, except that its roots were being eaten away by an
insidious blight called Soviet Communism. I would like both to
reclaim the tree as analogue, symbol and metaphor, and to thank
my parents, Selma and Gabriel Baumgarten, for their love, patience
and progressive politics.

Although women have been the majority of Americans since
1950, it was not their numbers but the Women's Movement, which
made many of them, including myself, aware of their exclusion
from studies of American history, politics, society and literature.
The Women's Movement, and especially one woman, are
responsible for this book.

In 1968, I was teaching my first US history class, and a student
asked why there were no books about women on my lengthy
supplementary reading list. Although I, unfortunately, cannot
remember her name, her question became the seed for my
(re)education. The various branches and fruits of the Women's
Movement also began as personal and social seeds. Feminist
theories and practices have grown from the roots of women's and
men's progressive values and actions, past and present. At the
same time, the 'women's tree' must continue to adapt to changing,
diverse and sometimes hostile political, economic and social
elements. Located in a larger landscape, the growth and
development of the Women's Movement is neither the complete
story of American women since the Second World War nor does it
represent the entire 'forest' of women's values and experiences
today.

This book begins with a brief introduction on women and the

xi

Second World War. It then traces not only the rise, composition, achievements and limitations of the Women's Movement, but also more than forty years of women's paid and unpaid work, political activity and education. I both describe and assess the relationship between cultural stereotypes of women and the thoughts and activities of women themselves. However, I do not claim that shared gender transcends women's racial, cultural and class diversity, or that women's history and experience can be abstracted from the larger context of American post-war society.

I have many people to thank in addition to the student in my first class and the hundreds of others from whom I learned in history, women's studies and social science courses. Without Bill Issel, dear friend, colleague and editor, this book would have been neither attempted nor finished. Bill provided me with the initial opportunity, worked with me for six years in trimming and shaping each chapter, and supplied the essential nourishment of encouragement and praise. I also wish to thank Chris Brookeman for his careful reading of the entire manuscript, suggestions for improving its readability, and his personal kindness. At Macmillan, first Sarah Mahaffy and then Vanessa Couchman supplied helpful guidance and understanding, along with a willingness to extend deadlines more than once.

Deborah Gerson carefully read and criticised the first six chapters; Irène Coustel of Université de Toulouse both suggested stylistic improvements in Chapter 6 and gave me fresh perspectives on American feminism. I first tried out the ideas in Chapter 5 on a thoughtful audience during Women's History Week at California State University, Sacramento. Chapter 11 owes much to Elizabeth Campbell, Jody Timms and the students in a graduate course on global feminism offered at the California Institute of Integral Studies (CIIS), San Francisco. Ofer Zur, Chellis Glendinning, Joanna Macy and Patricia Ellsberg contributed valuable material and insights for that chapter. Many others at CIIS provided a variety of support, ranging from just the right article to just the right word or act of encouragement. I especially wish to thank Vic Campbell, Ted Ciesinski, Tom Courtney, Lisa Faithorn, Michael Flanagin, Barbara Geisler, Jeff Gold, Ralph Metzner, Karen Roberts and Chris Wilson. Above all, I am grateful to Ron Silliman for his wit and compassion, as well as his feminist-socialist practice.

My brother Elias Baumgarten has been a true friend. Along with his keen mind, empathy and wisdom, his generosity made it possible for me to have that essential room of my own. My love and thanks to Jan Wilson, Paul Fortino, Cheryl Thompson, Paul Hudson, Batya Podos, Carol Roland, Clare Fischer, Judy Stamps – and especially to Ward Hoalton, who first presented me with Simone de Beauvoir's *The Second Sex* in 1962 and since then has given more than words, or whole books, can ever say.

ROCHELLE GATLIN
San Francisco
15 August 1986

Introduction: Women and the Second World War

In the 1930s, 75 per cent of American men and women were opposed to married women working. Public opinion shifted dramatically during the Second World War, so that 60 per cent of both sexes approved of married women's employment, at least as an emergency wartime measure. Women, especially married women, became the nation's largest 'reserve army' of labour. Although the US never adopted compulsory measures, the War Manpower Commission, set up in April 1942, made the mobilisation of women workers one of its highest priorities. The Commission launched major publicity campaigns to recruit women into the workforce and to persuade employers to hire them.

The result was not only a large increase in the number of women working, but also an important change in the age and marital status of employed women. Between 1920 and 1940, there had been only a 1 per cent increase of women in the labour force – from 24 to 25 per cent. In the five years of the war, this figure went up to 36 per cent. Between 1941 and 1945, 6.5 million women entered the labour force, for a 57 per cent gain in female employment. Even more striking was the change in the composition of this female workforce. At the wartime peak in July 1944, 72 per cent of the total increase was due to married women. The majority were not young women in their child-bearing years, but older women; 60 per cent of the women who took paid work between 1940 and 1945 were 35 or over.

Despite this shift from a young, single female workforce to an older, married one, there was no permanent change in the attitudes held about women's proper social and economic roles. Women workers, especially in the more highly paid, unionised war industries, were repeatedly told that their services would terminate

1

when their men returned. Government propaganda emphasised patriotic, rather than economic, motives for working, and described the new non-traditional jobs as similar to the domestic work middle-class women did in their homes. Running a drill press could be easily learned by women who had used electric mixers in their kitchens; following instructions for making shells was no more difficult than making cakes from recipes.

Continuing discrimination in the workplace and the lack of institutional support for working women with family responsibilities were even more important signs that no radical revision of sex roles was expected. Generally, women continued the pre-war pattern of filling the lower levels of the occupational hierarchy. They also received lower wages. In manufacturing, women earned 65 per cent of what men did. In 1942, the National War Labor Board endorsed a uniform pay scale for men and women doing the same work but, at the same time, the Board allowed a series of loopholes through which employers could discriminate against women. One favourite method was to call essentially similar jobs by different titles and then fill the lower paying ones with women.

The wage differential was greater when women's jobs were not identical with those of men. Sex segregation in employment continued to be supported by an ideology which assumed that any occupation done mainly by women had less value than work done by men. The National War Labor Board accepted the existing job segregation by sex, along with the low salaries assigned to women's work.

The record of labour unions was only slightly better than that of the federal government. Women were 9.4 per cent of all union members in 1940, but 21.8 per cent four years later. By 1945, they comprised 40 per cent of the United Electrical Workers and almost 30 per cent of the United Automobile Workers Union. Some unions sought to provide child care and other services; several negotiated contracts with maternity leaves without loss of seniority. But, by and large, union men used women's family responsibilities as a reason for not organising them. Labour unions did not strongly oppose separate seniority lists and separate job categories. One might say that the perpetuation of sex discrimination represented a tacit agreement between labour and management. Those unions, such as the United Electrical Workers, who fought for equal pay, did so in order to preserve the higher rate for returning male veterans.

Three-quarters of the female professional workers continued to be in sex-typed occupations, mainly teaching and nursing. The Army refused to commission women doctors until compelled to do so in 1943. Women were never elevated to top positions in the government. The Women's Advisory Commission, created as an adjunct to the War Manpower Commission, was a marginal group with no real decision-making power.

Women faced serious problems in combining paid employment with household responsibilities. It is not surprising that the mandatory six-day, 48-hour work week plus frequent overtime led to high rates of female absenteeism, more than twice that of male workers, according to a Seattle study. In contrast to the British, who provided considerable support services, American policy-makers were not especially helpful. The federal government, under the wartime Lanham Act, spent over $50 million on child care. Although this was the largest commitment to public child-care services in the nation's history, it was wholly inadequate. Only one child in ten could be admitted to the day-care centres, or less than one-third of the number of children cared for in Great Britain, which had less than half the population of the United States.

The Women's Bureau found that in wartime Seattle, Detroit and Baltimore, over half of the mothers relied on husbands, older children or other relatives for child care. One-fourth of the working mothers in Seattle had to leave their children unattended. Employed mothers were blamed for a dramatic rise in juvenile delinquency. Films and articles fed the public's fear that women's geographical and social mobility was leading to family disintegration.

Although divorce rates skyrocketed, so did marriage and birth rates. Single women moved to areas where servicemen were stationed to work and to wed. The public concern with delinquent youth focused on young women and led to renewed vigilance over their sexual behaviour. The targets of the stepped-up 'protection' campaigns were not prostitutes, but 'victory girls' who pursued sexual relations with servicemen out of a need for love, a hope of marriage or a desire for excitement. Adolescent girls were incarcerated and tested for venereal disease although they had broken no laws. Infidelity on the part of soldier-husbands was condoned as natural and inevitable, but the same conduct by servicemen's wives was equivalent to treason.

The wartime concern over female sexuality indicates that sexual values and behaviour among young people were beginning to move in the direction of greater permissiveness. However, the swift counteroffensive against any revision of the sexual double standard remained an important feature of the post-war years. Psychologists and social workers explained female 'sex delinquency' in terms of emotional maladjustment and assumed the primary responsibility for returning women to more conventional and repressive standards.

The war changed women's lives, but it did not result in any radical shift in the cultural definition of 'femininity'. Wartime manufacturing jobs provided an opportunity for working women to leave their poorly paid service and sales jobs. Black women made a significant move from farm and domestic service work to factory jobs. Clerical work, however, was still restricted to white women. Next to manufacturing, the greatest growth in women's employment occurred in the clerical sector. Over 2 million women went to work in offices, especially in federal government agencies. The Second World War caused a tremendous growth in government bureaucracy, and prompted what later became a permanent increase in the lower levels of white-collar female employment.

In 1944, three-quarters of the employed women surveyed in ten defence centres wanted to continue working after the war. In the late 1940s and 1950s, it would no longer be considered radical for older, married women to work, at least in female-dominated clerical, sales and service occupations. The materialism of the years after 1945 was of even greater significance than the war itself in removing some of the prescriptive barriers against married women's employment. After years of austerity and upheaval, Americans wanted stable, reunited families. They also dreamed of new cars and bigger homes stocked with consumer goods. Their material aspirations required more than one wage-earner per household. Yet for almost two decades, the contradiction between female wage-earning and the ideal of domestic femininity went unchallenged, even unacknowledged, by women themselves.

PART I: POST-WAR POLITICS AND WOMEN'S LIVES

From 1945 to the mid 1960s, women's lives and work changed faster than their consciousness. The three chapters in Part I discuss the economic, political and social experiences of American women prior to the emergence of the feminist movement.

Chapter 1 presents those elements of post-war political conservatism which hindered women's collective sense of themselves as a 'sex-class'. The demand for female workers, however, did not cease after the Second World War. Rather, a growing post-war economy needed women in its expanding clerical and service sectors. Although political and economic policies, as well as media images, emphasised women's domestic roles, it became socially acceptable for wives and mothers of school-age children to hold jobs outside the home. Chapter 2 describes their occupations in a sex-segregated labour market in which women were paid less than men. Chapter 3 covers both women's traditional unpaid work as wives, mothers and housekeepers, and some of the ways the post-war 'consumer' economy began to reshape this work.

Although white women did not consciously challenge the ideology of feminine domesticity or collectively rebel against their traditional subordination, they experienced contradictions between their paid employment and their unpaid family work. Also, by the early 1960s, politically active Southern black women and girls were presenting the nation with a new model of womanhood.

1. Post-war Conservatism and the Feminine Mystique

In 1947 Christian Dior introduced the 'New Look' in women's fashions, replacing the austere androgyny of wartime slacks with an ultra-feminine design shaped like an inverted flower, with a tight waist and flared skirt. The same year, he introduced (or resurrected) the nineteenth-century figure 8 or 'hourglass' and advised wearing a small corset to take two inches off the waist. Teenage girls in the 1950s wore half a dozen crinolines under full skirts, pulled in their waists with wide 'cinch' belts and pushed out their breasts with padded 'uplift' bras. Evening gowns for school dances were modelled after the movie image of the Southern Belle, occasionally complete with hoopskirts.

These fashions were part of the post-war feminine mystique,[1] which presented women with an ideal script against which they measured their performance. More important, this mystique was part of an ideology which masked women's subordination by calling it female 'nature' or 'duty'. It also became an effective device for depoliticising women's discontent.

Although the feminine mystique contained many elements of traditional misogyny, after the Second World War it was incorporated into a conservative political and social ideology which circumscribed options for both women and men. In this context, feminism, like communism, was demoted to the status of a simple-minded, outmoded and dangerous ideology. Social issues were turned into psychological problems. Political grievances could only be diagnosed as individual pathology, and feminism was merely a symptom of female neurosis. The debate about women's status existed within a narrow range. Liberal sociologists could speak of

7

the 'role conflict' women experienced, but they avoided a vocabulary which addressed the oppression of women by sexist institutions. On the other hand, the anti-feminists used and misused the most up-to-date medical terminology as a substitute for older moral and religious injunctions.

Anti-communism became a means to control sexuality. Government officials equated sexual nonconformity, particularly homosexuality, with political subversion. Women were told that communist ideology, under the guise of feminism, was advocating the destruction of the family. When Simone de Beauvoir's *The Second Sex* appeared in the United States in 1953, readers of *The Nation*, a liberal magazine, were warned of her 'political leanings'.[2]

Given this climate of opinion, the sexual romantics carried the day with their argument that since men and women are dissimilar, they should cherish and accentuate their differences. Created in the nineteenth century, this sex-role dichotomy had given women a distinctively female 'sphere' and assigned to them almost a monopoly over such traits as piety, purity, submissiveness and domesticity. In the mid twentieth century, sociologists of the 'functionalist' school led by Talcott Parsons upheld sexual differentiation as 'functional' in maintaining the family and the social order. Sociologists did see gender-appropriate behaviour as the result of 'roles' which had to be learned, but psychiatrists, especially Freudians, still clung to the idea of innate biological differences. Neither acknowledged that the doctrine of 'woman's sphere' consigned women to activities less powerful and important than those of men. Both the 'true woman' of the nineteenth century and the 'truly feminine woman' of the twentieth century were supposed to limit themselves to those activities and functions men defined as appropriate for women. Social conditioning taught women to accept their 'sphere', but women had never defined it themselves.

In addition to the influence of political conservatism and sexual romanticism, the feminine mystique was also a response to a mid-century masculinity crisis, as men became concerned about the decline of individual endeavour, self-employment and the absence of a Western frontier in which to test their ruggedness. Books such as William H. Whyte's *The Organization Man* and David Riesman's *The Lonely Crowd* documented the decline of 'inner-directed' and self-motivated achievers. Men turned to sports and revived the

Wild West in fiction, film and television searching for the pure models of competition, aggressiveness and skill absent in the bureaucratic world of corporations and professions. When they looked for tangible results of their achievements, they found them only in the suburban homes and consumer goods they could purchase.

Working-class men looked for proof of manliness outside the workplace. But in turning to the home and family for satisfaction, they ran the risk of being 'feminised' or 'domesticated'. The domesticated man was the butt of 1950s situation comedies on television. Jackie Gleason in 'The Honeymooners', Danny Thomas, Ozzie Nelson and Robert Young were 'pint-sized caricatures of the patriarchs, frontiersmen and adventurers who once defined American manhood'.[3] In cartoons, the male was shown as shorter than his wife who, monstrous in bathrobe and curlers, wielded a rolling pin over his head.

As political and economic centralisation made the traditional masculine role unworkable, men sometimes projected their frustration onto women. They even blamed their mothers for 'castrating' them. Ferdinand Lundberg and Marynia Farnham's *Modern Woman: The Lost Sex* (1947) is only one of the post-war works which blamed mothers for the over 2 million men rejected or discharged from military service during the Second World War for psychiatric disorders. Betty Friedan in 1963 pointed out that the 'immature' and 'self-sacrificing' mother would only be perpetuated by adherence to the feminine mystique. But no one admitted that motherhood had become the only vehicle by which most women could exercise control over others.

Certainly it was not women's power or presence in politics which caused male anxiety. After the Second World War not only women's issues but domestic concerns generally received low political priority. The main political arena was foreign policy. The fight against communism served as an excuse for higher military budgets, greater governmental secrecy and increased executive power at Congress's expense. Except for the President, the officials who made foreign policy were not elected. National security, the most important area of political decision-making, was sealed off from public scrutiny and influence.

Between 1940 and 1967, all the first- and second-level posts in the national security bureaucracy were held by fewer than 400 individuals who rotated through a variety of key positions. Only one of these individuals was a woman. Of the 91 people who held the very top jobs – Secretaries of Defence and State, Secretaries of the three military services, the Chairman of the Atomic Energy Commission, and the Director of the Central Intelligence Agency (CIA) – 70 were businessmen, corporate lawyers or investment bankers. Among this powerful and privileged elite, traditional masculine values still operated. Richard J. Barnet found that in the Pentagon, State Department, White House and CIA, 'toughness is the most highly prized virtue'. This style of *machismo* encouraged a willingness to use violence.

> The man who is ready to recommend using violence against foreigners, even when he is overruled, does not damage his reputation . . ., but the man who recommends putting an issue to the U.N., seeking negotiations, or, horror of horrors, 'doing nothing' quickly becomes known as 'soft.' To be 'soft' . . . is to be 'irresponsible.' It means walking out of the club.[4]

Not only were women excluded from this 'club' and told to cultivate the opposite virtues, but even in areas more accessible to their influence they were not successful. Federal support for child-care facilities under the wartime Lanham Act ended in March 1946. In turning to the states for funding, activists encountered both an old social welfare emphasis on mother's place in the home and new fears of communist influence. The *New York World Telegram*, for example, charged in 1947 that child care was conceived by leftists operating out of Communist 'social work cells'. All state aid to child care ended on 1 January 1948.[5]

The right to vote did not guarantee American women equal protection under the law. The 14th Amendment to the Constitution prohibited individual states from passing laws which abridged the 'privileges or immunities of citizens' or which deprived any 'person of life, liberty, or property, without due process of law', or denied 'any person . . . the equal protection of the laws'. However, states were allowed a wide latitude in interpreting the Amendment because the Supreme Court had not yet held that a law which classifies persons on the basis of sex was unreasonable and, therefore, unconstitutional.

In *Fay* v. *New York* (1947) the Supreme Court stated that women did not have a constitutional right to serve on juries; in *Hoyt* v. *Florida* (1961) the Court upheld a jury selection process which made men register to obtain an exemption from jury duty while women were automatically exempted unless they registered to be included. Not until 1957 was service on federal juries equalised for men and women, and as late as 1970, only 28 states applied the same criteria for both sexes.

In spite of married women's property Acts passed during the nineteenth century, wives did not fully control their own property. In Texas, for example, a wife's earnings were subject to the control of her husband. Some states restricted the right of a wife to engage in a separate business. In 1948, the Supreme Court upheld a Michigan liquor law which stated that no female could be licensed as a bartender unless she was the wife or daughter of the male owner of a liquor establishment.

Even the old English common law idea of a woman's virtual legal disappearance at the time of her marriage lingered on into the 1960s. Only four states recognised a married woman's unrestricted right to acquire her own domicile, independently of her husband. Six states in the mid 1960s still stated a preference for the father as the natural guardian of a minor child. Not until the Equal Pay Act of 1963 did it become illegal to pay women less than men for the same work, and enforcement remained a problem into the 1980s.

The image of women which emerged from the Supreme Court decisions and state laws mentioned above was based on an ideology of sexual romanticism. That is, women are weak and need male protection; women are and should remain wives, mothers and homemakers; women are not interested in learning and doing the same things as men. The Equal Rights Amendment, which assumes a similarity between the sexes and calls for their equality under the law, was deadlocked, even though the major political parties pledged their support in 1944 and 1948. Prominent women, including Eleanor Roosevelt, still insisted that protective legislation for working women would be harmed by the Amendment. When the measure finally passed the Senate in 1950, it contained a rider specifying that no protective legislation was to be affected. This rendered the bill meaningless. Interest in it would not be revived until the late 1960s when a new women's rights movement called for equality with men in all aspects of society.

The post-war period was also a low point for radical ideas and visions of women's emancipation. Due to the sex-segregated world of the late nineteenth and early twentieth centuries, feminists had created a female political infrastructure with its own hierarchy and independent base of support. By the mid twentieth century women lacked this potential for emancipation because they no longer had the social and physical space in which to develop their own values and identities apart from men. The 1920s 'sexual revolution' against Victorian prudery aimed at bridging the gap between men and women. 'Liberation' for young women no longer meant feminism, but rather sexual gratification and personal fulfilment. Movies demonstrated the new priority of attracting men, and girls became anxious about their popularity with the opposite sex. The bonds between women were replaced by what Mary Ryan calls a 'heterosexual imperative'. This, in turn, 'fostered a degree of distrust and competition between women such as had never been seen before'.[6]

In this regard, the 1940s and 1950s were even worse. While emphasising domesticity and family roles, the post-war feminine mystique did not revive female bonding. It fact, it intensified women's distrust of other women. Female friends were also potential rivals for male attention. Catching-your-man was the most popular theme of romantic fiction and movies in the 1950s. Both the sexy stars like Marilyn Monroe and the wholesome ones such as Doris Day and Debbie Reynolds were seeking a good marriage and children. One woman's success in the marriage market was often another's failure.

The woman determined to escape the sexual marketplace had to confront external and internal voices telling her that an 'independent woman' was a 'contradiction in terms'.[7] Furthermore, in the public world she found only the male model of success. No 'serious' woman artist or intellectual believed in the existence of a female sensibility or sought to create an alternative women's culture. Playwright Lillian Hellman, for example, depicted herself as an 'angry child', puzzled and irritated by her mother's feminine wiles.[8] But she never saw her individual rebellion as connected in any way with the predicaments of other women. 'Politics' had nothing to do with one's sex. Although Mary McCarthy wrote about women, her novel *The Group* (1954) was a caustic, even catty, portrait of college-educated women with little sympathy for or identification with its characters.

'I had tried very much *not* to identify myself as a female poet', admits Adrienne Rich, now widely known as a feminist writer. W. H. Auden praised her first book, *A Change of World* (1951), for its 'craftsmanship' and 'capacity for detachment from the self and its emotions', and found Rich's poems to be 'neatly and modestly dressed'. Randall Jarrell described her second collection, *The Diamond Cutters* (1955) as 'sweet'. Then came *Snapshots of a Daughter-in-Law* (1963), Rich's transitional book. During the eight years separating it from *The Diamond Cutters*, she had been raising her three sons and

> writing very little, partly from fatigue, that female fatigue of suppressed anger and the loss of contact with her own being; partly from the discontinuity of female life with its attention to small chores, errands, work that others constantly undo, small children's constant needs.

Years later, Rich thought the title poem was too cautious, but 'Snapshots' can stand as an early criticism of the feminine mystique in its expression of horror at the punishments meted out to bold 'thinking' women.[9]

One such woman was Sylvia Plath, who committed suicide the same year Rich's book appeared. Plath is more widely known in the United States than her husband Ted Hughes, but her fame has been posthumous. Many of the poems in *Ariel* (1966) were rejected by editors while she was alive. It is still difficult to know whether the attention she now receives is due to her poetry, her autobiographical novel, *The Bell Jar*, or her suicide. Unlike the male Beat poets of the 1950s, Plath's contribution to the increased self-expressiveness of 1960s poetry goes unacknowledged. She remains classed with the madwomen and suicides.

As a story of adolescence, *The Bell Jar* is a female twin to J. D. Salinger's *Catcher in the Rye*, even though it was not published in the United States until 1971. Growing up in the 1950s, Esther Greenwood had the 'mad' lucidity to say about marriage, 'that in spite of all the roses and kisses and restaurant dinners a man showered on a woman before he married her, what he secretly wanted when the wedding service ended was for her to flatten out underneath his feet like Mrs. Willard's kitchen mat.'[10]

Lucidity and ambition were not enough. Both Plath and Rich

married and had children, proving that they were 'normal' women. Pregnancy for Rich meant feeling 'for the first time in my adolescent and adult life, not-guilty'. The relief was short-lived: 'Soon I would begin to understand the full weight and burden of maternal guilt, that daily, nightly, hourly, *Am I doing what is right? Am I doing enough? Am I doing too much?*'[11]

For comic relief, there were best-sellers by women who wrote about domestic cares with self-deprecating humour. Betty MacDonald's *The Egg and I* (1945) or Jean Kerr's *Please Don't Eat the Daisies* (1957) – made into a movie starring Doris Day – may have provided a furtive outlet for frustration, but they also trivialised women and encouraged them to accept guilt and inadequacy as part of their fate.

Media 'escapes' only reinforced the feminine mystique by giving women a standardised message of heterosexual femininity. *Seventeen* magazine, designed for teenage girls, emphasised physical attractiveness. Advertising showed models in postures of sexual surrender to men and in competition with each other. Ads also told women how to refashion their bodies with diets, padded bras, deodorants, mouthwashes and body hair removers.

After 1948, television became the nation's most popular medium. There were 172,000 sets in operation in 1948, more than 5 million two years later, and nearly 50 million by 1960. Instead of attending afternoon movie matinees with friends, women turned on their television sets to watch morning quiz and game shows and afternoon soap operas. The energetic game shows provided excitement and prepared women for shopping. In addition to frequent advertising 'breaks', the game shows themselves functioned as vicarious shopping sprees. One of the most popular was 'Queen for a Day', which ran for nearly a decade. Female contestants told their hard-luck stories to the studio audience who then awarded prizes to the woman with the greatest need.

'Queen for a Day' had some of the earmarks of soap opera, a genre which became firmly entrenched on television in the late 1950s. The soaps reinforced the myth that America was a middle-class country because most of the families were headed by professional men. The women were usually housewives, but they were rarely shown doing housework. They had all the time real women did not have to deal with emotional problems and discuss them with the men in their lives. The soaps depicted the family as the sole repository of love, understanding, compassion, respect and sexuality. According to one scholar, soap operas took a 'hard line on any forms of communication that might break down the primacy of heterosexual couple love and the family'.[12] The commercials added to this familial ideology by emphasising that commodities would strengthen those essential intimate ties.

straight, heterosexual image.

While daytime television was designed for women and their children, evening 'prime time' programmes catered to male interests and were filled with male characters. On drama and adventure shows, especially crime programmes and Westerns, women were either victims or supporting players peripheral to the action. Only the situation comedies showed women as often as men. Like the soap operas, the 'sit-coms' stressed close family relationships and de-emphasised work. Some, such as 'Life of Riley' and 'Ozzie and Harriet', depicted a foolish, but lovable, husband and a sensible wife. 'I Love Lucy' showed another pattern. Lucille Ball played a frustrated housewife who wants to get into show business. Her husband disapproves of her working. In each episode, Lucy's silly pranks backfire and confirm her husband's view that she will never succeed outside the home. Older women and women of colour were rarely seen on any type of television show except in stereotyped roles as grandmothers and maids.

The romance magazines were one of the least subtle forms of social control. One study called them 'paragons of virtue, arguing with a traditional, cultural morality for the necessity of love and the family'. Merely living life as a woman was a punitive experience. Failure and swift punishment awaited those who ventured into the male world.[13]

'I Denied My Sex' (*True Romance*, April 1954) is the story of a girl who always wanted to be a boy. Although she tries to win compliments on her appearance, she beats her boyfriend at tennis, and her competitiveness is linked with her fear of sex (kissing). She decides to become a policewoman, fighting against her 'first instinctive reaction' which is 'one of complete surrender' to her boyfriend Butch. 'I wanted to be loved, to forget myself and be possessed by him.' As a new police 'rookie', she is told by a mother whose baby has been kidnapped how lucky women are to bear children. She single-handedly rescues the baby by using judo on the kidnappers, but faints as soon as two policemen arrive. The story ends with her vowing to Butch that she will no longer deny her femininity.[14] This example will seem less absurd as we turn to the psychologists and their popularisers who were constructing a myth of the female with all the authority of science behind them.

American popularisers of Freud took his hypotheses for certainties and believed that psychoanalysis was the most effective cure for social as well as personal problems. Helene Deutsch became the favourite authority on women. She described them in *The Psychology of Women* (1944) as passive, masochistic and narcissistic. Dissident women psychoanalysts, such as Karen Horney and Clara Thompson, who emphasised the social context for female behaviour, were not popularised as extensively. The result was the widespread belief that women's sexuality differed from men's in being both passive and linked to reproduction. Drawing upon Deutsch, Lundberg and Farnham stated that 'a mature woman without children is the psychological equivalent of a man without the male organ'.

Mothers were supposed to prepare girls for their adult passivity. 'If the girl has the good fortune to have a mother who finds complete satisfaction, without conflict or anxiety, in living out her role as wife and mother, it is unlikely that she will experience serious difficulties.' But Lundberg and Farnham found that most women were dissatisfied and injected in their daughters their 'own covert strivings toward masculinity'.[15]

A further obstacle towards appropriate expressions of femininity were co-educational schools which stressed achievement and individualism for both sexes. By the mid twentieth century it was acceptable for women to train for careers and for single women to work, but Lundberg and Farnham saw this as a serious danger to home and society. Sociologist Mirra Komarovsky less derisively labelled the problem as one of 'role conflict'. Women were now partially assimilated into the male world, but they still had to be prepared to relinquish 'masculine' pursuits for domesticity. Some 40 per cent of undergraduate women confessed to Komarovsky that they 'played dumb' on dates. Women were not expected to think logically, understand scientific principles or be good at mathematics. Secondary schools required girls to take courses in home economics, especially sewing and cooking. The president of Mills College, a prestigious women's school, argued that educational institutions had failed women by teaching them subjects unsuited to their domestic roles. Even Komarovsky, who rejected a separate female curriculum, agreed that: 'Women must be prepared to follow a pattern of economic and domestic activities which will, in general, differ from the masculine pattern.'[16]

Women's university attendance and aspirations show that, in fact, they were preparing for a pattern different from men's. In 1920 women had comprised 34 per cent of the undergraduate student body. After the Second World War their proportion fell to nearly 20 per cent, and not until 1970 did it return to the pre-war level. Two-thirds of all college women in the 1950s failed to receive their BAs. Less than one out of ten doctorates were granted to women in the mid 1950s as compared to one in six in 1920.

If women in the late 1940s and 1950s were heeding the feminine mystique by forgoing extensive ₍education, their choice was reinforced by The Servicemen's Readjustment Act (or GI Bill) of 1944. Of the 17 million persons who received educational subsidies, only 1.8 per cent were women. Comparable resources were not available to female students until the National Defense Education Act of 1958. Along with lingering fears of spinsterhood and the absence of financial aid for women, institutions of higher learning placed increasingly greater emphasis on research and less on teaching. Science received more attention, prestige and government funding during the Cold War than did the liberal arts. Women found that teaching, serving and nurturing others had less value in higher education than before the war. There was an increasing split between the institutional norms of post-war professions and the standards of 'femininity'.

Finally, women themselves saw high occupational aspirations and steady commitment to a career as competing with their family role. Those women who insisted on combining a career with motherhood were typically regarded as following a 'deviant' pattern which would create troublesome relations with their children. That few women were contemplating such 'deviance' is underscored by a survey taken of women college graduates as late as the mid 1960s. When asked how they defined success, the most frequent answers women gave were: 'to be the mother of several accomplished children, and to be the wife of a prominent man'.[17]

Although youthful marriage was common in other industrialised countries after the Second World War, it was particularly pronounced in the United States. By 1962 well over one-third of all brides were 19 or under, as compared to one-fourth in the United

Kingdom. The proportion of women who never married fell from close to 20 per cent in the late nineteenth century to about 5 per cent in the mid twentieth. While public opinion did not endorse Lundberg and Farnham's recommendation that 'spinsters' be outlawed from teaching children because they were 'incomplete' women, only 9 per cent of Americans in 1957 thought that an unmarried person could be happy.

With the exception of Simone de Beauvoir's *The Second Sex*, it is difficult to find a cogent criticism of marriage. Most studies, including those of Alfred Kinsey and his associates, took a marital perspective for granted. *Sexual Behavior in the Human Male* (1948) and *Sexual Behavior in the Human Female* (1953) were purportedly studies of sexual experience focused on orgasms, leaving out psychology, reproduction and most social values. Nevertheless, marriage remained the standard by which all forms of sexuality (masturbation, homosexuality, etc.) were assessed.

Along with encouraging early marriage and reproduction, the feminine mystique played a strong role in advising mothers. Despite the fact that by 35 or 40 these young mothers would have nearly completed their work, they were urged to devote themselves to mothering as though there was no need to plan for the remaining child-free half of their lives.

Dr Benjamin Spock was not the creator of child-centred or 'permissive' child-rearing, but he became its worldwide populariser. *Baby and Child Care* (originally published in 1946 and revised in 1957, 1968 and 1976) has sold about 30 million copies. Permissive child-rearing was a reaction against earlier 'behaviorist' theories with their rigid schedules and taboos against spontaneous affection. But, unlike the authors of earlier child-rearing manuals, Spock assumed that the mother had unlimited time and energy. By requiring her to be watchful, not only of a child's physical needs, but also of his or her emotional states, he expanded motherwork to include the role of home psychologist. In addition to letting the child set the pace and provide the cues, the mother had to monitor her own behaviour in order to provide the proper emotional atmosphere for her offspring.

Knowledge and discipline, however, were secondary to the oceans of unlimited and 'instinctual' love the mother was to bring to her tasks. Only through love and infinite patience could she develop an intuitive ability to identify herself completely with her baby's needs. In this merger, she would also find her own fulfilment, desiring no outside companionship or interests. Although in his 1976 revision Spock finally included the father and assigned him equal responsibility, the early Spock insisted that the mother be present all the time. Obviously, mothers should not go out to work, and women in the late 1940s and 1950s were urged to forgo taking jobs or to quit them in order to devote themselves to their children.

Spock did not recognise ethnic differences or economic necessity. As Nancy Pottishman Weiss has pointed out, permissive child-rearing techniques had a middle-class bias in requiring 'households with enough bedrooms and belongings for all members. . . . The larder is filled with food, the "feeding problem" being the recalcitrant child, not an inadequate food supply.' It was difficult for women to acknowledge such 'aberrations' as 'a husbandless home, a struggle making ends meet, and emotional trouble in pursuing model mothercraft'.[18] Spock's friendly and informal assurances to 'enjoy your baby' may have actually provoked more worry, guilt and anxiety.

If Spock at least tried to reassure women that they could live up to his exacting standards of motherhood, psychoanalytic theories assumed that most women would fall short of perfection. Two broad categories of 'bad mothers' were identified: the rejecting mother and the over-protective mother. The charge of over-protectiveness, or refusal to let children grow up, was hurled at mothers who had immersed themselves too much in child care. This included whole cultures such as Italians, Jews and Hispanics. The rejecting mother was guilty of 'maternal deprivation' when she experienced hostile feelings towards her children; working outside the home was equivalent to abandonment. According to John Bowlby's *Maternal Care and Mental Health* (first published in 1951), such maternally deprived children 'are a source of social infection as real and serious as are carriers of diphtheria and typhoid.'[19]

Fashions after 1955 glorified maternity. The waistless styles of Balenciaga's chemise or 'sack' dress, Dior's A-line and the 'trapeze' by Yves St Laurent all suggested advanced pregnancy. Yet mothers themselves became the prime targets of popular misogyny. As Betty Friedan put it: 'In every case history of troubled child; alcoholic, suicidal, schizophrenic, psychopathic, neurotic adult . . . could be found a mother. A frustrated, repressed, disturbed, martyred, never satisfied, unhappy woman.'[20]

Once motherhood, the very heart and *raison d'être* of the feminine mystique, was found to be full of pathology, it was obvious that the feminine mystique had begun to caricature itself. Even young, white, middle-class and heterosexual women could rarely attain it; older, non-white, lesbian and working-class women were almost certain to be 'deviant' or 'deficient'.

The public ignored lesbians except as cases of scandal. Only women who needed to find out more about themselves combed through the literature. What they discovered was frightening. Lesbians were sinful, criminal and sick. The sickness concept may have been a humane advance over the older religious and legal categories, except that the treatments included incarceration, electric shock, lobotomy and aversion therapy. Freud had considered homosexuality as a form of arrested sexual development and regarded it as incurable; American therapists were more optimistic.

Lesbian history, culture, life-styles and emotions were reduced to psychology. Since no concept of the 'normal lesbian' existed, some homosexual women did enter treatment hoping to be 'cured', without discerning that the real problem was socially induced feelings of guilt and worthlessness. Dr Frank S. Caprio, the 'expert' on lesbians in the 1950s, took it for granted that the 'vast majority' were 'emotionally unstable and neurotic'. Yet he found that many lesbians did not wish to make a 'heterosexual adjustment'. 'They prefer to think that their affliction is a congenital one so that they can use this as an excuse for not assuming the responsibilities associated with marriage and family life.'[21]

In the absence of social acceptance, many lesbians denied their sexual preference even to themselves or accepted it as a guilty secret. Since 'lesbian' meant 'deviant' and 'depraved', some felt they had to live out the stereotypes. Society had insisted that only men love women, so a woman new to lesbian life might imagine that she was a man trapped in a woman's body. Playing a masculine or 'butch' role is not inherently a part of lesbian life, but as contemporary lesbian critics point out, 'it is one that society has merchandised for its own reason – to keep Lesbians over there, bizarre and identifiable'.[22]

Partial awareness of the inappropriateness of socially constructed sex roles put lesbians in a unique position to demystify the feminine mystique. But the political climate of the 1950s was not auspicious for iconoclasts. All lesbians could do was form an organisation called Daughters of Bilitis (1955) for self-help and education.

Black women were more visible than lesbians, and psychiatrists could not 'cure' colour as they presumed to do with sexual preference. Nevertheless, 'deviance' was the model adopted by most social scientists studying non-whites. Blacks, in particular, were perceived as pathological because they departed from white, middle-class norms. Melville Herskovits' pioneering work, *The Myth of the Negro Past*, had outlined survivals of African culture in black life. Yet the most widely held view was that, unlike other ethnic groups, blacks had lost their culture and were left with no values or heritage of their own. This thesis allowed for the perpetuation of myths regarding the inferiority of blacks. It eliminated any positive explanation for the distinctiveness of black life, and it tended to blame the victims rather than the oppressive social structure.

Both the historical reality and the dominant image of the black woman as worker, even 'beast of burden', stood in direct contrast to the ideal of the fragile, domestic female. In fact, the black woman was stereotyped either as a 'matriarch' responsible for the psychological castration of the black man, or as a sexually 'loose' woman.

It was E. Franklin Frazier in *The Negro Family in the United States* (1939) who first called the female-headed black family a 'matriarchate'. This family structure was not typical, but the percentage was higher among blacks than whites: 25 per cent in 1964 compared to 9 per cent. That it was inextricably linked to poverty and public welfare rules which prohibited a man in the house, or that it had positive features, tended to be ignored. Rather, black family life was seen as 'deficient' or 'disorganised'. The 'Black Matriarch' was, in reality, a low-paid worker or welfare recipient dependent on a kin and friendship network for survival. The black community did not uniformly stigmatise 'illegitimate' births, and while whites saw in such children evidence of black women's 'immorality', many black people placed the children's needs first. Whites ignored the cultural strength this love of children represented and did not acknowledge the historical racism which had first prohibited legal marriage among slaves and then made achievement of marital stability difficult for urban blacks.

Not all social scientists condemned black people; some pitied them and claimed that white racism was responsible for black 'self-hatred'. This view, as Joyce A. Ladner has pointed out in *Tomorrow's Tomorrow: The Black Woman* (1972), inspired the 1954 Supreme Court decision in *Brown* v. *Topeka Board of Education* against racially segregated public schools. Separate schools caused negative self-images in black children; therefore, blacks would have healthier personalities if they were given the opportunity to assimilate into white society. In the 1960s, black critics would be joined by whites who had worked in the Civil Rights movement in offering rebuttals to the thesis of black self-hatred, but in the 1950s the assimilationist position appeared radical. Few black leaders outside The Nation of Islam (Black Muslims) questioned its legitimacy or the white, middle-class culture it upheld.

Long before the Civil Rights or feminist movements, however, black women knew that the feminine mystique was part of a white, middle-class ideology which excluded them. Judicial indifference to sexual crimes committed by white or black men against black women coupled with the lynching of black men for the least suspicion of raping white women had been the Southern system for 'protecting' white women since the nineteenth century. The black rapist and the 'bad' black woman were myths that justified terrorising black people. They also kept black and white women apart. In *Killers of the Dream* (1949), Lillian Smith described how politicians in the late 1940s were still using 'southern chivalry' and its code of 'protecting our women from the menace of Negroes'.

> Listening, many lonely [white] country women who have rarely felt esteemed or beloved, are suddenly caught up by a vision of themselves as Sacred Womanhood on a Pedestal, as Southern Madonnas, and though in a few hours they will be back totin' slops to the pigpen, milking cows, cooking supper, yet for one miraculously sweet breath of time they are transfigured by this image of themselves and they will never forget it.[23]

Black women dreamed, too. Too often, Maya Angelou wrote, we 'found ourselves ... unmarried, bearing lonely pregnancies and wishing for two and a half children each who would gurgle happily behind that picket fence while we drove our men to work in our friendly-looking station wagons.'[24] When Angelou briefly attained the status of a housewife out of a *Good Housekeeping* advertisement, she was disappointed. Most black women could never approximate the magazine ideal. To some degree they wished for it, yet being workers as well as mothers, they realistically chose to base their self-esteem on their own survival skills and looked to their kin and community for support and validation. As white women approached the labour force participation rates of black women, they, too, found the feminine mystique, with its rigid pattern of passive and domestic womanhood, untenable.

2. Women and Work: 1945–1970

Increasing numbers of women entered the labour force after 1945. Paid employment transformed their lives but rarely altered their thinking about sex roles. Women who worked outside the home still saw themselves primarily as wives, mothers and housekeepers. Family responsibilities limited women's employment opportunities, while sex discrimination in hiring, promotion and earnings was justified in terms of women's supportive and subordinate position in the family.

At the same time, the family and women's domestic labour in the home were also changing. Women's increased labour force participation was partly responsible, but so were long-range economic developments which affected both home and workplace. These included: more reliance on the market for commodities and services; the greater division and subdivision of labour which made many jobs less skilled; the increased demand for cheap, easily trained workers in the growing clerical and service sectors; and, finally, demographic factors such as longer life expectancy and smaller families.

Although economic and demographic developments pushed women out of the home, the feminine mystique followed them into the workplace. Men generally held the more prestigious and better-paid positions. Few protested against this sexual hierarchy because most women and men believed that men support families, women are economically supported by men, leadership qualities are inherently masculine, while passivity and nurturing are innately feminine. On the other hand, the presence of increasing numbers of women in the workforce helped to refute these beliefs and enhanced the possibility for sex equality.

The Second World War witnessed a dramatic increase in

24

women's employment: from 25 per cent in 1940 to 36 per cent five years later. Wartime propaganda stressed the temporary nature of women's work, and one out of four women employed in factories were let go or quit during the summer of 1945. Although highly paid, non-traditional work for women ended with the war, many women subsequently returned to work. They accepted jobs in the lower-paid clerical and service fields. During the immediate post-war period – from September 1945 to November 1946 – only 600,000 women actually dropped out of the labour force. The nadir for female employment was reached in 1947 when 29 per cent of women were working, but by 1960, 37.7 per cent of all women aged 16 and over were employed, constituting one-third of the total workforce.

More important than the overall increase was the permanent change in the age and marital status of women workers. Until 1940 women's participation in the labour force had been highest between the ages of 20–24. After the war, instead of a continuous decline in employment after the age of 24, a new pattern emerged. Women still left paid employment to bear and rear children, but they returned to work after their children reached school age.

By 1960, the highest work rates were occurring at ages 45–49, when 47.4 per cent of all women were working. The typical pattern until the late 1960s was for women to leave work when their first child was born and to return when their last child started school. In the early 1960s, 41.5 per cent of married women with children ages 6–17 were working. Married women in 1962 comprised 60 per cent of the female workforce.[1]

Class and race remained important factors in determining not only women's workforce participation, but also the kinds of jobs they held. Also, many women took part-time jobs or worked intermittently, so that their employment rates were never as high as those of men. Nevertheless, the female life cycle was altered by the impressive and permanent increase in the numbers of employed married and older women.

The ideology of the feminine mystique, which emphasised women's bio-social dependence on men and traditional family roles, appeared to be at odds with the growing numbers of employed women. Yet women made no collective protest in the 1950s. They had neither a sense of group identity nor feminist political organisations. In fact, the types of work women were paid to do and the socially acceptable reasons they gave for working converged, to some extent, with the premises of the feminine mystique. Women's passivity, dependence and even domesticity carried over into the world of work and served the needs of employers for a cheap, docile labour force.

Post-war federal policy assumed that the working head of household would be male and minimised government responsibility to guarantee women jobs. A Women's Bureau survey showed that over 80 per cent of employed women were self-supporting and/or financially responsible for members of their families. Yet Congressmen believed that women worked for unnecessary 'extras' and argued that only men had a fundamental claim to employment. One opinion survey showed that three-fourths of those questioned (including 70 per cent of the women) believed that an employer should discharge an efficient woman worker whose husband could support her in preference to an inefficient man who had a family to support.[2]

Such attitudes served to reinforce limited employment opportunities and to sanction lower pay for women. Despite their increasing labour force participation, women remained marginal and secondary workers. They were paid less than men even when they did the same work. Generally women did not work with men, but clustered in occupations dominated numerically by their own sex. 'Women's work' carried less prestige and lower pay than male-dominated occupations. At the workplace, there seemed little reason to question traditional sex roles.

Like the federal government, labour unions did little to protect women's wartime jobs, and they did not organise women workers in the expanding clerical and service sectors. Two factors are responsible for this: the traditional sexism of union men and the conservative post-war politics which made unions timid about organising new fields and anxious about their own political respectability. Political conditions after the Second World War did not encourage a reassessment of traditional trade union activity and ideology. In addition to the growth in bureaucracy and an increasing preoccupation with practical issues, unions had to contend with charges of communist influence. By the time the American Federation of Labor (AFL) merged with the formerly more radical Congress of Industrial Organizations (CIO) in 1955,

almost all left-wing influence in the American labour movement
had been eliminated.

The united AFL-CIO endorsed the principle of equal pay for
equal work in the mid 1950s. However, women's groups favoured a
federal pay law, because collective bargaining was too slow. In
1957 only a quarter of those workers with union contracts had
agreements containing equal pay clauses. More important, unionised
workers were only a minority of the labour force, and women were
far less organised than men. Unionised women were concentrated
in a small number of industries: the needle trades, electrical goods
and communications. The predominantly female clerical and sales
workers had been poorly organised even before the war, and union
organising efforts did not keep pace with the post-war increases in
employment. In 1960, only 9 per cent of all clerical workers were in
unions. The estimated 3 million women union members in 1957
comprised a little more than one-sixth of the total union membership
and accounted for less than one-seventh of the women in the labour
force.

Union conservatism not only perpetuated women's status as
marginal workers, but also made the union movement itself
'marginal'. The growing sectors of the economy, especially the
'tertiary' or service sector – transportation, communications,
wholesale and retail trade, finance, insurance, real estate services
and public administration – tended not to be unionised, and they
were employing women, not men.

Between 1950 and 1960, almost half of the total net increase in
the number of employed women occurred in occupations where
they were already at least 70 per cent of the workers. Some of these
occupations in 1950 were nurses (98%), telephone operators (96%),
private household workers (95%), stenographers, typists and
secretaries (94%), librarians (89%), operatives in manufacturing
apparel and accessories (81%), and teachers (75%). Within the
teaching profession, 91 per cent of the elementary school teachers
were women.

Educated, professional women were clustered into a small number
of occupations. According to the 1960 Census, almost one-third of
all female professional and technical workers were elementary
school teachers, compared to 3.2 per cent of all male professional
workers. Over the course of American history, the need for cheap

but educated labour has promoted the growth of a 'female labour market'. As more and more women have entered an occupation, its status and pay has declined relative to those occupations dominated by men. This happened to elementary school teaching in the nineteenth century and to clerical work in the early twentieth.

Between 1940 and 1962, the number of professional women workers increased from about 1.6 to 2.9 million, but the percentage of employed women in professional fields remained the same – 13 per cent. Women operatives represented a smaller percentage in 1962 than in 1940 – 15 as compared to 18 per cent. The percentage of women in private household employment declined from 18 per cent in 1940 to 10 per cent in 1962. The greatest expansion occurred in the clerical field. Clerical workers rose from 21 to 31 per cent of all employed women.[3]

Racial differences remained important. Between 1940 and 1960 clerical work replaced domestic service as the leading occupational field for white women, but not yet for black. While 41 per cent of white women in 1960 were clerical or sales workers, only 9 per cent of black women filled these occupations. Although the percentage of black women employed as private household servants had declined between 1940 and 1960, a disproportionate number were still in this occupation – 36 per cent, compared to only 4 per cent of white women workers. In 1960, 48 per cent of black women were in the labour force as compared to 37 per cent of white women. Black women were the lowest-paid workers, earning in 1960 a median income of $1391 compared to the white female median income of $2245. In that same year, black men were earning $3757 and white men, $7150.[4]

Clerical work is more skilled and better paid than domestic service, but the increasing numbers of women in 'white-collar' jobs also reflected the decline in skill, knowledge, responsibility, prestige and pay of office work over time. By 1971, the usual median weekly wage for full-time clerical workers in the United States was lower than that in every type of 'blue-collar' work. The only occupational category remaining below clerical was service work, also predominantly female.

Technological and structural changes in clerical work had facilitated women's entry into it; the preponderance of women clerical workers led, in turn, to further downgrading and deskilling of the work itself. As one writer expressed it:

The proletarization of white-collar employees does not have the same meaning at all if it is women, and not heads of family, who comprise the majority of the group. . . . The majority of white-collar tasks are less interesting, less prestigious, and bring lower remuneration, but they are carried out by women with reduced aspirations.[5]

Myths about female 'nature', especially women's innate lack of ambition, reinforced the fact that clerical jobs provided little or no opportunity for promotion. The growth of commercial courses in American high schools also contributed to the feminisation of clerical work. Even if women were only temporary workers, they brought their skills with them, thus sparing employers the expense of on-the-job training. With public and trade schools footing most of the bill, employers were more than willing to hire women. The schools could also be trusted to train a potential worker in dependable and punctual habits. The high school diploma certified a worker's reliability, and prolonged schooling socialised women into behaviour patterns of docility and obedience, as well as tact and patience.

Changes in the nature of clerical work, along with the increased demand for cheap office help, led employers to hire, even prefer, women, but demography explains the increasing numbers of married women in the workforce. Valerie Kincade Oppenheimer estimates that even if all unmarried women between the ages of 18–64, plus women no longer with their husbands, had been employed, their numbers were not sufficient to meet the growing demand for female labour between 1940 and 1960. Only when we include all women between 18 64, with the exception of younger women in school and married women with pre-school-age children, is there a large enough group.

Between 1940 and 1960, the percentage of single women between 20 and 24 declined from 47.2 to 28.4 per cent. Reduced fertility, especially during the 1930s Depression, had led to the overall ageing of the population, so that between 1940 and 1960 the proportion of women aged 18–34 declined from 29.3 per cent of the total female population to 21.5 per cent. Fertility increased during the 1950s, but these young mothers had been born during a period of very low birth rates.

The proportion of young women 18–19 years old enrolled in

school rose between 1940 and 1960. Slightly over one-third of 18-year-old women were in school in 1940; by 1960, almost half were. Less than 20 per cent of the 19-year-olds were students in 1940; this increased to almost 30 per cent by 1960. With the median age for marriage down to 20.3 years by 1962, many women experienced only a brief period of work before they married.

Now let us look at birth rates after the Second World War. Between 1950 and 1960, the average number of children born to married women rose from 1859 per 1000 in 1950, to 2038 in 1954, and up to 2313 in 1960.[6] Would not the increased burden of child care offset other factors? Working mothers did have fewer and older children than non-working mothers. Although married women made up almost 60 per cent of the female workforce in 1962, they represented only one-third of all married women. Most white women in the 1950s and early 1960s did not work outside the home during their child-bearing and child-rearing years. Also, one-fourth of the women workers in non-agricultural industries were working part-time, or less than 35 hours a week in the early 1960s. Three-fifths of all part-time work was being done by married women. Many others worked full-time but not the year around.

Despite these qualifications, there was a remarkable increase of married mothers in the workforce. In 1960, 39 per cent of married women living with their husbands and with children between the ages of 6 and 17 were working, compared to 26 per cent in 1948. While mothers of pre-school-age children showed a much lower workforce rate, their 18.6 per cent figure was also up from 1948's 10.7 per cent.

After 1957 the birth rate began to decline again, but even during the years of the post-war 'baby boom' the long-term trend towards smaller-sized families was not totally reversed. Rather than bearing many children, more women were having two or three instead of one or none. They also shortened the interval between children. By marrying young, entering motherhood quickly, and shortening the interval between successive children, women were still completing their child-bearing by the time they were 30. They could return to work five or six years later. Of course, this still meant an important sexual difference; while men participated in the labour force at all stages of the adult life cycle, women tended to drop out in order to devote full time to the care of infants and young children.

Leaving the workforce was not an option open to all mothers; it depended on their class, race and marital status. Employed mothers in 1960 were still over-represented in the lower and lower-middle classes. There was a close relationship between poverty, female-headed households and women's workforce participation. While the median income for families with male heads was $5857 in 1960, it was only $2968 for female-headed families. In that year, 10.5 per cent of American families were female-headed, but close to 20 per cent of full-time working mothers with children under 12 were not living with their husbands. Racial differences were especially noticeable; 8 per cent of white, but 22 per cent of black families were maintained by women in 1960. Both the higher proportion of female-headed black families and the lower earnings of blacks generally help to explain why more black than white women worked at all stages of their lives. Labour force participation rates during the child-bearing years of 25–34 show that half of the black women but only one-third of the white women were working, both in 1948 and 1960.

Not until 1975 did white women reach rates attained by blacks in 1948. After 1960 and still more after 1970, a sharp increase in labour force participation occurred for white women. But in 1960, 31 per cent of black women who were married, living with their husbands and pre-school children, worked, compared to 18 per cent of the white women in that situation.

Although employers had to overcome their prejudices about hiring married and older women, they still discriminated against them. A study of corporations in 1958 showed that 26 per cent of the firms in New York City, 40 per cent of those in San Francisco and 60 per cent in Houston, Texas, set maximum hiring ages between 35 and 45 years of age. This was at a time when the peak labour force rate for women occurred during the ages of 45–49. Employers said that young workers were more easily trained and willing to accept lower wages than older workers. Many also saw youthful attractiveness and potential sexual availability as job qualifications. A 1960 National Office Management Association study of 2000 firms revealed that close to 30 per cent seriously considered 'sex appeal' in the hiring of clerical workers.[7]

These employer 'preferences' meant that in the late 1950s the proportion of working mothers with school-age children in clerical and professional work was only half that of single women. Married and divorced women were concentrated in sales, service and operative jobs. Nevertheless, opportunities opened up for older and married women. This is especially true of teaching. In 1941, only 13 per cent of American school districts would hire married women; by 1956, 97 per cent accepted them. Demography, coupled with an expanded need for workers in traditional female occupations, provided the basis for the post-war increase of older, married women in the workforce. The average age of the American woman worker rose from 37 in 1950 to 41 ten years later.

With a longer life free from child-rearing responsibilities, some older women sought employment to 'fill time', but most women, married or unmarried, worked for the same reason as men: economic necessity. In the late 1940s, married women with college educations worked mainly because of the low income of their husbands. In the mid 1950s, over half of the female labour force was made up of women who supported themselves or provided the main support for a family. Yet, at the same time, nearly 40 per cent of the wives in families with a total income (before taxes) of $6000–$10,000 were in the labour force. This was a higher proportion than among families in lower income brackets.[8] Among white mothers of pre-school-age children, the employment rate was clearly and inversely correlated with husbands' income. But for married women with older children, the relationship between employment and husbands' earnings was becoming less clear.

The definition of economic 'necessity' expanded in the post-war period to include a 'higher standard of living'. Helping to buy a home, automobile or furniture, paying for the children's college educations or for family vacations – all these became acceptable reasons for married women's employment. The much publicised middle-class life style could be attained only through the contributions of an additional wage-earner. So women worked to bridge the gap between real and desired family income.

Paid employment did not free women from child care and housework. The growth in suburban home ownership after the war increased women's domestic tasks, as did the post-war standards of child care, discussed in Chapter 1. But society was now willing to condone a 'dual role' if women were individually willing and able to assume a double burden. When women experienced conflicts between work and family responsibilities, they expected to solve them individually.

Part-time work became one alternative for women with heavy

household obligations. In 1950, one-fourth of all employed women worked less than 35 hours a week; by 1960, this had increased to one-third of all working women. Married women workers, especially if employed part-time, saw their earnings as supplementary family income. The married mother worked not for 'selfish' reasons, but to give her children a better chance in life, such as a college education. She was merely extending the way she performed her traditional roles as wife and mother. Husbands could accept their wives as secondary or supplementary income-earners; women, in turn, were expected to play down personal ambition. The fact that women, even if they worked full-time, generally earned far less than their husbands minimised any threat to men's status as breadwinners.

The term 'career woman' had such unpleasant connotations that there was a relative decline in the percentage of women in high-level occupations which required long training. In 1932, 17 per cent of all doctorates were conferred on women; in the years 1955–60, only 10 per cent. Women comprised 30 per cent of university staffs in 1930, but only 22 per cent in 1960. Alva Myrdal and Viola Klein contended that women's increasing participation in the labour force was achieved 'though their willingness to accept low and medium-skilled occupations . . . in preference to more ambitious career plans which might in the long run conflict with their family role.'[9]

Nevertheless, improving their families' standard of living was not the only reason women sought work. A 1955 survey showed that while 48 per cent of the wives worked for financial reasons, another 21 per cent worked to fill 'a need for accomplishment' or to keep busy or to meet people. Even those who cited economic need mentioned other, subsequent benefits from employment, especially the companionship of co-workers and the sense of independence a paycheck represented. Almost two-thirds of the married women workers surveyed in 1958 referred to their jobs as their chief source of feeling 'important' or 'useful', while only one-third mentioned housekeeping.[10]

Generally, the more education women have, the more likely they are to be in the labour force. However, one group of women in the early 1960s broke the general rule. Fewer women between 35 and 44, with one to three years of college, worked than their contemporaries with less education. These women had no doubt been pressured by the post-war feminine mystique to leave school before earning their degrees, and they probably began their families soon afterwards. It is not educational level alone, but rather continued work in professional and managerial occupations which stimulates personal achievement and long-range work commitment.

Social factors, rather than voluntary personal choice, were responsible for young women's disinclination to view education as a means of preparing themselves for a lifetime of paid employment. Most teenage girls took it for granted that their future lives would be centred chiefly, if not exclusively, around homemaking responsibilities. The vocational guidance and counselling they received in high schools reinforced the conventional view of women's abilities. Bonnie Halascsak, the first woman security guard at US Steel, remembers being told by a guidance counsellor that she 'was very mechanical, very high in math. . . . But then they told me these were not women's fields, you know?'[11]

In 1956, 57 per cent of the male 17-year-olds but 63 per cent of the young women graduated from high school. On the average, the girls had achieved better grades than the boys did, although girls' grades dropped if they felt that academic success conflicted with their popularity or 'femininity'. More telling are the subjects each studied. In 1954, boys made up 60 per cent of the enrolment in chemistry, geometry and intermediate algebra and 80 per cent of those in trigonometry and physics classes. Over one-third of the girls, but less than 10 per cent of the boys, were enrolled in commercial courses which emphasised the development of clerical skills for immediate post-graduate employment.

Young women accounted for three out of five who had the ability to graduate from college but did not. At the universities women were only 28 per cent of those receiving BAs in the mid 1950s. However, they were 62 per cent of the graduates at teachers' colleges. Women earned their degrees within a narrow range of traditional feminine subjects. In graduate education, gender differences became even more striking. Four out of five women received MAs in education, English, home economics, nursing and the fine arts. Women were only receiving 10 per cent of the PhDs in the mid 1950s; one-third were in education and another third were in psychology, English, home economics, fine arts, chemistry and history combined. As late as 1970, women were earning less than 14 per cent of all doctoral degrees. In the early 1970s, women's major fields of study in college showed not only a continuation of the 1950s pattern, but also little change between 1966 and 1972.

Choosing acceptable female professions may have been not only a response to discrimination in male-dominated fields, but also a compromise between domesticity and desire for occupational achievement. Teaching remained a favourite for women because it did not involve extensive travel or excessively long hours. It could be combined with family responsibilities.

Women entered occupations both sex-typed and limited in opportunities for advancement. Rarely did they begin entry-level jobs which promised a well-defined route of promotion. If a woman reached the point where further advancement involved supervising male workers, she was typically passed over. Even in the field of education, men held the administrative positions.

Within corporations, managerial decisions regarding individual women were based on beliefs such as the higher turnover and absenteeism of women workers. These beliefs were, in turn, the result of conventional stereotypes about women, especially their primary desire for and commitment to domestic roles. Actually, the supposed low productivity and lack of job attachment on the part of female workers were more the result than the cause of their dead-end, low-paying jobs.

The employers' professed concern about the family did not lead them to reform working conditions. Adjustments to the work schedule were always expected to be made within individual homes, never in the corporate structure. Managers surveyed in 1959 rejected federal government funding for child care and did not believe the corporations had a responsibility to provide it. A survey in 1958 showed that 80 per cent of the children under 12 whose mothers worked full-time were cared for in their own homes. Of the 20 per cent cared for outside the home, only 2 per cent were in day care centres or nursery schools. Employers believed these child care arrangements were 'adequate as long as the mother comes to work'.[12]

Such corporate policies helped to account for women's marginal position in the workplace. The structure of work and the degree of commitment required in professional and managerial positions favoured men over women. Business management, particularly, has been dominated both by a 'masculine ethic' of rationality and efficiency and a single-minded devotion to the corporation. A study of female corporate executives (born between 1910 and 1915) reinforces the presumption that women who thrived in the board rooms of American corporations must have been exceptional individuals.

All were first-born and none of them had brothers. Early high-achievers who identified with their fathers and other men rather than their mothers, they usually had fathers who were business executives and actively encouraged their daughters' career plans. The women established a management pattern early and rejected traditional feminine goals. They did not try to combine work with marriage and motherhood, but concentrated solely on their careers. Not only did this choice set them apart from most women, but it also increased their dislike for 'traditional' women. As these executives allotted more and more time to their careers, their social lives declined, and not one married before she was 35. About half of them married after that age, but none had children.

In the 1940s and 1950s, unmarried women executives had to be more competent, efficient and motivated than their male counterparts. They translated their thoughts into male terms, talked shop, and 'sought to act in ways which would obscure the fact that they were women'.[13] No wonder they became fearful of any possible comparison between themselves and other women, such as secretaries or managers' wives. Even after becoming presidents and vice-presidents, these pioneers were unwilling to hire or sponsor other women.

Women who attained executive rank did so in a small number of professions. In 1950, when women were slightly under 30 per cent of the workforce, they were 40.1 per cent of all professional-technical workers. Yet only 1.2 per cent of the engineers, 4.1 per cent of the lawyers and judges, and 6 per cent of the physicians and osteopaths were female. In 1970, women were still only 1.6 per cent of engineers and 4.7 per cent of lawyers/judges. Although the percentage of women doctors had climbed slightly to 8.9 per cent, 98 per cent of the registered nurses were women.[14] Both in 1964 when women comprised 78 per cent of those in health service and in 1976 when they reached 80 per cent, the female jobs were low in the industry's hierarchy. Physicians, hospital administrators, insurance company directors, government regulators and medical school educators remained predominantly male.

Next to soldiering and police work, politics has been one of the most exclusively masculine occupations. The majority of American politicians have come from the legal profession where women are only a tiny percentage. Although the proportion of Americans who agreed that a woman is capable of being President rose steadily – from 31 per cent in 1937, 52 per cent in 1955, to 66 per cent in 1971 – this did not result in any significant increases in the number of women in national, state or even local government.

A total of 69 women were elected to the US House of Representatives between 1916 and 1969. Out of approximately 435 members, 17 was the largest number of women serving at any one time. The 88th Congress (1963–4) had 12 women members and the 91st (1968–9), only 10. The largest number of women in the Senate at any one time (out of 96–100 members) has been 3. Length of tenure is all-important in the national legislature, and the majority of Congresswomen have served three terms or less; 24 stayed no more than one term. Although there are signs that the pattern is changing, the largest group of female legislators has traditionally been widows of Congressmen, rather than politicians in their own right.

Most politically concerned women did not aim for public office. A 1974 study of a New York county concluded: 'In contrast to men, women's political participation is confined primarily to women's organizations or to party work at the lowest level of the party hierarchy.' Women themselves described their reasons for not running for local office: children at home, acceptance of the 'proper' role of women in politics, a realistic assessment of sex discrimination, and lack of acceptance by male colleagues. Apparently, the women's vote made little difference, or as political scientist Kirsten Amundsen aptly stated, '*if* there is a women's vote, it certainly has not been put to use on behalf of women'.[15]

The almost total absence of women in the top levels of business and politics has both illustrated and reinforced the belief that men are the 'dominant sex'. Even in the professions, women's jobs involve support, nurture, service, and de-emphasise exercising authority. To some extent, women's paid work has been an extension of and reflects the status of their unpaid work as wives, mothers and housekeepers. Moreover, women's opportunity for employment has been limited by their socially assigned responsibility for child care and domestic labour. Women's unpaid work in the home has put a stigma on work they do outside the home. Once an occupation becomes a 'woman's job', men leave it and wages decline. Family structure and hierarchy carry over and are reproduced at work. Nursing, for example, was specifically designed as an occupation for women because caring for the sick had been a 'maternal' function. The nurse continued to play 'mother' to the 'patient/child', but the doctor was the 'father', who had final authority over both. Secretaries have been expected to render 'wifely' services for their employers. This role, as well as the stigma attached to women's work, can be illustrated by Table 2.1 on the clerical sector.

TABLE 2.1   Women as percentage of all workers

	1950 (%)	1970 (%)	1976 (%)
All clerical	62.2	73.6	78.7
Bank tellers	45.2	86.1	91.1
Bookkeepers	77.7	82.1	90.0
Cashiers	81.3	84.0	87.7
Office machine operators	81.1	73.5	73.7
Secretaries and typists	94.6	96.6	98.5
Shipping-receiving clerks	6.6	14.3	17.3

SOURCE: Bureau of Labor Statistics, US Department of Labor, *US Working Women: A Databook* (Washington, DC: US Government Printing Office, Bulletin 1977), p. 9.

Between 1950 and 1976, the clerical sector as a whole became more predominantly female. The greatest shift was among bank tellers, an occupation which declined in skill and prestige, paving the way for cheaper female labour and continued male 'flight'. Secretaries/typists remained the category with the largest percentage of women. Of all clerical occupations, the secretary is the most analogous to the 'wife'. It is the elite position within the clerical ranks, but has low occupational mobility. A secretary's status is more a reflection of her boss's standing than of her own skills. The secretarial function retains personal characteristics inside the bureaucratic world. Secretaries are the 'human', caring side of the office 'family'. Within the service sector, private household work is most similar to women's unpaid housework. Even in the mid 1970s, over 97 per cent of these workers were female, mostly women of colour.

Some sexual divisions within occupations appear to be arbitrary. Women sell women's clothing, but men sell women's shoes. During the Second World War, women sold durable goods such as furniture and household equipment, but these high-commission jobs shifted back to men after the war. Women have generally sold the 'softer' and less costly items. They are waitresses and food handlers in snack bars, coffee shops and the less expensive restaurants, while men are the chefs and waiters in the more formal and costly establishments.

Manufacturing has operated according to a clear sexual hierarchy. Women accounted for one-fourth of the workers in 1950, but were only 7 per cent of the managers, officials and proprietors; 10 per cent of the foremen and less than 4 per cent of the skilled workers. Over half of the women operatives were in the food, textile and apparel industries. Since the Second World War, the segregated labour market plus union resistance has kept women out of the skilled, highly paid, blue-collar occupations – carpenters, electricians, plumbers and other crafts. In 1960, 21 per cent of white male workers, 10 per cent of black males, and only 1 per cent of all women workers were in skilled trades. By 1970, this had increased to 2 per cent for white women.

Most of the pay differential between men and women is attributable to occupational segregation, but women have earned less than men even when they have done the same or similar work. One company out of three in the early 1960s had dual pay scales for similar office jobs. In blue-collar occupations, wage discrimination was more overt. In the 1940s, the General Electric Company reduced wage rates by one-third if the job was performed by a woman; Westinghouse's female rate was 18–20 per cent lower than the male wage. After the Equal Pay Act (1963) and Title VII of the 1964 Civil Rights Act made it illegal to have separate female and male pay rates, General Electric simply changed the numbers signifying grades of work (and pay), so that 'male' became the higher numbers. This situation existed until a law suit was brought against General Electric in 1972.

In 1955, the median earnings for year-round, full-time workers were $2719 for women and $4252 for men. Women then earned 64 per cent of what men did. The gap widened over the next twenty years, from 61 per cent of men's in 1960 to 58.8 per cent in 1975. In contrast to the widening male-female wage differential, there was until 1974 a definite increase in Third World people's income relative to white, at least for year-round, full-time workers. Table 2.2 shows this was more dramatic among women than men.

TABLE 2.2   Earnings of black and other races to white[a]

	Among men (%)	Among women (%)
1939	45	38
1959	61	66
1964	66	69
1969	69	82
1974	74	94

[a] Year-round, full-time workers only.

SOURCE: Population Division, Bureau of the Census, *The Social and Economic Status of the Black Population in the United States: An Historical View, 1790–1978* (Washington, DC: US Government Printing Office, Current Population Reports, Special Studies, Series P-23, No. 80) p. 48.

However, black men and women were (and still are) more likely to be unemployed than white workers. Women are also more likely to be unemployed than men. The unemployment rate for black women was slightly below that for black men in the years 1954 and 1960, but since 1965 it has been higher. White women's unemployment has remained consistently higher than white men's. And the differential in the male-female unemployment rates has been growing since 1962.

The earnings gap between women and men varies by occupational sector. As shown in Table 2.3, it has been greatest in sales work and least in professional positions. In 1960, only male service workers earned less than any category of women. Women professional workers and managers, on the average, earned less than male clerical workers, salesmen and operatives.

In spite of legislation in the 1960s prohibiting employment discrimination on the basis of sex, government figures in 1970 still showed that women's median wage or salary was 66.7 per cent of men's among professional and technical workers and 56.4 per cent

TABLE 2.3   Wage or salary for selected occupations[a]

	1939		1960	
	Men ($)	Women ($)	Men ($)	Women ($)
Professional workers	2100	1277	6848	4384
Managers, officials, proprietors	2254	1218	7241	4173
Clerical workers	1564	1072	5247	3586
Operatives	1268	742	4977	2970
Sales workers	1451	745	5755	2428
Service workers (except private household)	1019	607	4089	2418
Private household workers	549	339	—	1133

[a] Year-round, full-time workers only.

SOURCE: Bureau of the Census, US Department of Commerce, *Current Population Reports*, P-60, No. 37, as cited in Esther Peterson, 'Working Women', *Daedalus*, xcⅢ, 2 (Spring 1964), 682.

among managers, officials and proprietors. Female clerical workers earned 64.4 per cent of the median wage paid to men. In sales work, women received only 42.8 per cent of what men did, and among operatives and service workers the figures were 59.2 and 56.8 per cent, respectively. Among scientists the gap was narrower; women in 1970 were earning 76.3 per cent of their male colleagues. More encouraging were monthly starting salaries for June 1971 college graduates; men in engineering received only $1 more than women; in liberal arts, the difference was $2.

This near equality is deceptive, however, for over the years a large gap opens up between male and female earnings, particularly between the ages of 35–44. This is usually attributed to women's intermittent labour force participation, since many women are re-entering the job market after a period of absence at the very time that men are hitting their occupational 'prime'. But even women with continuous work experience have earned less than men. Government figures for 1966 showed that women who worked year-round, full-time, 100 per cent of their adult lives earned 75 per cent of what men did. Those with four or more years of college actually dropped to 64 per cent of male earnings.

Corporations, labour unions, families and schools have all played a part in maintaining occupational segregation and salary differences. The legal system has reinforced the pattern. Until the 1970s, women were excluded from certain jobs, such as police work, and they are still barred from combat positions in the military services. Because women have not been subject to military 'drafts', veterans' preference statutes for government jobs have functioned as discrimination against women.

The domestic relations laws of individual American states have also contributed by defining marital roles in traditional ways: the husband as head of household and the wife as care-taker of husband, home and children. This has enabled employers to presume that the 'appropriate' wage for women workers can be lower than the 'family wage' paid to men. Such 'female wages' have meant poverty for single women and families headed by women.

Until the early 1970s, employment laws covering women contained more prejudice than protection. Presumably based on social concern for women's role as child-bearers, 'protective legislation' kept women out of jobs requiring night work or the lifting of heavy weights. But these laws have never been applied to women's work at home; neither have they regulated jobs traditionally designated as women's work, such as nursing or domestic service.

The American legal system is complicated by federalism. Often both federal (national) and state laws are needed to deal with a problem. State laws have tended to lag behind national legislation, and there has been little uniformity among states. In January 1965, only eight states had laws covering women's employment before and after childbirth; only four of these provided for maternity benefits. Twenty-five states in 1965 refused women unemployment compensation on the grounds that they had left their last job because of family obligations. From 1962 to 1965, the number of states refusing to pay unemployment compensation to pregnant women rose from 38 to 45.

Sixteen states in 1965 had no minimum wage law, and no state had set a maximum of 40 hours of work a week. Since 1938, however, the federal Fair Labor Standards Act (FLSA) has provided a minimum wage and overtime pay after 40 hours a week for all covered workers. Also, since 1963 women and men doing the same work must be paid equal wages. Not all workers are covered by FLSA. About 16 million non-supervisory workers in private employment were not covered in 1965, and these were disproportionately women. State statutes protected only 4 million. This left nearly one out of four women workers without any legal minimum wage. In 1961, a minimum standard of living cost $55–$60 a week. The median weekly earnings of women employed full-time, year-round as service workers was about $45; salesworkers earned $46 a week, and private household workers only $20.

Social Security (Old-Age, Survivors and Disability Insurance, or OASDI) is administered by the federal government uniformly in every state. Workers contribute to it out of their salaries, but the system was predicated on the patriarchal family with the husband as breadwinner. A married woman worker received little or no return on her own contributions. That is to say, she could not receive from her own share any more than the amount she would have gained from her husband's benefits as a non-working wife. Even a widow age 62 or older received an amount somewhat less than her husband was entitled to had he lived.

The largest category of public welfare assistance is Aid to Families with Dependent Children (AFDC), which essentially means female-headed households because they are poorer than households headed by men. In 1960, 15 per cent of male-headed households, but 42 per cent of those headed by women, were below the government-defined poverty level. Among households headed by women which also contained children under 18 years of age, 56 per cent were poor even by the government's parsimonious criteria.

Welfare policies have reinforced dependent and passive behaviour in women. Since its inception, the welfare system has supported the traditional wife-mother role and inculcated feelings of powerlessness in clients. Docile and resigned women, in turn, make the most cooperative and least challenging welfare recipients.

The welfare system has served another function which has sometimes contradicted the mother-in-the-home ideal. It was set up to ensure a supply of cheap labour to employers, and has done this by refusing aid to those who might be potential workers. 'Potentiality' has been determined in a racist fashion.

Instead of creating a comprehensive welfare system after the Second World War, the US trimmed its inadequate one. Southern states retained their low wage structure and racial caste system because welfare grant levels varied according to region. Despite long-standing poverty, there were substantially fewer blacks than whites on Southern welfare rolls. Black relief mothers received lower benefits than white mothers, and Southern welfare officials regarded these black women as 'employable', especially as seasonal 'field hands' in agriculture. Officials also conducted periodic purges of 'unsuitable homes' (defined as containing illegitimate children or male friends of the mother) whenever there was a need for low-wage workers. Frances Fox Piven and Richard A. Cloward have noted that: 'The especially vigorous enforcement of man-in-the-house rules in Southern states is directed almost exclusively at the Southern black, a pattern of discrimination that is justified on the grounds of the alleged defects in black family life.' A 1961 national study of welfare cases found that black welfare women were two or three times more likely to work than white women, especially in the rural areas of the South. These AFDC mothers were forced into very low-level jobs.[16] The relief system has played a direct role in keeping black women at the bottom of the occupational order, while at the same time ensuring that black mothers would find it harder to stay home.

The President's Commission on the Status of Women, established by John F. Kennedy in late 1961, showed a similar bias. The Commission's 1963 report reflected the ideological limitations of the 'liberal consensus' by assuming a rapidly growing economy rather than a redistribution of existing resources. This meant neglecting the socio-economic conditions which forced many poorly educated and minority women with young children to seek work. The Commission and its committees concentrated on white, highly educated, potential career women. Even with this group, there was no critique of the pattern which expected women (but not men) to interrupt their studies or careers for home responsibilities. The Commission suggested a 'drastic' revision in adult education so that married women could 'resume a field of study or a job', but also made it clear that widening choices for women 'does not imply neglect of their education for responsibilities in the home'.[17] While the Commission recommended construction of child-care facilities and larger tax deductions for child-care expenses, it did not call for changes in the sex-role division of domestic work.

With regard to equalising wages and employment opportunities for women, the Commission advised an Executive Order covering firms with government contracts. This was only a mild extension of a 1962 presidential directive that federal agencies make all selections for appointments, advancement and training without regard to sex. No more than 20 per cent of women workers would have been affected.

The Commission's stance in 1963 was far more conservative than the Civil Rights Act of the following year, which prohibited discrimination in employment, in all institutions, on the basis of sex, as well as race, colour, religion and national origin. The Commission had believed it would be politically detrimental to the cause of black civil rights if sex and race were linked at the same time. In fact, the Commission's assessment of the political climate was accurate, if not laudable. The inclusion of women in the Civil Rights Act was proposed by Representative Howard W. Smith of Virginia in order to obstruct the bill, and members of the House of Representatives initially treated it as a joke. Since organised feminism did not begin until 1966, the passage of the Civil Rights Act was not the result of feminist consciousness. It was, however, one step towards creating it.

The President's Commission on the Status of Women marked a political watershed despite its conservatism, for women became the subject of serious political discourse. Other signs of change had developed earlier when it appeared that the feminine mystique interfered with certain demands of 'national security'. In the mid 1950s, one study noted that the Russians were graduating 13,000 women engineers a year as compared to less than 100 in the United States. It expressed the hope that married women would return to the labour force, as they had during the Second World War, with the skills necessary to 'enhance the economic and military strength' of the country,[18] and recommended that college-bound women train for professions outside education, nursing, library science and home economics. However, the continued large demand for teachers and health workers in the 1950s and 1960s delayed any break with tradition.

Youth became another Cold War concern. The high post-war birth rate and prolonged years of adolescent schooling focused national attention on the 'teenager'. Business and advertising firms welcomed the new 'youth market' for records, clothes and automobiles; but parents, religious leaders and psychologists were becoming worried about adolescent 'alienation'. Youth heroes, such as James Dean of *Rebel Without a Cause* and Marlon Brando of *The Wild One*, were brooding, resentful 'loners'. Teenage 'delinquency' was no longer confined to youth gangs among the poor, but was becoming an attractive 'life-style' for suburban middle-class adolescents. Rock-'n'-roll music, particularly Elvis Presley's sensual performances, shocked conventional moralists. Educators and child-rearing experts, including Dr Spock himself, began to question the 'over-permissiveness' of post-war, child centred psychology. There was particular dismay when the Soviets launched the world's first orbital satellite in 1957. Were young Americans becoming too pampered and 'soft' to compete with the Russians on the scholastic 'front'? Perhaps mothers' employment, rather than constant maternal attention, would encourage more independence and toughness in their children.

About the same time, the myth of 'maternal deprivation' was being undermined by empirical studies. These studies found that maternal employment *per se* was not the overwhelmingly influential factor in children's lives that it was thought to have been. Family size and income, the father's work habits and emotional stability, the mother's attitude towards working, and even the sex of the child were variables which had to be considered.

Boys' reactions to their mothers' employment were somewhat more negative than those of girls. Some increase in delinquent behaviour was found among middle-class, male adolescents, while younger boys bcame more withdrawn and passive. The findings on marital relationships revealed some strain, but this varied according to economic level. Since wives went to work in lower-income families out of financial necessity, conflicts among these couples centred around money. In families with higher incomes, husbands and wives quarrelled more about marital roles.

When wives and husbands both worked, some shift in family power structure became inevitable. Although a wife's earnings ranged from only one-fifth to one-fourth of total family income, this monetary contribution gave her a greater share in major economic decisions. The earning wife also reduced, to some extent, her housekeeping activities and made fewer decisions about routine tasks. One researcher found that husbands' share of the housework increased from 15 to 25 per cent when their wives were employed. Of course, this still left the working wife with most of the housework. Also, not all tasks were equally shared; while husbands would take on some of the traditional female workload, such as dishwashing and cleaning, wives would actually curtail their normal sharing in 'masculine' tasks such as lawn care and repairs. In other words, women's work at home may have become more traditional in order to offset her 'unfeminine' behaviour outside the home.

While the reactions of sons and husbands were mixed and problematic, working women had a significant and positive effect on their daughters. Employed mothers embodied a concept of womanhood which included a wider range of activities and fewer restrictions. Their daughters, in turn, expressed a desire for independence and social mobility, and they chose traditionally masculine occupational goals more often than other girls did. Nevertheless, class distinctions were important.

Many working-class girls saw their mothers struggling with a 'double burden' of housework plus low-paid, often unskilled work. These young women worked part-time themselves while in school and were expected to help out at home as well. They had far less chance than middle-class girls – or their own brothers – of acquiring a college or university education. Although they were likely to be employed after marriage, work *per se* did not appear 'liberating' to them. Their jobs would never pay enough for them to hire servants or use commercial services. Instead, they hoped that their husbands could earn enough so they could stay home. A woman's attitude towards employment was not wholly a function of her social class, but not surprisingly, the jobs with higher pay and status tended to be better liked.[19] Middle-class women were more likely to pass on to their daughters both favourable attitudes towards employment (even careers) and the financial resources to pay for college educations.

The economic demand for masses of college-educated workers occurred sooner and went further in the United States than in other industrialised countries. Between 1950 and 1974, college enrolment for men increased by 234 per cent; for women the increase was 456 per cent. The ratio of women to men in college went from a low of 0.48 in 1950 (partly due to the GI Bill which favoured men) to 0.79 in 1974. College students became a politically conscious and active segment of the population in the 1960s, and the rise, or rather the rebirth, of feminism was partly the result of student movements.

The women workers of the 1950s had not been feminists, but

they certainly were the literal and metaphoric mothers of the women's movement. Working women posed possibilities for political change denied to homemakers. Paid work, even in the most stereotyped 'women's jobs', differed from work at home; measurable rewards, organisational hierarchy, clearly set hours of labour, and companionship with peers were found at most workplaces. Unpaid housewives, for example, could never demand 'equal pay for equal work'. And equal pay was a good point from which to organise because it touched basic American values. As President Eisenhower declared in his 1956 State of the Union message, 'the principle of equal pay for equal work without discrimination because of sex is a matter of simple justice.'[20]

Women's monetary contribution also led to some redistribution of authority within families, if not yet any major alterations in sex roles. On the other hand, working mothers still had to organise child care themselves. In the mid 1960s, social agencies began to favour publicly-funded day care, but this was mainly to encourage welfare mothers to seek training and jobs. As long as women have to carry the major responsibility for child care and housework, their relationship to paid work will continue to differ from that of men's. An understanding of women's lives must encompass not only what Marxists call the 'mode of production', but also the home and family, or the 'mode of reproduction', and the economic, demographic, political and cultural factors affecting both.

3. Women at Home: Changes in the Private Sphere

The 'frustrated housewife' began receiving media attention in the early 1960s. In 1960, three years before Betty Friedan would call women's work in the home 'The Problem That Has No Name', *Redbook* magazine ran an article entitled 'Why Young Mothers Feel Trapped' and invited readers to respond. The editors were shocked to receive 24,000 replies. It appeared that working-class as well as Friedan's middle-class women were suffering from the nameless malaise. One-third of the blue-collar wives questioned by Mirra Komarovsky wanted employment 'simply "to get out of the house"'.[1] But in the absence of a political movement which could interpret individual discontent as a collective phenomena, women's problems had indeed been rendered 'nameless.'

Post-war suburbanisation and a consumer economy provided the economic support for locating 'woman's place' within the home-family nexus. The family had been shrinking in size and in the number of functions it served for more than a century. No longer a self-sufficient production unit, the mid-twentieth-century nuclear family specialised in the consumption of mass-produced commodities. The socially valuable functions the family still performed, such as child care, were viewed as emotional relationships rather than as work tasks. When women made a 'career' of family life, they became socially invisible. Their activities as wives, mothers and housekeepers were not analysed as work by either liberals or socialists. Rather, female domesticity was regarded as something biologically and psychologically innate.

Rooted in biology, reinforced by psychology, this 'natural' division of labour was also socially 'functional'. According to post-

49

war sociologists, the nuclear family was the only unit in which children could develop into emotionally stable, loving adults. Sex-role differences within the family maintained social stability. The man's role was 'instrumental' and required the ability to earn a living in order to supply the family's material needs. In modern industrial society, this meant his absence from the home for most of the day. Woman's family role was 'expressive'. She divined and satisfied emotional needs and acted as a psychological director. Actually, most of her time was spent in housework and the physical chores of child care rather than in monitoring personal relationships. Instead of having a biological and psychological 'fitness' for domestic roles, it would be fairer to say that what women did in the home produced the kind of person called 'feminine'.

Mainly committed to family roles, women have not identified themselves primarily in terms of their jobs. Almost half of the 160 middle-aged women studied by Lillian Rubin in the mid 1970s were in the labour force, but *not one – including those who work at high-level professional jobs – described herself in relation to her work*'. A decade earlier, Helena Z. Lopata asked 568 urban and suburban housewives (including 100 employed urban women) what they thought were the most important roles for women. Four-fifths of the respondents limited women to roles in the home. 'The judgment', Lopata found,

> is that every woman should be married, that she should have children, and that none but family roles should be of even secondary importance to her before, during, or after the time she is intensely involved in these relations by virtue of the life cycle.[2]

These findings reflect the fact that women have been socialised for mothering and housework, not for careers. As Sheila Rowbotham has pointed out, paid work is something a woman might *do*, but the work of a housewife and mother is what she *is*. And it is always easier to stop doing something than to stop being who you are.[3] Not only did women find it difficult to locate their identity outside a family context, but also they did not separate the general role of 'housewife' into its constituent parts: wife, mother, housekeeper.

In fact, each of the roles – wife, mother, housekeeper – ought to be considered as a job which changes over the course of a lifetime. In addition, the family itself and women's work and status within it depends on class, race and ethnicity. The labour force participation of black women was vital for family survival. Among black, Hispanic and Asian people, the family was more than merely a consumption and emotional unit, for it also served to preserve and maintain cherished cultural values, history, and even language. Extended kin networks were often a more viable survival structure than the isolated nuclear family typical of the white middle class. Consequently, demographic, residential and economic trends did not equally and identically affect all women.

Demographic changes have altered both the structure of the family and the relative importance of each of women's family work roles. In the 1950s, the median age at first marriage reached an all-time low for the twentieth century. So did the percentage of women who never married – only 4 per cent, compared to 9 per cent in the 1910s. Women in the 1950 _____ the highest birth rate in many decades, and the percent_____ dropped from 20 per cent in the 1930s to 1_____ ot surprising then that marriage an_____ mportant to women in the 1950s tha_____

However, life expect_____ increased over the course of the twe_____ in 1900 to 72 years by 195_____ ancies because infant mortalit_____ 960, the rate for white infants w_____. Mothers were younger both at t_____st child.

Marriage becam_____p because husbands and wives_____riod together. By the 1950s, older_____nticipate a 13-year interval without children_____e two-person household increased from 15 per cent_____ per cent in 1950.

Because women outlive m_____y an average of eight years, the post-marital stage of life also became increasingly important. In one generation the percentage of single-person households doubled, from 9.3 per cent in 1950 to 18.5 per cent in 1973, and most of the gain could be attributed to older women living alone. Nine per cent of all men aged 55–74 were widowed or divorced in 1970, compared to 34 per cent of the women in this age group. Currently two-thirds of all married women can expect to spend the last 18 years of their lives as widows.

By 1970, these older women were nearly twice as likely to live alone or with unrelated persons than with family members compared to 1940. Despite an ideology of family 'togetherness', the 1950s was a time that both young people and older women began increasingly to live outside the family. Since the Second World War, the family has had less generational variety and has occupied a smaller portion of the life cycle.

While demographic changes have altered the shape and length of women's work in the family, economic factors are equally important. Women in the home are unpaid workers who reproduce and maintain labour power by bearing and rearing children and providing bed, kitchen and laundry services for male workers. Women act as buyers for the family unit, transform raw materials (meat, vegetables, etc.) into finished products (cooked meals), clean, maintain and produce durable commodities. Although exact figures are unavailable, one 1970 study estimated the worth of the homemaker to be $257.53 a week. The figure would be higher for less wealthy women who had more work to do (for example, mending clothes) and fewer modern devices in the home. From this study, one arrives at a total of between 500 and 600 billion dollars per year, or over half the gross national product.[4]

Because the labour of women at home is not counted as 'productive' work adding to the gross national product, the occupation of housewife appears to stand outside the money economy. Furthermore, women provide emotional sustenance to other family members, and these 'private labours of love' are rewarding and deserve more intense commitment than most of the paid work open to them. In the words of historian Gerda Lerner, women 'make human life caring and warm in a society which is mostly motivated by self-interest and competition'. Caring for the young and creating a livable environment are essential work, but also the root of women's problems in society.[5]

The housewife's work hides some of the social tensions in capitalist society and makes them bearable. Working-class men can maintain an illusion of power *vis-à-vis* their wives. Emotionally supported and 'patched up' by nurturing women, they are kept from full awareness of their powerlessness outside family relations. Women resuscitate adult workers physically and emotionally and rear children with the psychological capacities to become productive workers and efficient consumers. By reproducing and maintaining capitalism in this way, women at home have served as a conservative force.

Post-war suburbanisation and consumerism reinforced the ideology of the 'private' family and the traditional role of women in the home by further isolating women and children at home from men at work. Class distinctions did not disappear in the suburbs, but they were less obvious. The very rich and the very poor did not move to the new communities. Home ownership and total reliance on the automobile made suburban dwellers feel 'middle-class' and diluted ethnic identity. Most suburbanites were young, second or third generation descendants of European immigrants. Moving to the suburbs was a combination of upward economic mobility, a pioneering adventure, and a rebellion against the older generation. These new suburbs were not only more homogeneous in age than the central cities, but they were also designed for the two-parent, nuclear family. Single people and childless couples would feel 'out of place,' as would blacks outnumbered by a ratio of more than thirty-five to one.

Suburbanisation was as effective as anti-communism and popularised Freudian psychology in depoliticising women's discontent. During the weekdays suburbia became a world of women. They interacted as friends and neighbours more frequently than did urban women, but women's culture in the suburbs revolved around and reinforced traditional feminine work roles. Families moved to the suburbs for the 'good of the children' and to escape from racial minorities, but women discovered that suburban living suited their husbands better than themselves. Fewer women than men wanted to move to the suburbs, and women placed a lower value on owning a home than men. Suburban locations lacked the cultural amenities as well as the job opportunities found in the cities. Women ruled out commuting long distances to work because of family obligations. So while men enjoyed leaving the 'hectic pace' of the city after work, women at home all day felt depressed and isolated. The lack of options in the suburbs encouraged them to commit themselves to 'full-time' mothering.

Suburban home ownership also increased women's commitment to the home itself by adding to their housework. Suburbanisation facilitated the introduction of small-scale technology into the home. Placing household appliances in every single home was more profitable for manufacturers and advertisers, but housework remained an individual and isolated endeavour, even when eased by machinery. The suburbs also perpetuated the sexual division of labour. Women did not even gain greater control over domestic life. Rather, the 'private sphere' became permeated with market values and corporate authorities. Women's family role was glorified by advertisers to sell commodities, and the suburban home was the perfect consumption space – new, bare, needing to be filled with furniture, appliances and cleaning aids.

With the post-war suburban migration, the mass marketing of television, and the demise of any feminist or socialist sentiment, the consumer culture dominated American life. Lopata found that women mentioned magazines almost as often as they spoke of their mothers as a source of help in learning how to be houseworkers. Women talked about their favourite television programme with each other, rather than about their own experiences and hopes. Generally, the middle class turned to the mass communication media for child-care advice, while the working class relied more on 'traditional wisdom'. But as suburbanisation broke up old urban, ethnic neighbourhoods and the middle-class images on television became ubiquitous, the social reality of all women was increasingly dictated by the consumer culture.

Consumerism not only informed buyers what to purchase; it told Americans what to dream. As an ideology, consumerism mobilised individual desire or discontent into material aspirations rather than political or 'class' thinking. It created an illusion of change and freedom while encouraging passivity and 'private' solutions. Passivity and dependence on (male) authority were, of course, tenets of the feminine mystique. Women, therefore, were the perfect consumers. They were also the perfect commodities; their bodies and smiles were used to sell products. Advertising messages and images reinforced the stereotyped roles of women: sex object, wife, mother, housekeeper.

But like other facets of the feminine mystique, consumerism and its vehicle, advertising, had some unintended consequences. By following women into their own kitchens and laundries, advertising made the private 'sphere' into an arena for public manipulation. The traditional definitions of wife, mother and housekeeper were not always compatible with the commercial 'modernisation' of each job. Furthermore, women had been taught that 'housewife' was a single, 'natural' role, as inevitable in their life cycles as menstruation and menopause. Yet they found that each of their jobs conflicted with the others. When a child tracked dirt onto the newly waxed floor, the efficient housekeeper was expected to change instantly into the indulgent mother. An hour later, she transformed herself into the attentive, smiling and sexually 'willing' wife. Role conflict was felt not only by married women in the workforce, but also by those who stayed home.

The 'job qualifications' and 'job content' of 'wife' were more flexible and diverse than the other two home occupations. Marriage was supposed to be a partnership based on romantic attachment and was, theoretically, separate from housework and mothering. Yet in almost all homes, women assumed the responsibility for domestic tasks, and motherhood usually followed quickly upon marriage. On the average, women in the 1950s had their first babies 1.3 years after their marriages. For a sizable minority, motherhood was the reason for marriage.

An estimated 20–25 per cent of all births among married white Americans occurred as the result of pre-marital pregnancy. These pregnancies contributed to the low median age of marriage in the 1950s because they were concentrated among teenagers rather than women in their 20s. Of the 50 white working-class couples Lillian Rubin studied in California, 44 per cent had married because the woman became pregnant. This occurred in the early and mid 1960s, when 80 per cent of these young couples engaged in sexual relations before marriage. Although the birth control pill was available, over three-fourths of the women used no form of contraception because they believed that only 'bad girls' planned in advance. Instead, they let themselves be 'carried away on the tide of some great, uncontrollable emotion', and then took sole responsibility for the pregnancy. None of them considered abortion. Both men and women assumed that pregnancy meant marriage. Their attitudes were somewhat more conventional than those of middle-class youth because they had fewer alternatives. Without the opportunity for higher education, marriage was often the only way such working-class youth could leave their parents' home. Getting married and setting up a residence of their own opened the way to adult status.

Even among middle-class youth a modified 'double standard' of sexual behaviour operated. That is, women were saying by the late 1950s and early 1960s that 'coitus is all right for men under any condition, but is acceptable for women only if they are in love'. Women still needed to employ the rhetoric of love and marriage in order to justify pre-marital intercourse. The desire simply to 'experiment' with sex was not yet accepted as a legitimate desire.[6]

Whether it was love or love-plus-pregnancy which led to marriage, the result was not identical for women and men. Romance alone could not bridge the social distance between them. As Helen Hacker pointed out in 1951, marriage simply perpetuated the inequality between the sexes. Unlike their treatment of socially 'inferior' ethnic and racial minorities, men were willing to accept women at the level of greatest intimacy while rejecting them at other levels. That is, a man 'may be willing to marry a member of a group which, in general, he would not wish admitted to his club'.[7]

Sociologists who stressed romance and companionship as the distinctive features of modern marriage were being more prescriptive than descriptive, especially when it came to the realities of working-class marriage. Mirra Komarovsky found an absence of close companionship among working-class couples in the late 1950s. Men and women did not turn to each other for emotional support and friendship because of 'the persistence of some traditional values and definitions of sex roles'. Women considered the breadwinner or provider role of a husband to be of greatest importance, followed by his duties as a father. His accomplishments as a lover and companion received far less attention.

A 1970s study found that working-class wives did want intimacy, companionship and sharing in their marriages, but were still not finding them. Although men and women were spending more time together in activities involving the whole family and fewer husbands maintained the 'right' to a night out with the 'boys', less than one-fourth of these couples went out together without their children as often as once a month. The separation between women's 'world' and men's remained wide. All that really changed over the years was a rise in women's expectations. They had incorporated the middle-class, romantic-companionship ideal from afternoon soap operas and other media. Their husbands, on the other hand, were bewildered by this new demand for emotional intimacy and could not respond.

For poor black and Hispanic women marriage did not promise even financial security. Because emotional love could not surmount joblessness, women, whether pregnant or not, were more likely to appraise a potential husband strictly in terms of his earnings. As one Puerto Rican welfare mother put it: 'I needed a man . . . for money, not for love . . . I couldn't support myself and two children.[8]

Marriage among poor and working-class people has thus been more 'sex-segregated' and task-oriented than romantic. The working-class husband and wife have clearly defined and differentiated work roles; they also have separate leisure interests and activities. Conversely, the 'joint role' marriage has been more typical among middle-class people, including a minimum of task differentiation and a greater likelihood of shared interests, activities and decision-making. Yet among affluent couples the ideal of companionship did not transcend actual power relations.

Marriage has contained large hidden pockets of domestic oppression for women. There have been, as Jessie Bernard pointed out, two marriages – his and hers – and his has been better. Traditionally, marriage has been considered more important for women, and more married than unmarried women have reported themselves as 'happy'. But this 'happiness' is often the female 'adjustment' to marriage, which frequently involves psychological diminishment and damage. More wives than single women were found to be passive, phobic and depressed; wives also suffered more nervous breakdowns and reported more nervousness, inertia, insomnia, headaches and dizziness. On the other hand, marriage improved men's mental health as well as having beneficial effects on their careers.

Much of the poor mental health of married women can be attributed more to the role of housewife than to the marital relationship itself. Married working woman had far better mental and emotional health than did full-time homemakers. On the other hand, employed wives had far less leisure time. Compared to their husbands, fewer of them engaged in study or pursued hobbies Rather, they spent their time at home in child care and housework, an average of five hours a day to their husbands' hour and a half.[9]

We saw in the last chapter that generally women were less successful than men in the job market. Even professional women deliberately kept their ambitions and incomes down in order not to 'emasculate' their husbands. The childless career wife in the 1950s continued to accept home management as her responsibility and played down her accomplishments. But as one commented: 'It is interesting, though, that it doesn't work the other way; that is, that he never needs to play down some business scoop and never has to back up *my* ego by disparaging himself.'[10]

The ideology of 'femininity' and 'masculinity' undermined equality in more intimate ways. Sexual relations outside legal marriage were frowned upon (though obviously they were practised), but within marriage sex was supposed to provide romantic intensity and communication between partners. No longer a wifely duty necessary for procreation, sex could be enjoyed as a legitimate pleasure. However, the 'modern' emphasis on marital happiness through sexual relations ignored women's inequality in other areas. Not surprisingly, women did not become men's equals in the bedroom.

With the legal and widespread use of mechanical contraceptive devices – the diaphragm and condom in the 1950s and the birth control pill in the 1960s – unlimited intercourse was possible. Other forms of sexual expression were relegated to the category of 'foreplay', which, as women complained, never lasted long enough. The Freudian model of female sexuality created a new problem of 'frigidity' in women. It not only insisted the 'vaginal orgasm' must replace the 'immature' clitoral orgasm, but it also prescribed the wrong method for attaining it – passivity and 'surrender' to the male's needs.

The Freudian hierarchy of female orgasm was finally disproved by Masters and Johnson's *Human Sexual Response* in the mid 1960s. A recent study estimates that only 30 per cent of women can reach orgasm regularly from intercourse alone, without more direct stimulation of the clitoris. Because intercourse is designed more for the male's than the female's orgasmic potential, it is necessary for women to be assertive (get on top of their partners, move around, etc.). But such involvement was impossible under what Ruth Herschberger (in 1948) called the Total Responsibility Theory, which insisted that the man was responsible for both his and his wife's satisfaction. With the burden of sexual virility totally on him, it is no wonder that he resented the recalcitrant 'frigid' woman. It is also not surprising that women faked orgasms. Although they worried about pleasing their partners, married couples found it hard to be honest with each other.[11]

On some level, women knew that marital sex was often 'male sex'. They admitted that they occasionally 'submitted' to intercourse regardless of their own disinclination. Only 30 per cent of the women in Komarovsky's *Blue-Collar Marriage* expressed high satisfaction with their sexual relations, and this figure included women who were content with emotional intimacy – minus orgasm. When the ideology changed so that both sexual partners were expected to achieve orgasm, the responsibility still remained with the male. As one woman expressed it, 'it's not enough if I just let him have it, because if I don't have a climax, he's not happy'. Another woman kept reassuring her husband that it was her fault, not his. 'But it scares me because he doesn't believe it, and I worry he might leave me for a woman who will have climaxes for him.'[12]

Older women found that as the risk of pregnancy diminished, the pressures of motherhood lessened and the demands of their husbands decreased, sexual relations improved. But these wives also faced a new problem: the need to hold back and repress their desire so as not to make their husbands feel inadequate or anxious. In spite of their increased knowledge and self-awareness, older women still responded to their husbands' initiatives and subdued their own sexuality. Without other changes within and outside the institution of marriage, sexual relations between men and women remained unequal.

The post-war period had encouraged an increased domesticity among men, especially suburban men. The stern, remote patriarch was giving way to the 'family man' who helped around the house, played with his children, and did not 'boss' his wife. But no one thought it proper for the wife to dominate in a marriage, and traditional sex roles limited democratic task-sharing and decision-making. In suburban families, housework was still sex-typed along the lines of an older rural pattern. A husband mainly did the 'heavy' outside work, such as lawn care and automobile maintenance, and his 'breadwinner' role meant he was absent from the home a good deal of the time.

Women's involvement in their husbands' work was, at best, indirect. Among working-class couples the split between 'his' world and 'hers' was greatest, and so was the likelihood that economic deprivation would contribute to marital tension. Sexual relations became anxious occasions because of the dread of an 'accidental' pregnancy. The wives of 'poor providers' had an obvious weapon at hand in a moment of anger, but most did not use it. They preserved harmony and masculine esteem by not talking of 'sensitive' subjects, only to find that more and more subjects became 'sensitive' when bills went unpaid. Adherence to patriarchal convictions resulted in a slightly dishonest relationship, but a show of female strength and independence only deepened a husband's gloom and lowered his self-esteem. Most working-class wives found that their economic power was limited to persuasion and many further limited their role to that of providing physical services and emotional support for the male worker.

Corporate and professional wives were generally more involved in their husbands' careers, but only if they accepted the male's work-centred priorities. As one sociologist expressed it, the key to a successful marriage with an upwardly mobile man was 'the degree to which the wife actively adopted the corporate goals and skillfully aided the husband in that direction.'[13] Among other things, she became his unpaid assistant and hostess and gave up friendships when they no longer served his business interests.

Although paid employment gave women more decision-making power in the family, men's salaries were greater and husbands continued to control household spending. On the surface, however, it appeared that working-class women dominated in this area. Rubin found that in three-fourths of her working-class families the women managed the money and paid the bills. Among professional, middle-class families, the men did. When a paycheck covered bare necessities and went for regular, fixed expenses, its disbursement was a woman's job. But when income reached a level where real decisions could be made, men took over.

In addition to men's greater financial power, the legitimacy granted to male authority inhibited egalitarian decision-making. Both spouses tended to attribute more decision-making power to the husband than he actually possessed. Wives underestimated their power; husbands overestimated theirs. For example, men exaggerated their ability to help their wives overcome 'bad moods', while underestimating how much they had contributed to those 'moods'. Women, on the other hand, held themselves responsible for their husbands' emotional states to a greater degree than was required of them.

Because women were socialised to expect more from marriage and to shoulder the responsibility for making it 'work', they also expressed more verbal dissatisfaction with certain aspects of the relationship. One of their most frequent complaints centred around the lack of empathy and companionship. Women tried to cajole or pressure their husbands into more expressions of affection, but most had to adjust to the men's lower level of demonstrativeness. They could not undo the sex-role socialisation which had trained men, especially in working-class homes, not to express their feelings except when angry or during sexual intercourse. As one man put it, 'Guys talk about things and girls talk about feelings'.[14]

Women found self-disclosure easier with other women, especially their mothers and sisters, than with their husbands. The majority of young working-class couples had some joint social life, but as they grew older they increasingly turned to same-sex companionship. Many husbands and wives found each others leisure interests 'boring' or incomprehensible because recreation was as sex-typed as work.

The daily lives of women were essentially husbandless. Women spent the majority of their waking hours at home with their children. Difficulties and satisfactions with children, not husbands, came spontaneously to their minds whenever they were questioned about the general problems of being a 'housewife'. Of the suburban women in Lopata's study 38 per cent said their greatest satisfaction was in motherhood, while only 8 per cent mentioned being a wife. Until the children were grown, motherhood overshadowed wifehood.

During the 1930s, 15 per cent of married women had remained childless; in the 1950s, it was less than 7 per cent, and the next decade saw only 4.4 per cent of married women not bearing children. The average number of children born per mother in the 1950s was 3.5, the highest since the first decade of the century. The ideal number of children during this time was four, compared to two in 1941, and it was women, rather than men, who expressed the desire for more children.

Along with the feminine mystique, which was extremely pro-natalist, an expanding economy and the larger surburban homes encouraged bigger families. Religion also played an important part in family size. Catholic women in every income bracket had more children than non-Catholics. Among other religious groups, the active or devout also had larger families than the less devout.

According to the 1960 Census, Spanish-surnamed women (generally Mexican-American) in the southwestern states tended to be 41 per cent more fertile than Anglos. Although the percentage of black women in the labour force in 1950 was 14 points above that of white women, their fertility rates were also higher. Black and

Chicano cultures valued children, but their high fertility rates also reflected their maternal and infant mortality rates, which were twice that of whites in 1960.

The birth of the first child changed the marital relationship. Usually sex roles became more traditional, with an increased separation between husband and wife and a loss of marital satisfaction for middle-class, educated couples. However, in the already role-segregated working-class marriage, children actually brought the couple closer together. Marriage itself had been regarded more as the basis for family life than as a relationship in itself.

The presence of young children in the home was a major deterrent to women's paid employment. The arrival of children was also the reason women gave for moving to the suburbs. So, until the 1970s, suburban women were less likely to be employed than urban women. Over 40 per cent of urban women were in the labour force in 1960, compared to 34 per cent of suburban women. Distances to activities outside the home, the lack of public transportation, and the time schedules imposed by household duties and child care made involvement outside the home more difficult. Suburban mothers of young children were likely to feel 'tied down'.

Few suburban women in the 1950s could analyse motherhood as an institution or see that 'the problem that has no name' was a socially created one. They did, however, feel the strain. Told that they had almost absolute power over helpless children, they also received warnings against 'possessing' their offspring. They were expected to prepare children for the larger society in an environment 'protected' from the problems, population mix and cultural variety of urban centres. Mothering was the most important work they as women would ever do, yet they received neither formal training nor a salary.

It is not surprising that mothers expressed worry, self-doubt and guilt, or what Adrienne Rich calls 'an undramatic, undramatized suffering' experienced by women caught in a cycle of debilitating ambivalence. Some felt a desire to commit violent acts, but child battering was not an acceptable fantasy. Female violence was more commonly turned inwards, such as wishing to 'go over the edge' and relinquish sanity in order to be taken care of oneself.[15]

Reliable statistics on female alcoholism and drug addiction are hard to come by, but a recent estimate is that one out of four women are threatened by legal drug and alcohol abuse. Female and male patterns have differed. In one study done in the 1950s, 35 per cent of the middle-class female alcoholics and 56 per cent of the lower-class women had husbands who were alcoholics, whereas only 9 per cent of male alcoholics had wives with the same problem. Women have been more likely than men to abuse drugs through legal prescriptions. This is partly because women tend to make greater use of health services, but physicians have also been willing to prescribe tranquillisers to women, especially to housewives. A survey done in 1971 of 4000 women found that housewives (25 per cent of the population) comprised 36 per cent of the habitual diet-pill users.[16]

Even if housework, rather than mothering, has been the chief cause of women's depression and substance abuse, it was generally impossible for women to separate their two jobs. Motherhood was the reason women stayed home where they, of course, also did housework. And, in spite of anxiety and self-doubt, mothering was the most satisfying domestic job they did.

There were and are as many styles of mothering as there are mothers. Middle-class mothers were more 'person' or 'relationship-oriented' with their children, while the working-class mother was more 'product-oriented'. That is, she wanted her children to turn out quiet, clean and well-behaved. Working-class mothers had to worry more about the daily routine of physical life than their own or their children's emotional states. Financial problems, poor schools and the inability to protect children from physical and social dangers outside the home were overriding concerns for poor urban mothers. Women not only reflected their own class in their style of mothering, they also reproduced that class. Working-class mothers stressed discipline and respect because their children would have to cope with directly authoritarian situations at school and work. Middle-class mothers, on the other hand, provided their children with the social and interpersonal skills they would need in professional and 'creative' occupations.

The socialisation of children was a product not only of socio-economic class, but also of ethnic culture. Black mothers have had to teach their daughters to be 'providers' as well as homemakers. Yet whatever the income level and family structure (two parents, female-headed, kinship group), a more egalitarian pattern with more role-sharing existed among black families. Black and other ethnic mothers were also expected to prepare their children both to imitate the standards of the culture in which they lived and to take on those needed for upward mobility in the dominant culture. This was not always possible. In low-income black homes, for example, few objects were available for babies to manipulate. Instead, there was a high degree of human, non-verbal interaction. Black children became more feeling-oriented, people-centred and more proficient at non-verbal communication than white children. Unfortunately, this cultural style put them at an academic disadvantage in white-dominated educational institutions.

Unlike white working-class parents, black people believed in equal education for boys and girls. Overall, black educational attainment lagged behind that of whites, but black men were not favoured over black women. Racial discrimination in employment was one reason why black mothers passed on to their daughters high educational and career aspirations. Until clerical work opened up in the 1960s, young black women would typically have to do domestic or other menial service work unless they could make a big leap (via education) and enter a profession, usually teaching or nursing. On the other hand, those mothers who were domestic workers themselves did not have the resources to provide a college education for their children. As with white working-class parents, 'Concern that their children grow up to be good, decent, law-abiding citizens was a dominant theme' heard among black mothers.[17]

As noted earlier, unmarried pregnancy was not universally stigmatised by the black community, but it did inhibit a black girl's educational attainment. There is a correlation between high educational level and older age at marriage and/or first birth for both black and white women. The major cultural difference was that black women had a stronger tradition (based on necessity) of economically independent women. The model of the *resourceful* woman was an influential one in the lives of black girls, whatever their eventual marital status or occupation might be.

No income or ethnic group totally escaped the general social preference for male children. During the Freudian era of the feminine mystique, sons gave mothers the chance to live vicariously the adventurous life prohibited to females. As a result, many mothers and daughters were disappointed with each other. Daughters did not receive enough physical nurturance. Neither could their mothers provide them with power and status the way their fathers could. During the 1960s, when political and educational opportunities opened up for young women, mother-daughter bonds became frayed. Women who wanted knowledge and careers had to turn to men for role models and practical assistance. The younger generation was not refusing maternity *per se*, but only the mystique of full-time, all-encompassing motherhood. Older women, however, felt their daughters were ungratefully rejecting them.

Middle-aged women, who had been the young mothers of the 1950s, were also vulnerable to marital loss. In 1973, when one out of three marriages ended in divorce, the percentage of women over the age of 40 obtaining a divorce was 18.3 per cent, up from 14 per cent in 1960. There was a greater chance of losing a husband just about the same time the job of mothering ended. Divorce also meant a loss of income, as the median income of divorced women who were full-time, year-round workers in 1977 was just 64 per cent of divorced men.

Because of the culture's double standard of aging, ex-wives were far less likely to marry again than their ex-husbands. It is perfectly acceptable for men to marry women fifteen or even twenty years younger than themselves, but generally unacceptable for women to marry men more than four or five years their junior. While three-quarters of divorced men remarry, only two-thirds of divorced women do. In 1975, middle-aged and older men, divorced or widowed, were more than twice as likely to remarry than women of similar age and circumstances, and this gender discrepancy was true during the 1940s as well.

Widowhood, even more than divorce, has meant economic hardship for older women. Companionate-style marriage among the young weakens their obligations to parents. Elderly women fall outside the circle of domesticity. Most of them do not wish to live with adult children; when they have to, it is generally with a daughter. Middle-aged daughters, rather than sons, are expected to provide care and even a home for a widowed parent.

Women of the 'fifties generation' have had a particularly hard time. After expanded and isolated motherwork in the suburbs, they risk divorce and loneliness, caring for an aged parent, and/or continued responsibilities for their adult children, who have required more 'mothering' than predicted. In the 1950s, few young parents realised that having more children while maintaining a birthspacing pattern of two years would later produce unprecedented financial pressure on them. The social requirement of four or more years of university education for skilled occupations and the high unemployment rate for youth has meant a longer period in which parents must carry the economic responsibilities of child-rearing. Parents found themselves supporting two young adult children through college simultaneously. In 1969, child care costs were 97 per cent higher than ten years earlier, but the earnings of older men were only 15 per cent higher than those of younger workers.[18] Many mothers in the workforce are still fulfilling their traditional role of working for others.

Middle-aged employed women are, at least, making a better investment for their old age than married women who remain full-time housekeepers. As unpaid labour, housework carries no retirement pension or work credits toward old-age social security benefits. The older 'housewife' remains dependent upon her husband's benefits under a system which still assumes that marriage is a stable institution.

Housework, the third of women's domestic jobs, has no male equivalent. Men are husbands and fathers but not 'houseworkers'. Unlike any other job in modern industrial society, housework is associated with economic dependence on the part of the sex doing it. Although many tasks, such as growing food, baking bread, and making clothes, left the home, housework did not disappear. At a time when women were entering the paid workforce in increasing numbers, post-war suburbanisation, the consumer economy and the tenets of the feminine mystique entrenched women in the home and romanticised the 'housewife' role. Like motherhood, housework was regarded as an inherent part of gender identity, rather than a job. Unlike motherhood, women have not seen housework as more creative, interesting or important than other activities they might be doing. Even in the 1950s, they complained that housework was boring and menial.

Household technology lightened some of the physical labour, but did not decrease the hours women spent on housework because new tasks were created and standards of cleanliness were raised. Laundry is one example. The washing machine shifted this job from the commercial laundry back to women at home. Along with the electric iron, hot water heater and manufactured soap powders, the washing machine eliminated some of the drudgery of washday. But now, as advertisers urged, women could wash and iron more often.

Full-time, middle-class housewives, as recently as the 1960s, did not avail themselves of commercial services. Of the women in Lopata's study 85 per cent never called upon a housecleaner; over half never hired a babysitter or took clothes to a laundry. Most of them made only occasional use of repair shops, but over half went to the beauty shop at least once a month and one-fourth of them went once or twice a week. The frequency of this form of self-repair/improvement indicated not only the cultural importance of female attractiveness but also women's need for sociability and personalised service not found in other forms of shopping. Food purchasing, for example, was mostly done in large chain supermarkets.

In addition to having sole responsibility for higher standards of household cleanliness and personal 'upkeep', the housewife acquired several new tasks. Child care took up more time. Even before the post-war emphasis on the child's psychology, mothers were expected to prepare infant formulae, sterilise bottles, weigh the baby every day, transport older children to music and dancing lessons, and consult frequently with their teachers. Contemporary women spend about one full working day per week on travel time and in stores, compared to less than two hours per week in the 1920s. While food preparation and cleaning up after meals have become less time-consuming, women spend increased time in child care, shopping and laundry. The total amount of time spent on housework has remained the same. In 1924, full-time homemakers, urban and rural, devoted about 52 hours a week to housework; in the 1960s, it was 55 hours.[19]

There was one major change: married women in the 1950s and 1960s were entering the labour force. While labour-saving devices were not the direct cause, they did play an indirect and delayed role. Housework had become more menial by the shift from home production to maintenance and consumption chores and by the disappearance of servants. The middle-class housewife was no longer a household and personnel manager, but rather a chauffeuse, charwoman and short-order cook. The completely unspecialised and repetitive nature of housework caused dissatisfaction. Women spoke of feeling 'empty' or 'incomplete', as though they 'didn't exist'. In 1949, Edith Stein wrote that housewifery was similar to slavery, especially in the lack of pay and mind-numbing qualities. Housework meant 'hopping from one unrelated, unfinished task to another . . . nothing leads quite logically from one thing to another'. Stein, like Betty Friedan, was thinking mainly of the educated, middle-class woman, whose confinement to the home was a 'loss to society'.[20]

As housework became less satisfying as work, it was infused with sentiment. Like the consumer society, the emotionalisation of housework began after the First World War and was in full swing during the 1950s. Household tasks were not depicted as onerous chores to be accomplished efficiently, but as expressions of wifely and motherly love. Advertisements informed women that if they truly cared for their families they would launder and clean more frequently. Women in ads were portrayed as feeling guilty if their children went to school in scuffed shoes or soiled clothes, if all the 'germs' behind the bathroom sink were not eradicated, if 'tell-tale' odours lingered in the kitchen, if their coffee tables did not shine like mirrors. In order to earn her child's love and trust, a mother must even be free of 'bad breath'. 'The problem that has no name' was the outcome of this discrepancy between the emotional weight given to housework and the reality of the physically taxing, monotonous and isolated labour women were performing.

Employed women cut their housework in half. In contrast to the 52–56 hour week of the full-time housewife, working women spent only 26 hours on household tasks. Paid work allowed women to purchase labour-saving technology or commercial services as well as providing a legitimate excuse to lower housekeeping standards. In this way, they half-solved the problem of housework without directly confronting the domestic mystique. However, compressing housework into fewer hours still meant a total work week of about 65 hours for employed women. They enjoyed less leisure time than their husbands because housework was not shared equally. Husbands averaged 1.6 hours a day in housework whether or not their wives were employed, and this changed very little from 1955 to the early 1970s.

Domestic inequality did not inevitably lead to marital conflict because many employed women did not expect their husbands to do 'woman's work'. Working-class women felt they had no 'right' to complain. The male's breadwinner role was far more important than how much he helped with housework, although as one wife remarked, 'when I'm working, I sure wish I could have more help. With five kids and all, it's hard to work and do everything yourself.'[21] Housework was part of the marriage 'contract', and working-class women blamed themselves when they performed it poorly. They did not express the view, common to middle-class housewives, that they were too 'intelligent' to be doing menial work. This did not necessarily mean that working-class women liked housework. Rather, women in each class compared their work with their husbands', and working-class women found less discrepancy. If distinction is made between attitudes towards the *role* of *housewife* and *feelings* about *housework*, the working-class women were more likely to have a positive attitude towards the role and a more traditional attitude towards its 'appropriateness' for women than did middle-class women.

Housework is actually many jobs, and husbands were more willing to share the desirable ones. Men helped with shopping, cooking and laundry, but not with regular cleaning and ironing. Because men had greater power in the family, they were able to shirk the more monotonous and recurrent maintenance chores. Their assistance with child care was generally in the areas of 'play' and 'education' rather than in routine physical clean-up. While father romped with the children and told them bedtime stories, mother had time to wash and iron their clothes. The enlargement of the father's role, especially in middle-class families, deprived women of the most pleasurable aspects of housework and mothering.

Here, then, was further reason for female discontent with housework, but as we have seen, a number of factors made conscious, collective awareness difficult. Female domesticity was encapsulated within the myth of motherhood. As housework became less interesting, women invested more emotional commitment and time in mothering. The structure of the post-war suburban family isolated the mother-child unit from outside adult assistance and reinforced the myths of motherhood and the 'private' family.

The typical response to frustration remained individual. In addition to employment, women sought other activities to get them out of the house. Volunteer work attracted 22 million women in the mid 1960s. Six out of every ten American volunteers were women and three-fourths of them were married. The monetary worth of their volunteer work was estimated at US$14.2 billion. Voluntarism has been called 'a vast but hidden subculture of

American women's lives', and it has contributed immeasurably to social welfare and community maintenance. The work itself can range from traditional feminine nurturing/mothering tasks in service and religious enterprises to struggles for political and social change.

Women of the upper class have a long history as both patrons of culture and directors of social welfare projects. They have provided the more 'human' and 'soft' side of capitalism by taking 'some of the roughest edges off a profit-oriented business system that has cared little for specific human needs'.[22] Wealthy women maintain 'elite' culture by serving on the boards of trustees for museums and orchestras. They organise special programmes, such as educational series for children, raise funds, and serve as unpaid guides in cultural institutions. Some have taken on patron functions by underwriting the expense of a new opera or by demanding that museums display contemporary work.

The volunteer work of upper-class women is usually well publicised, but most women's community work, like their work in the home, has remained hidden. Studies have tended to overlook women's neighbouring and informal community involvement. They have neglected the settings in which women gather, such as parks and beauty parlours, and have over-emphasised men's spaces: bars and street corners. Then, they characterise working-class women as 'non-joiners', inextricably bound to the home.

It would be more accurate to say that working-class women in the 1950s had a low *institutional* participation. Komarovsky, for example, in *Blue-Collar Marriage*, found that almost one-third of the women belonged to no organised group and another third were only in church-affiliated groups. Yet she noted that these women maintained frequent visiting relationships with relatives and neighbours, far exceeding that of their husbands. Middle-class suburban women tended to be 'joiners', but only if they were college graduates.

Young suburban women frequently turned to each other for help. They shared household and child-rearing knowledge with each other. In new communities, there were arrangements for borrowing and lending tools and exchanging babysitting, transportation, shopping and other services.

We can, in retrospect, point to these informal suburban networks as potential bases for feminist 'consciousness-raising' groups, but the post-war period itself, from 1945 to the mid 1960s, was a low point in female political activism. While this reflected the prevailing conservatism discussed in Chapter 1, there were also less obvious institutional reasons. Education and social work had become increasingly professionalised. Educational reform, a traditional concern for women, was rendered inaccessible to them. Although women joined parent organisations, such as the PTA (Parents and Teachers Association), the organisations themselves had adopted policies and procedures that prevented parents from altering administrative decisions.

Women's volunteer activities during the anti-communist 'McCarthy' era were, understandably, more in the nature of service-oriented work which maintained the status quo than in change-oriented activities. Nevertheless, non-political organisations provided a training ground in which women might learn political attitudes and skills.

Women Strike for Peace provided one organisational bridge to the women's movement. Thousands of women became politicised in the early 1960s because they were concerned about their children's future. This peace movement began before the war in Southeast Asia had generated widespread public protest; its primary concern was to stop nuclear testing. The women who became involved were not feminists, but middle-class mothers worried about the contamination of their children's milk by strontium-90. The House Committee on Un-American Activities believed that the women's peace movement was communist inspired. But the women themselves insisted that they were 'simply mothers who want their children to grow up and live in peace'.[23]

Women Strike for Peace indicated the political potential of traditional feminine concerns. Its organisational form was also prophetic. It was (and remains) a grass-roots network with rotating leadership, not an organisation with a formal hierarchy. While this arrangement was a practical response to women's lack of time and home responsibilities, by the end of the 1960s 'leaderless' groups and grass-roots organising would become important feminist principles.

Welfare mothers provided another example of increasing political consciousness growing out of traditional concerns and networks. The core of poor black and Puerto Rican women's social interaction has been with each other: sharing goods and time and exchanging child care. This sharing has been a survival strategy in poverty-level communities, a form of 'insurance' that something will come one's way in times of scarcity. Such social networks also had the potential to generate and sustain community action.

In the early 1960s, a number of small neighbourhood groups of welfare mothers existed in the larger cities of Minnesota. Initially led by social workers, not welfare recipients, they were limited to discussing members' welfare and personal problems. There was no overt criticism of the welfare system. But between 1964 and 1972, a welfare rights movement formed out of groups like these. The movement replaced the emphasis on self-help with criticism of the system. The Minnesota Welfare Rights Organization and others around the country challenged the notion of welfare recipients as passive 'clients' and insisted on their rights as 'citizens'. Although these groups were not specifically feminist, they allowed women not reached by other movements to become activists for personal and political change.

Participation in church activities was another way working-class women developed self-confidence and leadership skills. The black domestic worker, ignored by the white world, achieved a different status in her own community as president of her church's missionary society. In the South, the black church became one of the principal institutional bases – along with the black colleges – for political change through the Civil Rights Movement.

In the Movement's early stages, black women and girls were at the forefront. Although Martin Luther King, Jr, is always credited as the national leader, it was the arrest and conviction of Rosa L. Parks for purposely violating a bus segregation ordinance which led to the Montgomery (Alabama) bus boycott at the end of 1955, and to eventual integration of Montgomery's buses. Autherine Lucy Foster, in February 1956, became the first black student to sit in a University of Alabama classroom. However, after she was physically attacked by a mob, the university expelled her.

Young women and girls were in the front line of desegregation efforts at Southern elementary and high schools: Central High School in Little Rock, Arkansas (1957) and elementary schools in New Orleans and Atlanta (1960). Girls along with boys faced mob violence outside the schools and suffered verbal and physical abuse from their white classmates. Although vastly outnumbered, the high school girls in Little Rock found ways of fighting back. Carlotta Walls described her retaliation against a white girl:

> I turned suddenly and stepped on her foot. But hard! I smiled at her and called her a few choice names, and I told her what I'd do to her if she didn't leave me alone. And each time I saw her after that, I smiled, pretty like. And you know what? She didn't come near me anymore today.[24]

Minnijean Brown, another Little Rock student, was suspended by the school authorities, after she emptied her lunch tray on the heads of two boys who had tormented her. The boys admitted they deserved it.

These young black women and others like them, rather than upper-class cultural workers or white middle-class volunteers, became the preferred role models for numerous activist women during the 1960s.

PART II: THE WOMEN'S MOVEMENT: ROOTS AND BRANCHES

The revival of feminism in the second half of the twentieth century has developed into one of the world's most important liberation movements. The five chapters in Part II are devoted to the origins and activities of the Women's Movement in the United States.

Contemporary American feminism has its roots in the Black Civil Rights Movement and the New Left of the 1960s, the subject of Chapter 4, as well as the youthful Counterculture, covered in Chapter 5. Women's participation in these political and cultural movements provided them with non-traditional political experiences, radical ideas about themselves and society, opportunities to create alternative institutions, and finally, an awareness of the discrepancy between articulated egalitarian ideals and unquestioned sexist practices.

The politics of the Women's Movement (Chapter 6), especially those of radical feminists, not only drew upon women's experiences as Civil Rights and New Left activists, but also questioned women's roles in these movements and in American society generally. The Counterculture's emphasis on sexual relationships and alternatives to the nuclear family, as well as its diverse experiments in art, media and religion, influenced both feminist sexual politics (Chapter 7) and women's culture (Chapter 8), particularly in the areas of education, art and spirituality.

The politicalisation of gender has been one of the major contributions of the Women's Movement. Feminists have not only included women's values and needs in public policy formation, but they have also transformed formerly 'private' and 'personal' areas of life into social concerns.

On the other hand, the conservatism of American politics, the persistence of patriarchal attitudes and economic inequalities, and the limitations of the Women's Movement itself have prevented any radical resolution of institutionalised sexism. It is, therefore, appropriate to use the present tense in Chapters 6, 7 and 8, even though the Women's Movement is currently being transformed in two important directions: increased awareness of class and race issues within the US, and greater attention to global problems and perspectives.

4. Women in the Political Movements of the 1960s

The Civil Rights Movement became the catalyst and model for other movements, including women's liberation. During the 1960s women became politically active, first on behalf of others and then for themselves. This chapter will trace the political roots of women's liberation in the Civil Rights Movement and the New Left.

A liberal political climate which accepts reform appears to be a prerequisite for more radical social movements. Although Betty Friedan's *The Feminine Mystique* (1963) was a slighter and less radical work than Simone de Beauvoir's *The Second Sex*, its appearance coincided with more propitious attention paid to women. The report of the Commission on the Status of Women, the Equal Pay Act and the 1964 Civil Rights Act sustained Friedan's message by providing women with some legal weapons against sex discrimination. The National Organization for Women (NOW) was founded in 1966 in order to integrate women into the public-political sphere. As a lobby for women's rights, NOW was dedicated to providing women with employment and political opportunities equal to those of men. Like the early Civil Rights Movement, NOW expected to accomplish its goals within the existing liberal political framework. By the time it was founded, however, the black and student movements had moved beyond liberalism. Not much attention was paid to the liberal wing of the women's movement until the more radical women's liberationists emerged a few years later. A few of those who became radical feminists gained their first political experience in NOW, but most had their apprenticeship in the Civil Rights and New Left movements.

The Civil Rights Movement and especially the New Left were peopled mainly by the young. Both movements, in the beginning, articulated liberal, reformist ideas. Movement participants saw their actions as goads to the national conscience; that is, they challenged public opinion and political elites to live up to accepted American values – equal opportunity, fair play and individual 'fulfilment'. They used direct action tactics to get existing laws enforced and court decisions implemented. By the mid 1960s, each movement was disenchanted with the liberal state as a source of redressing social wrongs. As the ideology and practice of movement leaders grew more radical, they became increasingly out of touch with their less politicised potential followers. Later in the decade, the black and student movements also experienced internal conflicts and divisions, partly due to increased government surveillance, infiltration and repression.

Women's involvement in the 1960s political movements both provided a necessary stage in political evolution and limited the early feminist movement mainly to white, middle-class women.

During the first half of the 1960s, economic growth seemed to substantiate the liberal tenet that social problems could be solved without class conflict or redistribution of existing wealth. From 1961 to 1965 the gross national product grew at more than twice the rate of 1956–60. Unemployment declined steadily; the weekly buying power of a worker with three dependants increased by 13 per cent from 1961 to 1965. Also, this expansion was not yet accompanied by inflation.

The demand for more skilled white-collar workers in service and professional jobs coincided with an increase of the youth population. In 1960, 15 per cent of Americans were between 14 and 24; by 1970, the figure was 20 per cent. Institutions of higher education were training not only the future members of the corporate and government elite, but also the middle-level and technical staff under them. With the help of government loans and scholarships, new groups of young people were going to college – more women, blacks and working-class students. At the end of the Second World War, slightly under one-fifth of the 18–21 year olds were enrolled, but by the early 1970s, roughly half of that age group were found in post-secondary educational institutions. The 1960s began with close to 3,800,000 people in college and ended with over 7,800,000.

In addition to increased education, the more affluent students reared in comfortable suburbs had received a great deal of loving attention from their mothers. Spockean child-bearing imbued the younger generation with the belief that they were 'special' and talented, and the world would be good to them. They had also grown up in an atmosphere of moral rhetoric, directed at the evils of communism. Upon discovering the extent of the gap between American ideals and actual institutional practices, many reacted with shock and moral outrage.

Thousands of young women experienced a further discrepancy between ideals and actualities. The social role of the housewife which they were expected to fill not only conflicted with their new intellectual confidence at school, but also with their political ideals of 'freedom' and 'equality'. Young women who were displaying 'unfeminine' traits of self-assertion and initiative as students and organisers disliked being treated as sex objects and housekeepers by their 'brothers' in the movement. The reproduction of traditional feminine roles in radical circles clashed with the ideals of liberation and autonomy found in those same groups.

Women's experience in the Civil Rights Movement and the New Left represented in microcosm a more intense version of the dilemma affecting many other women. That is why formerly non-activist women responded to feminism when it emerged as a separate movement. Due to their changing circumstances in the 1960s, middle-class women felt a sense of 'relative deprivation'. They were not poor, or absolutely deprived, but they perceived a gap between what they believed they were rightfully entitled to and what they could attain under existing social conditions.

In 1950, only 24 per cent of bachelor's and professional degrees went to women; by 1968, women were earning 43.5 per cent of these degrees. Most of the increase occurred between 1960 and 1965. Nonetheless, while the educational preparation of women began to approximate that of men, their share of occupational rewards declined. Raised with higher expectations and more education than their mothers, women found themselves having to accept the same jobs as clerical, sales and service workers.[1]

The younger generation, however, came of age in a more politicised decade, when reliance on psychological 'adjustment' and private solutions was changing to a more political approach and confrontational style. The activists of the 1960s, more middle-class than working-class, did not intend simply a revival of Marxist ideology or the organised left. Their ideas were eclectic; they rejected 'revolutionary discipline' and top-down authority, and set out to change not only social institutions but also personal consciousness. They also favoured direct action as a means of 'bearing witness' to social wrongs.

Such Christian imagery pervaded the work of women in the Civil Rights Movement, and they carried it over, in a more secular form, into the New Left. Of the three main groups of women who were active in the Southern Civil Rights Movement – white Southern women, black women (mainly Southerners), and, later, Northern white women – the first two generally had religious backgrounds. Sara Evans found that virtually every white Southern woman who participated in the early years of the movement 'came to it first through the Church'.[2] The Methodist Student Movement, the Young Women's Christian Association (YWCA), and a number of campus ministries provided avenues for Southern white women to meet black students and to question Southern mores from a religious perspective. In many rural Southern communities, the church was the only independent black cultural institution. Unlike educators, black ministers were not under the jurisdiction of white-run school boards and racist state legislators. Black churches were often the only places where Civil Rights activists could meet.

The religious content of the Civil Rights Movement was clearly expressed in the work of the Student Nonviolent Coordinating Committee (SNCC), founded in 1960. 'Moral radicalism' is the most accurate way to describe SNCC's ideology before 1965. SNCC's Founding Statement began by affirming the 'philosophical or religious ideal of nonviolence as the foundation of our purpose, the presupposition of our belief, and the manner of our action'. Non-violence 'seeks a social order of justice permeated by love', in which, 'Acceptance dissipates prejudice; hope ends despair', and, 'The redemptive community supersedes immoral social systems'. The activists themselves were the nucleus of this 'beloved' or 'redeemed community', whose actions and example would free others from the 'sin' of segregation.

Non-violence had strong emotional appeal because it was used militantly in sit-ins and other forms of direct action. Diane Nash, an SNCC leader from Fisk University (Nashville, Tennessee), saw the sit-in movement as an attempt to create a 'beloved community' in which there was 'appreciation of the dignity of man and in which each individual [was] free to grow and produce to his fullest capacity'.[3]

Nash's emphasis on individual potential and self-realisation was congruent with mainstream liberal ideals. Early movement leaders could easily move between religious and liberal rhetoric. Although the liberal goal of legal equality did not fully incorporate the movement's vision of community or recompense activists for their bravery and sacrifices, liberalism was the only political language they had. Most black students shared the prevailing anti-communist sentiments and few espoused Black Nationalism before the mid 1960s.

The mixture of moral and liberal values, backed by direct action, was intended to expose the discrepancies between the American ideal of 'equality of opportunity' and the realities of life for American blacks. Such exposure would prod liberal conscience and speed the pace of social change. When it soon became obvious that white Southerners were not being converted to the cause of black civil rights, movement activists addressed themselves mainly to the federal government. Civil Rights workers first insisted that the Justice Department enforce existing legislation, implement court decisions, and protect citizens exercising their constitutional rights. Subsequently, they organised the Mississippi Freedom Democratic Party in an attempt to replace the all-white Democratic Party in the South with an interracial alternative.

The Southern Civil Rights Movement was largely a black-led movement. Although SNCC was a racially integrated organisation until the mid 1960s, the large influx of Northern whites occurred only during the summer of 1964. Initially the protesters were the most advantaged group of blacks – college students. As one early leader said: 'In really analyzing it, the only people in the black community at that time who were free to take on the Establishment were college kids.'[1] Despite the physical risks involved in Civil Rights work, young black women participated almost as often as men. Almost one-half – 48 per cent – of the early protesters were women. Students such as Diane Nash and Ruby Doris Smith (Robinson) were early leaders, engaging in the most dangerous activities and getting jailed for their efforts. However, not all the black women leaders were students. Women such as Fannie Lou Hamer of Sunflower County, Mississippi, Amelia Boynton in Selma, Alabama, and Carolyn Daniels in Terrill County, Georgia, were only a few of the movement 'mamas' who sheltered younger Civil Rights workers and provided active support. The strength and perseverance of these older women, as well as the daring of the younger ones, produced new role models for Southern, and later Northern, white women.

The resourcefulness and survival skills which had been part of black female heritage were missing in white female socialisation. Casey Hayden, Jane Stembridge, Mary King, Dorothy Dawson Burlage, and other Southern white women who were pioneers in the Civil Rights Movement had to create a new meaning of womanhood for themselves. They first had to battle the enemy within: the image of Southern ladyhood. Southern notions of white womanhood, especially the 'defence' of female sexual 'purity', had been traditionally used to justify violence against blacks. The passivity and delicacy admired in the 'lady' were the opposite of the qualities needed for movement work. These customary attitudes blocked social change, so white Southern women had to break both with traditional sex roles and with disapproving parents and communities.

They had few older role models of their own race. Lillian Smith was too old and ill to be active herself, but she tried to inspire younger women by pointing out that 'Southern women have never been as loyal to the ideology of race and segregation as have Southern men'.[5] One of the most important of these 'disloyal' women was Anne Braden. 'I always considered I had a mission in life to get women out of the kitchen and involved in things.'[6] Long before the 1960s, she and her husband Carl had been committed to liberal and labour causes as well as racial justice. The Bradens had had to endure a great deal of 'red-baiting', but this did not keep younger people away. Many of the whites who worked with SNCC before 1964 had close ties with the Bradens.

Young black women found more support from their elders and sanctuary within their communities. The courage of the young aroused the older people and made them impatient for change. Yet there were generational differences among blacks and within the Civil Rights Movement itself. The uneasy relationship between Martin Luther King's Southern Christian Leadership Conference (SCLC), dominated by ministers, and the student-led SNCC was one illustration. Ella Baker, an older black activist, was the executive secretary of SCLC, but she felt uncomfortable in the male-dominated organisation and with King's leadership style. Baker's theory was that 'strong people don't need strong leaders'. She was, therefore, pleased with the tendency toward 'group-centred' leadership she found in SNCC, and in August 1960 she left SCLC and went to work for SNCC.[7]

SNCC did have elected leaders and an organisational structure, but local projects enjoyed a great deal of autonomy. The open and fluid character of SNCC and its lack of ideological rigidity allowed ideals and projects to be shaped and changed by the actual experience of activists. SNCC workers were supposed to be brothers and sisters. Some of this community spirit did exist, growing out of shared experiences in protest and organising. There was even a kind of 'counterculture' based on voluntary poverty, communal living and protest songs adapted from black spirituals.

Because the Civil Rights Movement existed in order to combat the system of white supremacy by empowering black people, sex oppression seemed a secondary, if not trivial, issue, and its emergence was overshadowed by increasing racial division in the movement. The disparities between women's and men's position became clear only during the Freedom Summers of 1964 and 1965, when 650 Northern white women went to work in the Southern Civil Rights Movement. Such awareness, however, coincided with the ascendancy of 'Black Power', as black anger at whites was surfacing within the movement as well as in society generally. On SNCC projects, black hostility was directed more at white women than at men. One form it took was that black men tested their 'manhood' by breaking the most potent Southern taboo against sexual access to white women.

Volunteers for the summer projects were counselled during orientation sessions to be discreet in their sex lives, both to prevent alienating the religious black rural communities in which they were going to live and work and to lessen the chance of retaliation by white bigots. Nevertheless, interracial sex was widespread during the summers of 1964 and 1965. Not all of these sexual liaisons were exploitive. Voter registration, community organising and setting up alternative 'freedom schools' in the deep South were all highly dangerous activities. Movement workers suffered from homesickness, exhaustion, despair, frustration and fear — all the signs of 'battle fatigue'. They needed and sought comfort and warmth from each other. Some couples also believed that physical intimacy was a way of practising the ideal of the 'beloved community'.

Unfortunately, many of the sexual encounters were not motivated by love or even desire. White women volunteers were put in a painful double bind, making it almost impossible to pass the 'sexual test'. If they refused black men, they were called 'racists' – the worst epithet of all. They were then more vulnerable to subsequent advances and unlikely to see them as sexual harassment. Women who yielded risked not only being thought 'loose' and 'not serious', but were open to charges of being a 'danger' to the safety of their co-workers. The new white volunteers bore the brunt of male chauvinism, but they were not in a position to combat or even name it.

Black women did not support them; instead, interracial jealousy and resentment surfaced. Cynthia Washington contends that she and other black women 'did the same work as men. . . . But when we finally got back to some town where we could relax and go out, the men went out with other women. Our skills and abilities were recognized and respected, but they seemed to place us in some category other than female.' Or, as another black woman said: 'We became amazons, less than and more than women at the same time.'[8]

Although racial solidarity had a moral and political priority that shared womanhood lacked, it was black women, followed closely by 'long term' white Southern women, who first challenged male chauvinism. In 1964, black women in the Atlanta SNCC office held a half-serious, half-joking sit-in to protest against the assignment of almost all the typing and clerical work to women. That same year the first feminist position paper was presented at a SNCC staff retreat. It was actually written by two white women, Casey Hayden and Mary King, but everyone thought the unsigned paper was the work of Ruby Doris Smith Robinson. Black women had been such important role models in SNCC that most white women 'believed that if anyone could be expected to write such a paper, it would be black women'.[9]

Sexual exploitation was only one of the problems women faced. In the 'freedom houses' where Civil Rights workers lived, almost all of the housework fell to the women. In the 'field' the work was often assigned by sex. Women, especially if white, were given the less dangerous tasks as freedom school teachers, librarians and project office workers. Voter registration was more of a 'man's job'. Canvassing plantations in order to register black sharecroppers was almost a paramilitary operation. The owner was usually a powerful and prominent white citizen who viewed voter registration as an invasion of his land. Only the best drivers were picked to go down the private road leading into and out of the plantation, and all the drivers were men. No women were sent to register voters on plantations during the summer of 1964. The following year women were canvassing, but this resulted from the expansion of local control over projects, not from a conscious decision to widen women's work in the movement.

The failure of the black-led Mississippi Freedom Democratic Party to unseat the regular all-white Mississippi delegation at the Democratic Party's 1964 convention marked a turning point in the Civil Rights Movement. Increased racial polarisation and the rise of 'Black Power' dissipated the opportunity to form an interracial feminist movement. Equally important were long-standing differences between black and white women which preceded their involvement in Civil Rights work. The problem of sexism and its relative importance was perceived along racial lines.

Both the 'sexual test' mentioned earlier and the sexual division of labour on Civil Rights projects affected white women more than black. In fact, black women complained that while white women were doing domestic tasks 'in a feminine kind of way, . . . [we] were out in the streets battling with the cops'.[10] Because black women had never been put on a pedestal, they did not see political work as a break with traditional concepts of womanhood to the same degree as whites did. It was still assumed in the mid 1960s that young women should be 'settled' into their 'true vocations' as wives and mothers by their early 20s. Many white women felt they had only a brief time to act on their political beliefs. Unlike black women or even white men, full-time political activism was permissible only as a 'phase' of their youth. None of the white female radicals could yet challenge or discard what seemed to be the inevitability of the traditional wife-mother role. At the same time, their feminism was being nurtured by the contradictions they were experiencing: on the one hand, their new strength, confidence and rebelliousness, and, on the other, the expectation that they would continue to play the old roles, even in the very movement where new possibilities for personal growth were being opened to them.

Black women perceived independence and dependence differently. They defined themselves simultaneously in relationship to men and as independent beings. For white women, nurturance and autonomy were polarised; one meant the loss of the other. Independence in the form of political activism or career commitment was incompatible with the privatised wife-mother role. The division between 'public' and 'private' was not as sharp for black women. They were taught to maintain and preserve both their families and their communities. One might say that the survival of the black community was a 'family matter'. Black women could extend the maternal role to supportive work in the movement, without experiencing conflict in female identity.

This meant, however, that black women were restricted to internal affairs. Gloria Joseph has described the sex division in the Civil Rights Movement: 'Black women were very active on a local level and assumed positions of leadership within this sphere. However, when the situation called for face-to-face encounters with White society, it was the men in the groups who were called upon.' She added that the reason prominent and popular black leaders during the 1960s were men was due to 'a conscious and willing decision on the part of women as well as men to send the men forth'.[11]

Racial tension was already high when the unsigned position paper on women appeared at SNCC's staff retreat in November 1964. Although male supremacy was documented with concrete examples, the authors compared women's position in SNCC with that of blacks in white-dominated society. 'Assumptions of male superiority are as widespread and deep rooted and every much as crippling to the woman as the assumptions of white supremacy are to the Negro.' Stokely Carmichael ridiculed them by remarking that 'The only position for women in SNCC is prone'.

The following year King and Hayden wrote their 'memo' on 'Sex and Caste', an invitation to politically active women to change a sexual 'caste system which, at its worst, uses and exploits women'. 'Having learned from the movement to think radically about the personal worth and abilities of people whose role in society had gone unchallenged before, a lot of women in the movement have begun trying to apply those lessons to their own relations with men.'[12] The paper was not a call for a separate feminist movement, but an 'in-house' memo to activists in the black liberation and student movements.

Although black women had been the first to challenge sex-role stereotypes by their deeds and example, they could not turn away from the struggle against racial oppression. White women could deal more simply with sexism. When feminist consciousness surfaced a few years later in the New Left, it was not only due to the groundwork which had been laid by women in the Civil Rights Movement, but also because the New Left was not multiracial.

Black Nationalism forced white activists to create their own politics. First students and then women drew the implication from Black Nationalism that each group had to analyse its own particular oppression. Next, it had to create its own organisations. Although predominantly white, the women's movement learned from the example of 'Black Power' the necessity of creating a new consciousness and identity. An oppressed group had to move beyond seeking 'integration' into a white or male 'mainstream' or appealing to liberal conscience for redress. Rather, black people (and later, white women), in the words of Stokely Carmichael and Charles V. Hamilton, had to 'redefine themselves, and only *they* can do that'. Redefinition involved reclaiming 'their history, their culture' and creating 'their own sense of community and togetherness'.

Black Power also challenged traditional habits of dependency. It was necessary 'to establish a viable psychological, political and social base upon which the black community can function to meet its needs' before entering into coalitions with other groups. By replacing an internalised sense of inferiority with pride, Black Power encouraged a reassessment, and even rejection, of 'white' values and norms, including individualism.

> The power must be that of a community, and emanate from there. . . . The goal of black self-determination and black self-identity – Black Power – is full participation in the decision-making processes affecting the lives of black people.[13]

The Women's Movement, unlike, for example, the Black Panthers, did not emphasise armed self-defence or teach that 'political power grows out of the barrel of a gun'. In contrast to black people, white women found the family to be a primary source of oppression. A further important difference was that of economic status, but the Black Liberation movement itself did not clearly analyse class structure in capitalist society. The early feminist critique of 'patriarchy' also left the area of economic class somewhat undeveloped. Although the New Left had, in its late stage, incorporated a Marxist perspective, it was too derivative of foreign models to be of much help to the Women's Movement. The genuine contributions of the New Left were its innovations in organisational process and its connection of the personal with the political.

The developing theory of a relationship between 'personal' and 'political' emerged as a three-stage process. In the first stage, political action changed the involved individual. By connecting with a larger community, the person gained a new source of strength and a different relationship with history and society. Black people active in the Civil Rights Movement gained a new knowledge of society and a changed concept of themselves. The black writer Alice Walker is only one of many who felt that the movement gave her a new life. 'It has been like being born again, literally', she wrote in 1967.[14] Many white female Civil Rights activists also felt themselves personally changed as a result of their political involvement.

The second stage had two parts: first, acknowledging that personal feelings – hope, frustration, anger – are legitimate motives for political involvement; then, integrating these feelings into political history and practice. This stage was found in the Civil Rights Movement, but it was especially obvious in the New Left. Politics became subjective as well as objective. Women in the Old Left had subordinated personal feelings to that of the 'greater cause' as it was defined by the Communist Party. Women who joined the New Left were seeking personal fulfilment. The New Left incorporated psychology into politics by stressing how 'late capitalist society creates mechanisms of psychological and cultural domination over everyone'.[15]

Older radicals could not see the youthful emphasis on personal feelings as 'politics', only as a sign of extreme and irrational alienation from society. Neither did they understand why the younger generation gave as much attention to fighting university restrictions as they did to protesting against American involvement in Vietnam. The students, however, saw a connection between the policies of the institutions in which they lived and worked daily and those of more distant ones which also affected their lives.

C. Wright Mills, in *The Sociological Imagination* (1959), provided a bridge between old and new. He wanted to end the separation between individual life and social institutions in order both to minimise individual alienation and to increase political democracy. 'In essence', he said, 'democracy implies that those vitally affected by any decision men make have an effective voice in that decision.'[16] When politics were connected to and rooted in personal life, then political structures would have to be responsive to the needs of individuals. Politics would not mean sacrificing or repressing one's personal life for the sake of a 'greater cause'.

The third stage of the 'personal is political' was an expanded definition of the political realm. Politics was located not only in government, schools and workplaces, but also in the most 'private' areas of life – sexual relationships, leisure and consumer 'tastes', even physical appearance. The New Left and especially the Counterculture paid increased attention to these 'private' areas, but did not fully develop a political sensibility around them. In the Counterculture the 'personal' tended to become a substitute for politics. In the New Left personal-political connections were limited by masculine assumptions. Men drew the line when 'politics' were applied to their own desires and behaviour. They refused to confront the 'patriarchy' within themselves.

Like the Civil Rights Movement, with which it was closely affiliated, Students for a Democratic Society (SDS) and the New Left generally went through a series of ideological and organisational changes. During its ten-year life span (1960–70), SDS went from believing in the possibility of reform within the liberal system to active resistance against that system. In 1965, for example, SDS broke with its parent organisation, the League for Industrial Democracy (LID), over the issue of anti-communism. Paul Feldman, a member of the LID Board of Directors, accused SDS of suffering from 'ideological confusion' because it would not 'judge the Communist side in the war by the same standards applied to the American role'. SDS, for its part, felt that LID's anti-communism made it simply part of 'the liberal wing of the Establishment'.[17]

Kirkpatrick Sale covers the political shifts of SDS in his detailed history. We shall concentrate only on those ideas and activities

which were important for women and led to the subsequent
development of the Women's Movement. Foremost among the ideas
were 'the personal is political' and 'participatory democracy'. Both
were first articulated in the Port Huron Statement (1962), probably
the most widely distributed document of the American New Left in
the 1960s. It was a middle-class document, concerned more with
the world of the white student than with that of the poor and black.
Its opening chapter was devoted not to class and race but to values.

Social institutions produced widespread loneliness, estrangement
and alienation. Politics as currently practised lacked vision and
idealism. The older generation had not exercised the 'moral
leadership' expected of it. 'The goal of man and society should be
. . . finding a meaning in life that is personally authentic; a quality
of mind . . . which easily unites the fragmented parts of personal
history,' and so on. While the reforms suggested were still mainly
within the purview of welfare capitalism, the Statement's emphasis
on humanism, individualism and community was designed to pose
an alternative to personal malaise. For example, there was a need
to change human relationships, 'to go beyond the partial and
fragmentary bonds of function that bind men only as worker to
worker, employer to employee, teacher to student, American to
Russian'.

The 'personal is political' was more fully spelled out in the
demand for participatory democracy. Society should be organised
to ensure 'the individual share in those social decisions determining
the quality and direction of his life'. Participatory democracy would
bring people 'out of isolation and into community, thus being a
necessary, though not sufficient, means of finding meaning in
personal life'. The political order should connect 'men to knowledge
and to power' (rather than prevent individuals from acquiring
them), 'so that private problems – from bad recreation facilities to
personal alienation – are formulated as general issues'.[18]

Nothing was said about gender relationships, and unlike SNCC,
the northern student movement reinforced traditional gender roles
by its competitive, intellectual style. No one questioned the cultural
assumption that intellectual work was primarily a male domain.
Although Casey Hayden and other women were vocal at the Port
Huron Convention and the idea of 'participatory democracy' came
out of her experience in SNCC, her husband received the credit for
'writing' the Statement.

The membership of SDS was generally 32–39 per cent female, but no major office was held by a woman until 1966. In 1968, Jane Adams penetrated the top ranks by becoming national secretary. The local campus chapters lacked clear structure and lines of authority, but this did not improve women's position. Men talked politics at their residences, made decisions without including women and, in general, exercised informal leadership.

Ironically, women's status had been somewhat better in the old authoritarian Left than in the new 'democratic' one, for the Communist Party had recognised the 'woman question' and made various efforts to combat 'male supremacy'. The purges of the McCarthy Era and the resulting gap between radical generations meant that the 'woman question' enjoyed no historical continuity. It was only a peripheral, if not divisive, issue within the New Left.

Women themselves did not initially feel oppressed in the movement. Many were part of an elite: educated, middle- and upper-middle class women whose class privileges had given them confidence in their own abilities. Secondly, they were having experiences within the movement which provided them with further personal and political growth. As part of a visible, growing movement, they did not feel invisible; they felt collectively powerful and personally empowered.

The Economic Research and Action Projects (ERAP) was a relatively early SDS effort that allowed women to demonstrate their effectiveness. In the process, they gradually became conscious of their own subordinate status. Applying the SNCC model to northern communities of the poor, ERAP-ers lived among them and organised around issues affecting their daily lives. The work was hard, tedious and frustrating. Unlike Southern blacks, northern poor (especially whites) were often not conscious of the social nature of their problems. Northern oppressors – absentee landlords, city councils, welfare departments were more invisible and impersonal than those in the South. Because the students alternately romanticised and patronised the local people, they were met with some hostility. ERAP's high points were the summers of 1964 and 1965, which ran parallel to the Civil Rights summer programmes. The summer of 1964 began with ten projects; in 1965, there were thirteen. Most were short-lived.

In the ERAP communities the practice of participatory democracy was somewhat better than within SDS's national organisation. The staff members developed a sense of community, at least among themselves, without a hierarchy or authoritarian leadership. Sara Evans found that the 'parallels are striking between the fused ideology and practice of SNCC and SDS-ERAP ... and the women's movement ... that emerged several years later'. The anti-leadership bias and emphasis on internal process created by the 1960s movements were soon found in such feminist practices as rotating chairs, intensely personal meetings, and distrust of public spokeswomen.[19]

'Consciousness raising' was also developed in the ERAP. People might change if they talked together and discovered that their 'personal troubles' were shared by others. Out of this process would come an understanding that these collective problems needed collective action. The 'consciousness raising' done among welfare mothers helped to lay the groundwork for a national welfare rights movement. On the whole, 'women's issues' such as welfare, better garbage collection and housing improvements enjoyed greater, more lasting success than the male-dominated projects of organising around unemployment or working with youthful street gangs. Two of the most successful ERAP endeavours focused on welfare and were directed by women: Marya Levenson and Pat Hansen in Boston and Carol McEldowney and Sharon Jeffry in Cleveland. McEldowney and Jeffrey also assumed leading roles when the woman question first came up in SDS.

Women's involvement on these and other projects was crucial and their style was more effective than the men's in reaching community people. Women organisers were more patient, willing to listen and to 'chat' about everyday matters. The men, on the other hand, tended either to maintain their 'intellectual hegemony' or to over-identify with the exaggerated macho subculture of unemployed street youths. ERAP men thought their 'work' of hanging out and drinking with the gangs was more 'important' and 'exciting' than women's work with teenage girls and welfare mothers.

Although these men were trying to break with traditional middle-class values and avenues of success, they had brought their socialised aggressiveness and competitiveness into the movement. They relied on sexual conquest instead of occupational prestige to prove their masculinity. Women's experiences in ERAP were similar to those of their sisters in the Civil Rights Movement. In practice, the rejection of the 'bourgeois' code of sexual morality, including the 'double standard', meant that women were coerced into adopting male sexual standards. When a woman became involved with a leading man, she moved into the inner circle – until he got tired of her. Women experienced a growing contradiction between this sexual oppression and their own growth as capable project leaders and workers. After SNCC activists, Casey Hayden and Mary King, wrote their 'memo', a number of ERAP women decided to bring up women's issues at the December 1965 SDS conference.

The workshop on women led by ERAP workers 'constituted the real embryo of the new feminist revolt'.[20] But the 'baby' was delayed for almost two years, largely because of changes in the movement. Community work was downgraded in favour of campus issues and anti-war protest. After 1965, the military draft became the central issue on campuses. As only men were drafted, women found themselves relegated to auxiliary roles. They were supposed to support men in every way, as in the widespread slogan, 'Girls Say Yes to Guys Who Say No!' Sexual availability became a revolutionary duty.

The anti-war movement became permeated with machismo. Unlike the SNCC projects, the possibility of jail was reserved for men only. They were the heroes who formed a 'brotherhood' based on common risk and danger. Draft resistance did make the personal political, and the growing movement of veterans against the war allowed working-class males (who were more likely to be drafted) an important role. But women could not be full participants.

In July 1967, Jane Adams and other SDS women presented an analysis and set of demands to the SDS national convention. Using the colonial analogy popular in New Left circles, the Women's Liberation workshop claimed that women in the US 'are in a colonial relationship to men and we recognize ourselves as part of the Third World'. The workshop demanded for women the same status as any other 'legitimate' group, and called both for women 'to fight for their own independence' and for men to 'deal with their own problems of male chauvinism in their personal, social, and political relationships'. The most original point made by the Women's Liberation workshop was its indictment of the 'family unit' for perpetuating 'the traditional role of women and the autocratic and paternalistic role of men'. It asked that the traditional family be replaced by 'new forms', including communal child care centres, dissemination of birth control and increased availability of abortion. It further demanded that 'every adult person living in the household' assume an equal share of housework. As yet, women were not separating from SDS. In fact, they ended their statement with: 'We recognize the difficulty our brothers will have in dealing with male chauvinism and we will assume our full responsibility in helping to resolve the contradiction. Freedom now! we love you!' The men's answer was not encouraging. Alongside the women's statement printed in *New Left Notes* was a cartoon of a 'girl' wearing a babydoll polkadot dress and visible matching panties, carrying a sign which demanded 'Our Rights. . . . Now'.

The SDS convention was one example of male intransigence; the August 1967 National Conference for New Politics held in Chicago was another. The chair kept refusing to recognise women who wanted to speak on women's problems. Finally, he patted Shulamith Firestone on the head and said: 'Move on little girl; we have more important issues to talk about here than women's liberation.' Firestone did 'move on' to write *The Dialectic of Sex* (1970), in which she insisted that the 'sexual class system' is 'the model for all other exploitative systems'.[21]

The women who met together after the Chicago conference were ready for feminist autonomy. After seven years of movement activity, they had experience in community organising, demonstrations and committee work. They were accustomed to questioning authority and no longer fitted the accepted image of proper young women. Most important, they had in the 'radical community' a ready-made communications network through which they could reach each other. They used the infrastructure of underground newspapers and 'free' universities to spread news about the Women's Movement.

As women began meeting in small groups without men, they talked about themselves. The 'personal is political' became the basis upon which to create a politics which expressed their own needs and hopes. White women, especially, felt 'released' from fighting for someone else's freedom; they were finally fighting for themselves. But who was the enemy? 'When "chauvinism" was the enemy', remembers one woman, 'we still thought we could solve the problem by trying to reform individual men.' But soon she and others became aware that: 'The problem went much deeper. By male supremacy we meant the institutional, all-encompassing power that men as a group have over women. . . . Slowly we came to realize that we had to confront and attack male supremacy as a whole system.'[22]

Like the Civil Rights Movement's growing awareness of institutional racism, feminists evolved an analysis of a 'patriarchal' system which both excludes women from social power and devalues all the roles and traits assigned to women. However, the early writings of what came to be known as 'radical feminism' were also filled with personal anger because women were writing about their recent experiences with New Left men.

Marge Piercy's 1969 essay, 'The Grand Coolie Dam', is one example. She accused men of creating in the movement 'a microcosm of that oppression' found in the larger society. The male leaders used rhetoric about the oppression of 'colonialized people' to silence women, insisted that women's revolutionary role consisted of doing the 'shitwork', and defined 'sexual liberation' as a man's right to sleep with and discard any woman he chose. Piercy also criticised the use of Marxist-Leninist jargon as a sexist practice. 'Women in the Movement . . . have trouble talking jargon.' A woman might not have had the practice or she might simply refuse to engage in 'elitist bullshit'. But, the 'male ideological clique' see it 'as a pitiful weakness. She is crippled. If she cannot talk their language, they cannot hear her, although she speaks the language of the kind of workers they are attempting to organize.'[23]

Some of the early feminists equated Marxism itself with male chauvinism. Robin Morgan, editor of one of the first important feminist anthologies, Sisterhood Is Powerful, came to believe 'that it was the politics of the Left, not solely the men who mouthed them, which were male supremacist'. When she said 'Goodbye to All That', in early 1970, she included 'those simple-minded optimistic dreams of socialist equality all our good socialist brothers want us to believe'.[24] This initial angry 'No' to leftist sexism delayed for some years the development of an autonomous socialist-feminist perspective.

Actually, the Women's Movement was not the decisive break it appeared to be at the time. Rather, it was a logical continuation of 1960s political principles and experiences: the personal is political (or can become so); the process of decision-making ('participatory democracy') is as important as the final outcome or action itself; one must begin 'living the revolution' in one's daily life and personal relationships; and a change in consciousness is a prerequisite for social and political transformation.

The Civil Rights Movement and the New Left provided social spaces in which women could develop a sense of self-worth. Many white middle-class women developed new female role models and communication or friendship networks through which new political interpretations could spread. Because the Civil Rights Movement and the New Left were not traditional, centrally organised, disciplined left-wing organisations, women were able to claim the movements' moral idealism for themselves. They could, for example, judge the gap between the New Left's words and deeds, values and practices, in much the same ways that the New Left had judged American society. Feminists now acknowledge that rather than being a break with 1960s politics, the Women's Movement embraced the best elements of those earlier movements.

5. Women and the 1960s Counterculture

The Counterculture of the 1960s set the stage culturally for the Women's Movement much as the New Left and Civil Rights Movement had done politically. The Counterculture challenged all the conventional social realities: sexual relations, art and media, religion, and the family. In its own alternatives, it espoused female values and a feminine way of being while it oppressed women in practice. The Counterculture broke down the liberal distinction between the public/political and the private/personal. It treated as primary and public those values and characteristics traditionally assigned to women and children in the private sphere. The Counterculture emphasised spontaneity and dependence on others, rather than self-control; intuition and feeling, instead of detached rationality; cooperation and consensus over competition and efficiency; and a preference for face-to-face relationships rather than bureaucratic structure. The Counterculture also devalued those social priorities and motivations which had been traditionally masculine – aggressiveness, toughness, material success – and which had rewarded men more than women.

The new culture posed a contradiction for women. Although its values were similar to what Dorothy Dinnerstein calls the 'Things that women have always informally and deeply known', the Counterculture was not led by women. Rather, it was 'the beginning of a redefinition, by young men themselves, of the traditional male role'. Men were willing to become more 'feminised' but they did not encourage women to assume traditional masculine characteristics and roles. Instead, men asked women to become mere assistants in what had formerly been their special domain.[1]

The Counterculture made psychology its axis or base, but it rejected the popular Freudianism of the 1950s in favour of a radical

97

critique of all theories of social 'adjustment'. The Hippies believed that each person could create a new self without the help of traditional experts or techniques. Their own techniques included 'mind-expanding' drugs, sexual and sensual pleasure, various forms of meditation and radical changes in habits and living patterns. This psychological approach contained a feminist potential because it reversed the hierarchy embedded in such dichotomies as public/private, mind/body, and reason/feeling.

The new enhancement of the body affected women more than men. Cultural values surrounding menstruation, pregnancy and childbirth had equated women with 'physical nature'. Advertising images had turned female bodies into consumer objects. Women internalised the media standard of flawless beauty and tried to emulate the impossible. The Counterculture gave women their bodies back by favouring physicality rather than rational detachment. It advocated the 'abolition of repression' in favour of 'play'. Norman O. Brown imagined that: 'The human body would become polymorphously perverse, delighting in that full life of all the body which it now fears.'[2]

The emphasis on physical acceptance provided women with an alternative to consumer standards of beauty. The Hippie appearance rejected packaged flawlessness and the expense involved in achieving it. Self-expressiveness, naturalness, variety and even sloppiness were encouraged. With the abolition of a single standard of female attractiveness, women with big noses, frizzy hair and large bodies could be 'beautiful'.

Another reversal of Western patriarchal values involved the primacy of feeling over rationality. The Hippies rebelled against what Theodore Roszak called 'the myth of objective consciousness', which divided reality into two spheres – the subjective 'in-here' and the objective 'out-there' – and made the latter the only acceptable means to gain knowledge and power. Objective consciousness meant studying something as if one's feelings were not aroused by it, encouraged the use of jargon and technical terms rather than plain or sensuous language, and created the need for experts who used 'professional standards' to avoid personal responsibility.[3]

Instead of detachment from and control over the world 'out there', the Counterculture sought identification and participation. Hippies experimented with a different epistemology which would permit sensuousness/subjective knowledge of a reality potentially full of wonder and mystery. They used sex, drugs and meditation both for immediate gratification and as a means of transcending what the scientific/materialist world view called 'reality'. Their temporality was geared more to the present moment than to the clock and calendar. The Counterculture's sense of time was closer to that of the housewife than to the employed worker, except that the housewife enjoyed little leisure. Leisure, rather than work, was central to the Counterculture. Its ultimate aim was to break down the distinction between the two by emphasising play, pleasure and self-cultivation.

While *symbolic* sexual stimulation was accepted, widespread and profitable in American culture, direct gratification was supposed to be restricted to a single, legal heterosexual relationship. 'The idea that pleasure could be an end in itself is so startling and so threatening to the structure of our society', noted Philip Slater, 'that the mere possibility is denied.'[4] If women have, in turn, remembered the sexual 'pleasure' of the 1960s more as exploitation, it is not only that their memories have been coloured by feminist awareness. The model for sexual liberation *was* a masculine one. Ellen Willis, for example, admits that she was initially in favour of the campaign against obscenity laws and conventional sexual morality. But she also realises that 'the sexual freedom movement was full of contradictions'. The libertarians 'took for granted that prostitution and pornography were liberating. . . . No one suggested that men's isolation of sex from feeling might actually be part of the problem, rather than the solution.'[5]

Singer Janis Joplin provides an extreme, but not unique, example of the sexual conflict engendered by the Counterculture. Her sexual relationships with women were trivialised (even by herself) as a sign of her 'liberation' – she was so 'free' she could 'make it' with anyone. Her constant boasting of her heterosexual prowess, on the other hand, was an attempt to hide her desperate need for love. According to her biographer, Joplin 'identified with men as she thought they acted and sometimes did. She defined men sexually, as she defined herself, and then went at her one-night stands and sometimes orgies under the cover of a liberated style of life.'[6] Joplin's emphasis on sex, even equating music and sex, came from the male-dominated Counterculture which, in Ellen Willis' words, 'defined freedom for women almost exclusively in sexual terms. As a result, women endowed the idea of sexual liberation with immense symbolic importance; it became charged with all the secret energy of an as yet suppressed larger rebellion.'[7] The early feminist consciousness-raising sessions, according to one participant, 'produced a great emotional outpouring of feelings against the way women had been used sexually and revelations of sexual shames and terrors we had all lugged through our lives.' In the late 1960s, the first major actions of women revealed 'how central was the new feminist analysis of sexuality to our collective struggle for justice'.[8]

This 'feminist analysis of sexuality' owes much to the gap women perceived between the Counterculture's promise of heightened feelings, love and community, and the more masculine prerogatives which continued to operate. A commercial version of sexual liberation, which arose about the same time, violated no promise, but rather unabashedly promoted the masculine ethic for both sexes.

In 1962, Helen Gurley Brown announced the 'new woman' in her book *Sex and the Single Girl*. Since 1965, her magazine *Cosmopolitan* has promoted an image of the 'single girl': 'She took the pill and lived in an apartment with a double bed. She spent money on herself and men spent attention on her. She was the old feminist ideal of the independent woman with a new twist – she was sexy.' The 'singles culture' has had a longer life than the Counterculture because it opened a profitable new market for travel, liquor, sports equipment, cosmetics and furniture. 'Singles culture' has been based on what Barbara Ehrenreich and Deirdre English call 'marketplace psychology', which promises to liberate women from loving and caring for others, in favour of 'a philosophy of ruthless self-centeredness'.[9] Business terminology permeates private life. Relationships are 'contracted' when they are emotionally 'profitable' and terminated when they cease to be so. In the 1970s, this version of the 'sexual revolution' distorted feminist demands, just as it had earlier attempted to channel the Counterculture's desire for 'sexual freedom' into safe commercial expressions.

Although the Counterculture espoused anti-capitalist values, it could not detach itself from commercial culture. One reason was rock music, which is inherently commercial, part of the music industry and 'show business'. It is a mass-produced commodity, dependent on advanced technology and, not surprisingly, male-dominated. Rock and drugs (especially marijuana and LSD) were essential features of the Counterculture which do not appear to have been absorbed into the Women's Movement. Yet rock music affected women, both positively and negatively.

Rock musicians challenged both the existing hierarchy in the music industry and accepted musical standards. They broke down the boundaries between 'art' and 'non-art' and blurred the distinction between 'high' and 'low' culture.

Rock music of the 1960s was eclectic; it incorporated elements of blues, country, folk, soul and 'psychedelic rock'. It was also democratic; members of the audience began to play instruments and sing, rather than simply listening to professionals. 'People now sang songs they wrote themselves, not songs written *for* them by hacks in grimy Tin Pan Alley offices', wrote Ralph J. Gleason in 1967. Rock musicians were artists as well as entertainers. One need not agree with Gleason's opinion that Bob Dylan's lyrics 'did what the jazz and poetry people of the fifties had wanted to do – he took poetry out of the classroom . . . and put it right out there in the streets for everyone',[10] to realise that the song lyrics of the 1960s were more complex, self-expressive and self-consciously poetic than those of the previous decades. They were also more sexually candid. Unlike the 1950s, sex did not have to be referred to as 'rocking' or driving a car. But sexual frankness and the reversal of the old bad girl–good girl dichotomy also exposed the male chauvinism in the lyrics.

'It ain't me babe', was Bob Dylan's reply to a woman who wanted more than a quick sexual encounter. The Rolling Stones were not the only male singers who thought a woman was either a 'stupid girl' who belonged 'under my thumb' or else a 'honky tonk woman' whose place was 'in between the sheets'. Few songs portrayed autonomous women or spoke of equality between the sexes. The Beatles' 'Norwegian Wood' (1965) and 'We Can Work It Out' (1966); the Jefferson Airplane's 'Somebody to Love', and Otis Redding's 'Respect' (1967), especially Aretha Franklin's version, were exceptions; both women and men needed love and respect and both were vulnerable to rejection and pain.

The music of the 1960s looks less male dominated if we include black women who drew upon the earlier work of Bessie Smith, Ida Cox and Billie Holiday. Aretha Franklin, Nina Simone, Nancy Wilson, Esther Phillips, Tina Turner and Diana Ross possessed the pride and survival strength Janis Joplin lacked.

Grace Slick, of the Jefferson Airplane, was the only really well-known woman in the 1960s white rock scene besides Joplin. Like Joplin, Slick was famous for her escapades, costumes and use of drugs. But Slick was also realistic, aggressive and cynical. These traits were survival tools in the male world of rock. She felt 'natural' singing rock and roll with men because she thought of herself as 'kind of masculine'. In the white rock scene of the 1960s she stood alone.

A San Francisco Bay Area group less famous than the Jefferson Airplane featured two women. Terry Garthwaite and Toni Brown wrote songs, sang and played instruments in the Joy of Cooking. The group had begun playing in 1968, but did not cut its first record until 1971. Garthwaite recalls that there were men who refused to audition for Joy of Cooking and that the men in the band became resentful when Joy of Cooking became known as a 'women's band'.

Overt male resistance was not the only problem. Women also found the life of a rock singer difficult, especially if they had children. The constant travelling, the ambiance of drugs and glamour, the intense competition and pressure to 'be cool' conflicted both with their socialisation as females and their desire for intimate relationships. Bonnie Raitt, who like many other women achieved success in the 1970s rather than the 1960s, located the problem less in the musical work than in her personal life. 'Guys may pick up girls on the road, but I don't know many women who get into that kind of scene. . . . Horniness aside, it's the tenderness and being close to someone that I miss and those kinds of relationships are not made overnight.'[11]

The very form white rock took may have intimidated many women. The general belief was that women were not intelligent enough to understand electronic technology and were too weak to play drums. Female stars such as Joan Baez, Judy Collins and the early Joni Mitchell were folk, not rock, musicians. Although more white women gained musical recognition in the 1970s – Linda Ronstadt, Rita Coolidge, Maria Muldaur, Carly Simon and Bette Midler, to name a few – they did not play music with a high decibel level. Women's music, whether feminist or mainstream, has continued to be performed more by individuals than groups. It is generally softer and acoustical rather than electronic.

Rock and roll in the 1960s presented a paradox for its female listeners; 'music that boldly and aggressively laid out what the singer wanted, loved, hated – as good rock-and-roll did – challenged me to do the same', wrote Ellen Willis, 'and so, even when the content was antiwoman, antisexual, in a sense antihuman, the form encouraged my struggle for liberation.'[12] The sheer sensual power of rock music, especially in concerts accompanied by light shows, did not numb or pacify its female audience. Rather, it provided women with some of the energy they needed to create their own cultural alternatives.

Women gained more direct experience working with the Counterculture media. The most important of these was the underground press. Strictly speaking, the Counterculture press was not underground. Although many papers suffered from legal and extra-legal harassment, their staffs and readers were not consciously risking their lives. 'Underground' was a metaphor of rebellion. The underground press was an alternative structure to and disseminated values different from those of the established mass media.

Movement people did seek to get their message across in the established media. They even organised events to catch the media spotlight. The Yippies (Youth International Party) were expressly committed to staging audacious stunts to attract publicity, such as tossing dollar bills onto the floor of the New York Stock Exchange in 1967. By creating dramatic and colourful confrontations, they hoped to use the mainstream media to transmit radical values to millions of Americans. In 1968, New York Radical Women staged one of the first feminist demonstrations by using Yippie 'guerrilla theatre' tactics to ridicule the Miss America pageant. Robin Morgan described one of the actions and the media distortion of it:

> The demonstrators mock-auctioned off a dummy of Miss America and flung dishcloths, steno pads, girdles, and bras into a Freedom Trash Can. (This last was translated by the male controlled media into the totally invented act of 'bra burning,' a nonevent upon which they have fixated constantly ever since, in order to avoid presenting the real reasons for the growing discontent of women.)

WITCH, an offshoot of New York Radical Women, continued 'doing actions' such as protesting against a Bridal Fair by wearing black veils and singing 'Here come the slaves/off to their graves' to the prospective brides.[13]

The Yippies were short-lived and the Women's Movement soon stopped such tactics because they alienated other women. But these examples illustrate how media priorities entered into the internal life of the movement. Media publicity helped to recruit many young people into both the Counterculture and the New Left. However, the knowledge of the newcomers was based on what they had read and seen, that is, the more flamboyant and dramatic actions. They expected the movement to live up to its media image and pushed it in that direction.

The unequal contest between established media and radicals is not the whole story. The movement created its own alternative media: newspapers, film (especially Newsreel, a documentary group), radio, video, 'guerrilla' or street theatre, and small book presses. Of these, the alternative newspapers were the most widespread and successful. Despite the economic concentration of the mainstream press, newspapers and magazines had more open distribution channels, freer access, and required less initial capital than television.

Hundreds of short-lived Counterculture papers existed all over the country, with circulation figures (in 1968) ranging anywhere from 330,000 to 5 million. The importance of the underground press does not lie in the longevity or circulation of any one publication, but rather in the amazing diversity of publications which emerged after 1965, the anarchic and participatory staff structures which evolved on most of them, and the relationship these publications attempted to create with their readers. The underground press not only indicated the shortcomings of the established media, but also created an audience for other types of alternative, local and special-interest media, including feminist publications, in the 1970s.

The underground papers provided both a service and work environment for the radical community. They covered events the regular press ignored, and their reporters did not write 'objective' or 'balanced' accounts. These alternative papers, like later feminist publications, reported on and for their community. They also helped to expand that community.

Along with news and opinion, the papers offered many young people a means of subsistence outside mainstream employment. Work and 'life' became one on those underground papers which consciously aspired to be radical institutions themselves: the *Rag* of

Austin, Texas; the Chicago *Seed*; *Space City* of Houston, Texas; *The Great Speckled Bird* in Atlanta, Georgia; and the *Kudzu* of Jackson, Mississippi, to name a few. On these papers, the staff worked and sometimes lived communally, without hierarchical structure. All tasks were rotated. Collective ownership and participatory democracy would replace the 'alienated labour' of the capitalist workplace. Yet, even among small and committed staffs, collective decision-making and work rotation were difficult practices to maintain. Constant personality clashes and rapid turnover jeopardised the survival of many alternative organisations.

Because women were active workers, the underground press became aware of and began discussing the Women's Liberation Movement before the mass media covered it. Women on the *Seed* stimulated the paper in new directions and insisted on equality with male workers. The *Rag* took no sexist advertising. On the other hand, the *Los Angeles Free Press* gave space to the women's movement amidst its pages of sexist advertising. The *East Village Other* ran a cartoon of a man performing oral sex on a bound, naked woman. When the issue was removed by the Brooklyn District Attorney on the ground of obscenity, the artist retaliated by redrawing the cartoon with the man kicking and stamping on the woman.

Women on *The Bird* (Atlanta) formed their own caucus in the latter part of 1969 in order to act collectively in the generally male-dominated staff meetings. The *Rat* women went further and seized the paper in January 1970. It was the first time women had taken over a male-run newspaper and transformed it into a women's collective.

By the time of the *Rat* takeover, women had also begun to publish their own papers. In January 1970, *It Ain't Me Babe* appeared in Berkeley, staffed by female veterans of the New Left. Six weeks later, New Left women started *off our backs* in Washington DC. The early feminist publications served the double purpose of providing reliable information about the emerging Women's Movement and creating networks of like-minded women around the country. Like the underground press, the feminists' style was angry and personal. Nearly all the papers were collectively edited and produced. Hierarchy and competition were criticised as part of what the Women's Movement now called 'patriarchal culture'. In their functions and structure, as well as in many of their values, the feminist publications are direct descendants of the underground press.

While some young rebels were creating alternative ways to communicate with each other, others were seeking new ways to communicate with God. In one sense they were following a familiar American pattern of individuals and groups, like the nineteenth-century Transcendentalists, who broke with established churches and formed their own spiritual alternatives.

Henry David Thoreau's *Walden Pond* and 'On the Duty of Civil Disobedience' were widely read by political and cultural radicals in the 1960s. Margaret Fuller showed the feminist side of Transcendentalist thought in her *Woman in the Nineteenth Century* (1845). Just as 'man' (as human being) should not set himself above 'nature', but rather exist in relationship with it, so 'man' (as the male sex) must not separate himself from and dominate 'woman'. 'By Man I mean both man and woman; these are the two halves of one thought.' Fuller's androgynous vision was in opposition to the commonly held doctrine of 'separate spheres', based on 'innate' differences between the sexes. 'Male and female', she wrote, 'represent the two sides of the great radical dualism. But in fact they are perpetually passing into one another. . . . There is no wholly masculine man, no purely feminine woman.'[14] Although Fuller discussed the need to widen women's economic, educational and political options, her emphases, like those of the other Transcendentalists, were spiritual and aesthetic.

The Transcendentalists were one of the precursors of Counterculture spirituality. The 'Transcendentalists' of the 1960s also rejected Western acquisitive and economic values, were concerned with the mystical and transpersonal, and wanted to develop communal and cooperative styles of living.

Despite some of the authoritarian cults that emerged, the Counterculture encouraged a search for new definitions of personal and social power, distrusted traditional authorities and dogmas, provided an enhanced sense of individual autonomy, and simultaneously increased a desire for closer relationships with other people and with the natural world. To this extent, the Counterculture revived pantheism and paganism and created modern versions of pre-Christian or non-Christian nature religions. This aspect of Counterculture spirituality benefited American women, because the structure, ritual and values of neo-paganism provided a basis for women to challenge traditional sex roles.

Misogyny is an inherent part of both Christian dualism and the scientific view of nature. Culture, the province of the male, is separated from nature, which is identified with the female. Women are either equated with nature, or they are 'seen as representing a lower order of being, as being less transcendental of nature than men are'. This begins with the body 'and the natural procreative functions specific to women alone',[15] or rather with the cultural view that devalues reproduction, childbirth and even child care as merely 'natural' processes.

Even Simone de Beauvoir in *The Second Sex* retains this dualistic view. Transcendence is opposed to immanence, and women have been doomed to immanence, that is, nature and death. 'In all civilizations and still in our day woman inspires man with horror: it is the horror of his own carnal contingence, which he projects upon her.' Woman becomes for man 'the privileged object through which he subdues Nature'. De Beauvoir's solution was transcendence for women, too, so that they not be required to 'subordinate existence to life, the human being to its animality'.[16]

The Counterculture's view of 'animality' and 'carnal contingence' differed from that of de Beauvoir. A sense of connectedness between human projects and natural processes replaced the divorce of transcendence from immanence. Neo-pagans saw nature as alive rather than an object to be controlled. Human beings were both divine and natural. They could become gods and goddesses (as well as animals) in rituals and fantasies. Gods were not 'out there' but were potencies within the psyche. As goddesses, women could challenge traditional sex roles, at least in spiritual practices.

The female goddess is related to the neo-pagan belief in a world of multiplicity and diversity. No one god or set of beliefs contains the absolute truth. This pluralism leads to tolerance for others rather than a zeal to convert them. It also contrasts to the Judeo-Christian view that God (the Father) is male and that His priestly interpreters must be the same sex. Instead of being restricted to the Virgin Mary, female neo-pagans could choose from a rich variety of divine role models: Artemis, Persephone, Athena, Changing Woman, etc.

Neo-pagans, like the Counterculture generally, emphasise

traditional 'feminine' qualities of peacefulness and gentleness. Sacred rituals take place around everyday life-maintenance tasks such as bathing, preparing and eating food. The most valued 'way of knowing' is close to 'feminine' intuition and stresses feeling and imagination rather than reason and logic. Neo-pagans do not believe the body is 'unclean'. Feminists have taken this to mean that female physical processes such as menstruation and childbirth are inherently sacred. Their interest in holistic health practices and ecology are also grounded in the Counterculture neo-pagan respect for nature.

Within the Counterculture, there was a particular fascination with Native Americans (American Indians) as a people of the land. These youthful 'Indian lovers' often had only a superficial knowledge of Native American cultures, and they were criticised by both the mass media and by Native American spokespeople for their naïve romanticism. Yet the Hippies helped to arouse new scholarly and political interest in what was by the 1960s the poorest, least visible minority group in the country. *Akwesasne Notes*, which began in 1969 as the newspaper of the Mohawk Nation, soon surpassed *Green Egg*, *Gnostica* and other neo-pagan journals in circulation figures.

There may have been as many as 600 different Native American cultures in the Continental United States before the white invasion. Of the estimated 300 Indian languages spoken in the area north of Mexico, at least half are still in use. In spite of the enormous diversity of their cultures, most Native Americans have stressed a respectful relationship with the natural world, rather than an artificial, technological conquest of it.

A sexual division of labour prevailed among Native American peoples, and the actual status of women varied greatly from one culture to the next. However, most tribes acknowledged female deities, important personages, or personifications of natural phenomena. The Earth Mother is one of the two primary images in the Navaho and Pueblo pantheons. These Southwestern tribes also have Changing Woman, Dawn Woman, Corn Mother, Spider Woman and Deer Mother, to name only a few. White Buffalo Cow Woman brought the sacred pipe to the Lakota, telling them: 'With this sacred pipe you will walk upon the Earth; for the Earth is your Grandmother and Mother, and She is sacred. Every step that is taken upon Her should be as a prayer.'[17] This reverence for the

Earth, personified as female, along with the circle as a cosmic, natural and organisational symbol, has been important to both Counterculture and feminist spirituality.

In addition to Native American sources, feminist spirituality owes most to the modern revival of wicca or 'the Craft'. Robert Graves' *The White Goddess* (1948) has had an enormous influence on women, but neither Graves nor neo-paganism generally has been free of sexism. The Goddess and even the Witch can become stereotypes, limiting women's capacities. This is because mixed male-female covens tend to work with sex-typed polarities, such as sun-moon, sky-earth, light-dark, active-passive. The first of each pair is associated with the male, as are the symbols and elements of sword and wand, air and fire. To the female go the second of the pairs, along with cup and pentacle, water and earth. Although all of these elements and symbols are supposed to be equally accepted by both genders, it is impossible for practitioners to be free of the sex hierarchy culturally embedded in these dualities. As Barbara Starrett expressed it: 'Dualism always poses an ethical choice, an either/or; one opposite is always preferable to the other. . . . Dualities reinforce linear, cause-and-effect, hierarchical thinking.'[18] She and other feminists have tried to claim all the symbols – those of the dark as well as the light – for themselves, and find it easier to do so in all-female spiritual groups.

Until the Women's Movement, it was mainly men who spoke about and for the Craft and, with the exception of Sybil Leek, wrote the books. Women's power as witches and priestesses did not necessarily lead to their greater autonomy outside Craft rituals. Yet neo-paganism, especially wicca, has been better for women than other forms of alternative spirituality. Unlike many of the Westernised forms of Eastern religions led by male gurus, women have held strong positions in neo-pagan circles, participating in rituals on an equal footing with men.

Feminist consciousness, in turn, has politicised neo-paganism, often to the dismay of more 'traditional' wiccans. As early as 1968, a group of feminists calling themselves WITCH declared that any woman could proclaim herself a witch; no special ritual or initiation was needed.

There is no 'joining' WITCH. If you are a woman and dare to look within yourself, you are a Witch. You make your own rules.

> You are free and beautiful. . . . Your power comes from your own self as a woman, and it is activated by working in concert with your sisters.

WITCH believed that witches 'were the original guerrillas and resistance fighters against oppression – especially the oppression of women', and, as we have seen, they engaged in political 'hexing' activities.[19] As the influence of the Counterculture waned, feminist witches became less flamboyant. Yet they continue to emphasise the Goddess in their rituals, even to the point of excluding any 'male' symbols. In secular activities, too, such as women's studies courses and political meetings, feminists usually sit in circles, favour consensus rather than authority, and evolve techniques so that all who attend can participate.

Some of the active spiritual, media and political circles in the 1960s also experimented with group living, but most Counterculture communes were based less on shared spiritual or political values than on a need to find alternatives to the nuclear family. The intrusion of consumer culture into the private sphere, followed by the politicalisation of 'private life' in the 1960s, led many radicals to argue that the family was not a 'natural' arrangement, but rather a social institution whose function was to reproduce willing workers and consumers for the capitalist political economy. The nuclear family both reflected the dominant values of the culture and transmitted them to a new generation, or as Jules Henry put it, 'the family merely distills into a lethal dose what exists in the culture at large'.[20]

There were also more positive motivations behind the formation of communes. The Counterculture believed that love should be 'free', not a 'scarce commodity', and communal life allowed emotional and erotic relationships to be extended beyond marriage and blood ties. Additionally, at least some 1960s communitarians were convinced, like their nineteenth-century predecessors, that these alternative family structures were also model political institutions. However, the proliferation of rural Hippie communes in the late 1960s was also a sign of political failure. Neither the New Left nor the Counterculture had succeeded in changing mainstream American institutions and values.

The Counterculture could not even sustain large-scale urban 'alternatives' of its own. The Haight-Ashbury neighbourhood of

San Francisco, for example, became a Hippie community between 1965 and 1966. Initially, it represented not simply a place, but a changed consciousness based on emotional, sensory and aesthetic expression: sex and music, sidewalk and body painting, every imaginable assortment of clothing and hairstyles. The streets were a continuous festival populated with characters living out their dreams and fantasies.

On the other hand, the Haight lacked coherence and stability as a community. Its intellectual and political values were excessively 'laissez-faire', and Hippies placed little value on organised projects or institutions. Never a planned community, the Haight could not exclude anyone or train potential residents for neighbourhood commitment and participation. By 1967, it was already devolving into a violent slum full of 'bad vibes' from hard-drug pushers, the Hell's Angels (a violence-prone motorcycle club), young runaways and numerous 'crazies'.

Many young people treated their experiences in the Haight and other urban Hippie neighbourhoods as a vacation from 'straight' society; they soon returned to school or work. Others, less fortunate, became drug addicts and lived a derelict life on the streets. A third group wished to continue a craft-based and spiritually-oriented life in more stable communal arrangements. They began to leave the cities for rural areas in California, Oregon and New Mexico.

Sociologist Rosabeth Moss Kanter calls these rural experiments 'retreat communes'. They specialised in domestic or family relationships, in contrast to 'service communes' which interacted with the wider society by providing a religious or welfare service. One thing the rural communes did not 'retreat' from was traditional sex roles. As one woman put it, 'even though we had complete freedom to determine the division of labor for ourselves, a well-known pattern emerged immediately. Women did most of the cooking, all of the cleaning up, and of course, the washing.'[21]

Both the short-lived and the more enduring experiments found it all too 'natural' to revert to a traditional sex-based division of labour. Men dominated in leadership and administrative roles. Women might learn carpentry and they were often needed as farm workers, but it was always more difficult to get men to 'help' in the kitchen and with child care.

In 1969, Stephen Gaskin, a former English teacher, led his Haight-Ashbury followers to Tennessee. Here he established one of the most successful rural communes, called simply The Farm. In order to survive, it rejected Counterculture values for more traditional ones: hard work, evangelical religion and the patriarchal family. Unlike the outside society, personal ambition is not encouraged. Rather, The Farm's way of life is based on religious communism under a strong, unquestioned male leader. The Farm has retained the nuclear family and traditional sex roles. Midwifery is the only leadership position to which women can aspire. Ina May Gaskin, author of a highly regarded book, *Spiritual Midwifery*, heads a team of midwives who have respect and authority in the community. Many feminists, too, have come to prefer midwives over depersonalised male-dominated hospital births, but the feminist critique of medicalised childbirth does not confine women to their reproductive function.

New Buffalo, launched in 1967 as one of the first Counterculture communes in New Mexico, did not have an official leader. But by 1970 a number of 'head men' had emerged. Theoretically, male and female roles were 'co-equal', that is, women could voice their views and act on the basis of their spiritual visions. However, a male reporter noted that most of the women 'develop an honest fascination for almost classically feminine functions'. He goes on to quote one of the commune's men: 'A girl just becomes so . . . so *womanly* when she's doing something like baking her own bread in a wood stove. . . . I can't explain it. It just turns me on.'[22]

With the exception of The Farm, rigid sex roles were the result of a lack of structure and served, to some extent, as a substitute for more conscious planning. In contrast, Twin Oaks, organised in 1967 along the lines of B. F. Skinner's *Walden Two* (a utopia based on his behaviour modification theories), relied on order rather than spontaneity to achieve its goals. As Kathleen Kinkade, one of the founders, expressed it: 'What behavioral psychology has to do with it is that we set up our institutions in such a way that the kind of behavior we want is reinforced by those institutions. For example there is nothing to reinforce competitive behavior.'

Twin Oaks embraced technology and instituted a system of managers and 'labor credits' which awarded points for specific tasks. Unpopular work received more credits. Twin Oaks also responded positively to the Women's Liberation Movement. As Kinkade explained in the early 1970s: 'We have no sex roles in our work. Both men and women cook and clean and wash dishes; both

women and men drive trucks and tractors. . . . Managerial
responsibility is divided almost exactly equally.'[23]

The Women's Movement did not originate in rural communes;
in fact, most of the men resisted feminism. On one farm when
women began holding meetings in the woods, the men considered
this to be 'a declaration of war'. The women then decided to chop
and collect wood instead of cooking, and the community divided
into two hostile camps. Although the women did not intend to
humiliate the men or separate from them, but rather to shift the
division of labour, their experiment was 'a colossal failure'. Half the
women eventually compromised, the other half left.[24]

Vivian Estellachild, who had lived on two communes, felt by
1971 as other feminists did. 'The hip man like his straight
counterpart is nothing more, nothing less, than a predator.' While
she still believed that 'communal living appears to be a step in the
right direction', she had seen that 'the hip commune uses women in
a group way the same as the fathers did in a one-to-one way'.

Despite this bleak assessment, collectivising family functions did
have feminist potential. When women shared kitchen work and
child care, sociability, friendship, and even bonding developed
between them. It was the first time many women had lived
communally with non-related members of their sex, and they
learned to value other women. Even Estellachild admits that the
'only good thing' that resulted from her experience 'was my
beginning awareness of women's problems. . . . I became very
interested in the women.' Another woman expressed this more
fully. 'Cooperative living for us also means that there are other
women around so we can confront men, receive support, and get
further in touch with our feelings without being isolated and
alone.'[25]

When confronting men did not get the desired results, some
women took the next step. They left and started communes of their
own, such as the home women formed in 1970 near the University
of Iowa which excluded men, or the rural lesbian Woman Share
Collective in Oregon.

Feminist ideas also led to new sexually mixed communes,
especially in urban areas. Before 1969, few urban groups created
communes solely for domestic purposes. In 1974, the Boston area
alone had over 200 identifiable communal households. Not
surprisingly, there were more fights about housecleaning than

anything else, because commitment to equal work-sharing meant a radical change from traditional family patterns. Although only a minority of people ever lived in communes, and most of them for a short time, these arrangements were part of a general trend away from a single model of family life based on age and sex hierarchies.

These two chapters on the 1960s have covered some of the ways in which participants in the New Left and the Counterculture went beyond liberal politics by treating 'private life' as a political issue. Sexuality became a central question among radicals. However, the Counterculture's answers did not reflect women's needs or directly improve their status. As radical women began to discuss these matters among themselves, especially their treatment as sex objects, they started to see the 'political' in those areas which had remained 'private' or 'natural' in the 1960s movements: orgasm, heterosexuality, motherhood and housework. Along with liberal feminists, they embarked on a campaign to end all forms of sexual discrimination and exploitation – at the workplace, on the streets, in the home, and within the legal-political system.

6. The Politics of the Women's Movement

From the late 1960s to the late 1970s, the Women's Movement has been composed of three main branches: liberal, socialist and radical. The organisations of the movement have been numerous and varied, but many women who consider themselves feminists have never joined any group, and countless others have changed their lives even though they do not support the movement or call themselves feminists.

Among the three political branches, liberal feminism has the longest history. It goes back to the women's rights movement of the nineteenth and early twentieth centuries which won the vote for women. After 1920, however, women's rights does not have a continuous history of achievement. By the mid 1960s, the only existing group with connections to the earlier movement was the National Woman's Party (NWP). Since 1921, it had worked to remove all legal discrimination based on sex and kept the Equal Rights Amendment alive at a time when other women's organisations and trade union women saw it as a threat to their hard-won protective labour legislation.

The National Organization for Women (NOW), formed in 1966, became the first new broad-based women's rights organisation since the passage of the suffrage amendment. NOW's initial concern was legal equality for women, and it called upon the Equal Employment Opportunity Commission (EEOC) to treat sex discrimination as seriously as it did race discrimination. In other words, NOW demanded that the federal government enforce Title VII of the 1964 Civil Rights Act. Very soon NOW insisted upon more than enforcement of existing legislation.

Liberal feminists differ from socialists or radicals in their willingness to work within the existing political and economic framework. NOW's 1966 statement committed the group 'to take action to bring women into full participation in the mainstream of American society *now*, exercising all the privileges and responsibilities thereof in truly equal partnership with men'.[1] Liberal feminists demand that women be included in the 'mainstream' of society rather than relegated to its domestic periphery. They want equality with men, not subordination to them. Liberal feminists wish to enter the existing economic and political institutions on the same terms as men do. Their model, like that of the early Civil Rights Movement, is that of an integrated society.

periphery outskirts of minor importance

Liberal feminists must de-emphasise sex differences. If men and women are basically more alike than different, then human rights, heretofore granted only to men, can be extended to women as well. Liberal feminists assume that men will cooperate. NOW, for example, is an organisation for women, but men are welcome as members.

The liberals' emphasis on sex sameness and their hope that equality for women can be attained through a mixed gender movement differ from the views of both radical feminists and more traditional female reform groups. While both liberals and radicals reject the traditional 'femininity' based on the wife-mother role, radical feminists emphasise a distinctive 'woman's culture' grounded in sex differences. The radicals share with the 'traditionals' a preference for homosocial rather than mixed-sex organisations.

Women Strike for Peace (WSP) is an example of a more traditional type of political 'femininity' rather than feminism. In the early 1960s, WSP identified itself as an organisation of *mothers* not citizens. Calling themselves 'housewives' (although many worked at paid jobs, too), WSP activists used sex-role stereotypes to oppose Cold War politics. Their only difference from other middle-class 'full-time' mothers of the post-war period was in seeing motherhood 'not only as a private function, but also as a contribution to society in general and to the future'.[2] Although WSP criticised both male politics and the isolation and privatisation of women, it was not a woman's rights organisation. Unlike feminists after 1966, WSP relied on and used 'feminine nature' to work for peace.

Betty Friedan, the catalyst and one of the founders of NOW, criticised the kind of 'femininity' WSP espoused. In *The Feminine Mystique* (1963), Friedan located the key problem for women in their role as unpaid housewives-mothers-consumers. Her solution was paid, meaningful work outside the home – a chance for women to achieve prestige and power the same way men do. Individually held attitudes, women's image in the mass media, sex-role socialisation in families and schools, and discriminatory institutional practices needed to be changed. Although liberal feminists were primarily concerned with 'public' issues – employment opportunity, legal rights and political power in government – these had a way of spilling over into more private or psychological areas. NOW drew up a women's Bill of Rights for 1968 which demanded that child care facilities be established 'by law on the same basis as parks, libraries, and public schools'. Publicly funded day care was a prerequisite for women to compete equally with men in the job market.

NOW's stand on reproductive issues came even closer to making personal life a political issue. The Bill of Rights demanded: 'The right of women to control their own reproductive lives by removing from penal codes laws limiting access to contraceptive information and devices and laws governing abortion.'[3] This controversial reproductive plank, especially abortion, caused a split within NOW and the formation of a more conservative women's rights group.

The Women's Equity Action League (WEAL) deliberately restricted itself to economic and educational issues. Essentially a political pressure group, it appealed to powerful leaders and cultivated a conservative image. The organisation played an active role in removing sex discrimination from colleges and universities, institutions unregulated by the 1964 Civil Rights Act. WEAL was instrumental in securing the passage of Title IX of the 1972 Education Amendments which prohibited discrimination against students, faculty and staff in educational institutions receiving federal grants.

The National Women's Political Caucus (NWPC), formed by Bella Abzug, Gloria Steinem, Betty Friedan and Shirley Chisholm in 1971, worked to raise the proportion of women delegates to the Democratic and Republican Party Conventions in 1972. It was particularly successful with the Democrats. In 1968, the year that Chisholm became the first black woman elected to the US House of Representatives, women comprised only 10 per cent of the Democratic delegates, but four years later 40 per cent were women. NWPC has also tried to get more women elected and appointed to public office. It has supported women's political issues, especially the Equal Rights Amendment (ERA), which finally passed both houses of Congress in 1972 and was sent to the states for ratification.

In addition to WEAL and NWPC, there have been many special interest liberal feminist groups. Federally Employed Women (FEW), founded in 1968, has fought to end sex discrimination in government employment and to secure child care centres and other benefits for government employees. By 1971, women had also formed caucuses or autonomous organisations in almost every professional association and academic discipline.

Not all liberal feminist organisations have been middle-class or professionally based. The Coalition of Labor Union Women (CLUW, 1974) has acted as a feminist pressure group upon male-dominated unions. Reformist rather than radical, it works within the established AFL-CIO union structure and is open only to union members. This has restricted CLUW's efforts to organise non-union workers and to develop programmes incorporating women's issues outside the area of production. Union restraint on women's activities predates CLUW. The United Auto Workers has had a Women's Department since 1944, and UAW women were among the founders of NOW. However, union women could not support the ERA because the UAW was opposed to it. In 1970, the UAW reversed its stand and supported both the ERA and the repeal or reform of abortion laws, becoming one of the first unions to do so.

Women of colour have been active CLUW members. At the founding convention in 1974, 20–25 per cent of the 3200 women present were black and several of them assumed leadership positions. CLUW has been more successful as a working-class and multiracial feminist organisation than the National Black Feminist Organization (NBFO) formed in 1973. Although created to combat racism in the Women's Movement, the NBFO was, according to its critics, too concerned with the reaction of white feminists.

Race and class differences among women have caused many significant and lasting problems for the movement. However, the most explosive early conflicts concerned whether 'open' lesbians should be accepted and whether sexual preference should be considered a feminist issue. Lesbians had been active in the Women's Movement from its inception, but many of them had kept their sexual preference hidden. Then in 1969, a fight between the police and gay men occurred at the Stonewall Inn, a gay bar in New York City. This widely publicised event marked the beginning of Gay Liberation, and lesbians and gay men began to 'come out' publicly, proclaiming themselves a proud minority group with a legitimate culture of their own.

Almost immediately, however, lesbians who had been active in the Women's Movement found Gay Liberation and its organisations too male-dominated. Like the radical women who had bid goodbye to male-dominated leftist organisations, some long-time homophile activists, such as Del Martin and Phyllis Lyon, joined with younger lesbians to seek their 'community' in the Women's Movement.

They did not find a warm welcome. Friedan even resorted to McCarthyite scare tactics in her zeal to purge NOW of what she called the 'lavender menace'. In 1970, at the second Congress to Unite Women, lesbians staged a protest. Carrying signs proclaiming, 'Women's Liberation Is a Lesbian Plot', and wearing 'Lavender Menace' T-shirts, they made their case in a paper entitled 'The Woman-Identified Woman'. Some of the protesters who felt that the Women's Movement was itself sexist seceded. They organised a new group, Radicalesbians, the first all-lesbian group since the founding of Daughters of Bilitis fifteen years earlier. While 'woman-identified' women are more likely to be part of the radical than the liberal branch of feminism, outspoken lesbians did push NOW, if not Friedan, away from its initial homophobia.

The turning point was probably the media-baiting of Kate Millett. As Chair of the Education Committee of New York's NOW, Millett has spoken of her bisexuality to the 1970 Congress and other gatherings. Just as her book *Sexual Politics* appeared, *Time* magazine, which had featured her on its cover in August 1970, discredited her in an article in December. Although Millett was disturbed that *Time* had made her an instant leader only to dismiss the entire movement, she correctly predicted: 'I have pulled a coup whereby the women's movement will officially support Gay Liberation.' In the fall of 1971, NOW acknowledged 'the oppression of lesbians as a legitimate concern of feminism'.[4] By 1977, the National Women's Conference, sponsored and funded by the federal government, included sexual preference as a feminist demand, along with the ERA, employment and reproductive freedom.

The lesbian issue is only one example of how the liberal or

moderate branch of the Women's Movement has been able to incorporate or 'co-opt' radical demands. Consciousness-raising, a feminist tactic and process begun by radicals, provides a similar case. NOW initially had viewed consciousness-raising groups with disdain, for it feared that women's energies would be diverted to solving personal problems rather than political ones. Due to members' demands, NOW chapters eventually began to include consciousness-raising sessions in their programmes.

In spite of partial radicalisation on issues, NOW's structure has remained traditional. It is a national organisation with a hierarchy, written by-laws and elected officials. Ti-Grace Atkinson, President of the New York chapter, was one of the early critics of NOW's unequal power relationships and traditional hierarchical structure. After she failed to persuade the New York chapter to initiate a 'lot system' to replace elected officers, she resigned from NOW in October 1968. Her new group, The Feminists, divided 'shitwork' equally and developed a technique to allow equal speaking time for each member at meetings.

Between 1967 and 1974, NOW grew from 14 chapters to over 700, and from 1000 members to 40,000. NOW members have not been drawn equally from all segments of the female population. In a survey done in 1974, only 17 per cent listed their primary occupation as that of homemaker. NOW members worked disproportionately in professional occupations and were more highly educated than American women generally. Almost half were under the age of 30, but only 5 per cent were black and another 5 per cent were other women of colour.[5]

Most of the early activists in the radical branch of the Women's Movement were also young, highly educated, white and middle class. In spite of important ideological differences, the two branches have shared a common constituency and culture. This has facilitated close friendships and effective coalitions around a number of feminist issues – the ERA, abortion rights‚ and employment opportunity – but has also limited the movement's influence.

Liberal feminism has been the most popular type in the United States because it seeks to extend already accepted American values and practices to women. Liberals ask for civil rights and equal opportunities – not equal results. They usually accept existing social, political and economic arrangements. Even when they do want more than merely to include women in the 'male model' of power and success, they generally do not attack the power of men as a class or demand the destruction of the 'patriarchal system'.

At its best, liberal feminism promotes a vision of androgyny, which was first set out by Alice Rossi, a charter member of NOW, in her article, 'Equality Between the Sexes: An Immodest Proposal' (1964). 'An androgynous conception of sex role means that each sex will cultivate some of the characteristics usually associated with the other in traditional sex role definitions.' For example, men would try to be tender and women, assertive. Of course, Rossi assumed that 'by far the majority of the differences between the sexes . . . are socially rather than physiologically determined'.[6]

The androgynous perspective suggests that men and women should be equal to each other, not that women should emulate men. Androgynous feminists are a bridge between liberals and radicals; they are concerned with such issues of 'personal politics' as eliminating sexism in language and religion, freeing female sexuality from learned passivity and dependence on men, and developing child-rearing practices free from gender-role conditioning. Yet, in assuming that men and women are equally willing to change social attitudes and institutions, androgynous theorists ignore the facts that men hold much greater power over social resources and are likely to resist any possible loss of their supremacy. Because androgyny moves liberal feminists to the point of questioning existing models of politics, work and culture, it forms part of what Jo Freeman calls an 'inherent logic' in feminism.[7] Simply trying to include women equally in existing institutions may involve changing those institutions thoroughly.

Liberal feminists, then, are potential radicals. However, many liberals, such as Friedan, are not conscious of this and they deny that the liberalism they espouse is a political ideology like any other. They are often unaware that the liberal values of individual rights and equality of opportunity actually contradict their feminist recognition that women are a sex-class whose common condition is socially and not individually determined.

Initially, socialist-feminists shared the liberal separation of public and private problems. Socialists have traditionally focused on economic inequality. They aim to change or overthrow capitalism and its class system. But socialists have not seen women as a class in themselves, only as part of the proletariat engaged in wage labour. Due to the feminist movement, socialists have begun to analyse housework, motherwork and other aspects of 'private life' within capitalism.

The American Women's Movement, unlike its British or Continental counterparts, did not begin with a strong socialist-feminist component. This was due first to the absence of a continuous and powerful socialist movement in the US and second to the particular conflicts women had with the 1960s New Left. The 'socialist tradition' most politically radical young women were familiar with was the small, government-persecuted Communist Party whose ideological rigidity had been rejected by the 1960s radicals. Most of them were unaware of the anarchist Emma Goldman (1869–1940) or of the work done by the Socialist Party of America during the first twenty years of the century.

Founded in 1901, the Socialist Party supported women's suffrage and published Margaret Sanger's articles on birth control. Between 1908 and 1915, a Woman's National Committee (WNC) operated within the Party, though it was never an autonomous group. Women were just 10 to 15 per cent of the Party's membership and only a few were able to play more than supporting or auxiliary roles. In addition, the Party was suspicious of the women's movement outside its ranks.

Women in the 1960s faced the same ideological and organisational resistance as their radical foremothers; those who parted with the 'male left' in the late 1960s lacked an alternative socialist or labour tradition to inspire them. Most of the American trade unions had become conservative and vehemently anti-communist and the New Left had few close ties with them. The early important reassessments of socialism were done by European, especially English, feminists. American women benefited from the work of Juliet Mitchell and Sheila Rowbotham.

Mitchell's 'Women: The Longest Revolution' (1966) was the first new feminist critique of socialist theory. Mitchell claimed that women's condition is the result of historical changes both in production and in three areas of 'reproduction': reproduction itself, sex, and the socialisation of children. The liberation of women 'can only be achieved if *all four* structures in which they are integrated are transformed'.[8]

Mitchell's longer work *Woman's Estate* (1971) and Sheila Rowbotham's *Woman's Consciousness, Man's World* (1973) were able to incorporate some of the radical feminist critiques of sexuality and 'patriarchy'. Rowbotham had already been asking herself questions about what relationship her 'personal experience' had to a social movement, for she had discovered areas of her experience not addressed by her political class consciousness. At the same time, she was aware that capitalism 'does not only exploit the wage-earner at work, it takes from men and women the capacity to develop their potential fully in every area of life'. A movement concerned only with 'the specific oppression of women cannot, in isolation, end exploitation and imperialism'. Juliet Mitchell set up a chart in *Woman's Estate* with the views of 'Radical Feminists' on one side and those of 'Abstract Socialists' on the other. Finding both inadequate, she called for a larger theory. 'We should ask the feminist questions, but try to come up with some Marxist answers.'[9]

American feminists did not immediately take up the task of synthesising Marxism and feminism. Instead of analysing the oppression of women within the historically specific context of advanced capitalism, radical feminists developed theories based on their own experience of oppression in contemporary patriarchy.

The radicals' emphasis on patriarchy rather than capitalism was in part due to the struggle between themselves and female 'politicos' during the early years of the Women's Movement. The politicos took their priorities from the male-led New Left and did not wish to separate from it, despite the Left's niggardly acknowledgement of women's issues. In 1968, SDS 'argued that inasmuch as women's liberation was "an integral part" of the battle against capitalism', women should remain within the organisation rather than form separate women's groups.[10] This was less than what the Socialist Party had offered women in 1908. Women's groups which were forming outside SDS met a hostile reception.

In order to develop a woman-centred theory and practice, the early radical feminists felt they had to make a clean break with 'male' thought. Barbara Burris, who had been involved in the Civil Rights Movement and SDS, joined with five other women in 1971 to write 'The Fourth World Manifesto'. The authors wanted to develop a new definition of imperialism which would include women as a 'colonized group'. Rape was called 'an individual male imperialist act . . . while the abortion laws are male group control over . . . female territories'. They argued that women, like other colonised people, have a culture of their own, a 'female culture of emotion, intuition, love, personal relationships'.[11] Although this approach could merely glorify women's oppression and perpetuate sex differences, it was a necessary declaration of female independence and pride. It was also an early step towards forming a theory of patriarchy which was not based on previous definitions of class or imperialism.

In this painful process of separating from the male Left, feminists found themselves at odds with those who remained in SDS, the Socialist Workers Party, Progressive Labor or other groups. The conflict broke out in early 1968 during a protest against the Vietnam War, when members of Radical Women, a New York group, refused to work with the Jeanette Rankin Brigade. Instead, they planned their own demonstration – 'The Burial of Traditional Womanhood'. It was the first public action where women proclaimed, 'Sisterhood is Powerful'.

Feminist-politico splits continued to surface: within New York Radical Women and other groups, at a conference held in Chicago in late 1968, and at later conferences and feminist actions. The arguments often centred around the issue of sexuality and the value of consciousness-raising. Although most radical feminists were anti-capitalist, it seemed more important at the time to oppose the politicos' emphasis on class and imperialism than to find common ground. Until the politicos themselves evolved into autonomous socialist-feminists, they attacked the radical feminists for ignoring working-class and Third World women.

Although both radicals and politicos insisted upon including all women, neither side recognised and confronted class and race differences among women. Constance Carroll, a black educator, wrote that the Women's Movement 'attempted to transcend rather than confront the racial tensions and complexities resulting from the Black woman's involvement in the movement'.[12]

'Sisterhood', according to early radical feminists, meant that all women were a single class oppressed by men. As economic class differences did surface in women's groups, they were usually dealt with on an *ad hoc* basis. The Furies, for example, a lesbian-feminist collective, published a collection of articles on class conflict based mainly on their personal and group experience. Women were an oppressed class, but they could still oppress each other. A 1971 issue of *Women: A Journal of Liberation* took a similar, personal approach to the question of class. Besides articles on women's experience in various working-class occupations, one appeared which listed the ways that middle-class women deny their own privileged positions and patronise working-class women. Also included, with some editorial reservations, was an angry letter from an anonymous welfare mother who complained that 'women's liberationists' ignored the needs of the very poor altogether. While this kind of confrontation and dialogue in movement publications was valuable for already committed feminists, it did not recruit working-class women into the movement. The Furies' *Class and Feminism* (1974) ignored not only racism, but also economic issues such as employment, trade unions and women's unpaid work in the home.

There had been a few early articles on housework written by socialist women, such as Mary Inman's 'In Woman's Defense' (1940) and 'A Woman's Place' by Selma James and another woman who used pseudonyms (1953), but it was not until the late 1960s and 1970s that the socialist-feminist analysis and debate on the subject really began. The more orthodox Marxist-feminists call for the collectivisation of housework and child care and the participation of women in the paid labour market. Another group, which sees housework as 'productive' work, demands 'wages for housework' in order to eliminate the role of the housewife. The first American discussions of housework treated it as a personal-political issue within contemporary patriarchy rather than as an economic problem. Pat Mainardi's witty and widely reprinted essay 'The Politics of Housework' (1968) dealt mainly with the arguments men put up to avoid sharing domestic chores and how women, in turn, can overcome this male resistance.

As American feminists became more interested in the history of women's work, they began to include housework and reproduction. About a year after Ann Oakley's *Housewife* (1974) appeared in Britain, Barbara Ehrenreich and Deirdre English published an essay in *Socialist Review* called 'The Manufacture of Housework'. They traced the effects of industrialisation on family life at the turn of the century and postulated that middle-class uneasiness over the future of the home led to a 'domestic science movement'. Investing housework with 'the grandeur of science' in order to keep women at home, the 'domestic science movement' was also 'an effort to discipline and Americanize' the urban immigrant poor by teaching them middle-class values and family roles.[13]

By the mid 1970s, an emerging socialist-feminist consciousness in the United States was coupled with a growing theoretical sophistication. Socialist-feminists now drew upon the work of both the earlier 'housework' feminists and the ideas of radical feminists. *Capitalist Patriarchy and the Case for Socialist Feminism* (1979), the first volume of socialist-feminist writings primarily by American women, explores the influence of both patriarchy and capitalism on women's lives. Yet, for the most part, the articles lack a synthesis of feminism and Marxism. Heidi Hartmann argues that historically women's participation in the wage-labour market had been 'as clearly limited by patriarchy as it was by capitalism', but she concentrates more on the former than the latter. Batya Weinbaum and Amy Bridges, on the other hand, look at consumption as work women do for capitalism. However, they also note that consumption is based on household and community needs and may embody 'values antithetical to capitalist production'. Nancy Hartsock takes a third approach by considering how the feminist emphasis on everyday life rather than abstract theory might lead women 'to oppose the institutions of capitalism and white supremacy as well as patriarchy'.

This anthology was partly the result of ideas generated at the first organised conference of socialist-feminists held in Yellow Springs, Ohio, in July 1975. Although the conference itself was more Marxist than feminist, it stimulated both a more integrated analysis of capitalism and patriarchy and the formation of small, autonomous socialist-feminist groups.

One of these, The Combahee River Collective in Boston, is a black lesbian group. Unlike the National Black Feminist Organization, the members of Combahee proclaim themselves to be socialists. They want to extend Marx's theory to cover the specific economic conditions of black women. Like radical feminists, they have used the technique of consciousness-raising, but as black women one of their major concerns has been 'racism in the white women's movement'.[14]

While the evolution of and debates on socialist-feminist theory can be traced through books and articles, it is more difficult to assess how much influence socialism has had on women's political activity. Barbara Epstein claims that 'socialist-feminism had always been an intellectual wing of the women's movement'. However, socialist-feminists have been active in the reproductive rights movement, especially in those organisations such as the Committee for Abortion Rights and Against Sterilization Abuse (CARASA) which are committed 'to reproductive issues as a whole rather than abortion as a single-issue politics'.[15] Many socialist-feminists are devoted to peace, anti-nuclear and anti-intervention work.

As economic and specifically workplace issues became more central in the 1970s, women workers began organising. Most do not call themselves socialists, but their demands and activities are a challenge to the institutions of patriarchal capitalism: corporations, trade unions and the state. Unlike the Coalition of Labor Union Women (CLUW) discussed earlier, most of the new working women's groups have their roots in the Women's Movement rather than the trade unions. Not surprisingly, many are organisations of clerical workers. Although one-third of all American working women are in clerical jobs, only 9 per cent in 1976 belonged to unions. Trade unions have a history of neglecting clerical workers because they are women, so in the 1970s office workers began forming independent organisations, usually on a city-wide basis. These include: 9 to 5 in Boston, Women Employed in Chicago, Women Office Workers in New York, and Cleveland Women Working. Most have combined direct action with education and research in order to improve the condition of working women and to enable women to organise within their own workplaces.

In contrast to the individualism of middle-class feminists, the office-workers movement has generally emphasised better conditions for all women (even household workers) through collective action. Union WAGE (Women's Alliance to Gain Equality), in particular, takes a class-conscious stand. Joyce Maupin, one of the founders, has written that Union WAGE does not see the problem of working women 'in terms of the advancement and promotion of individuals'. Rather, the goal 'is to change the lives of all file clerks, factory workers, farm workers, and waitresses'.[16]

Some unions have recently shown signs of cooperating with the Women's Movement. In 1977, Karen Nussbaum, one of the founders of 9 to 5, helped to form Working Women, a national organisation of local clerical groups. In 1981, 9 to 5 joined the Service Employees International Union (SEIU) and created District 925, a nationwide SEIU union to organise clerical workers. The public employee union, American Federation of State, County and Municipal Employees (AFSCME), not only supported its San Jose (California) local in its successful 1979 strike to re-evaluate jobs and their monetary worth along gender lines, but has also adopted the issue of 'equal pay for comparable work' as an organising tool to recruit women in the public sector. In 1979, the AFL-CIO accepted Joyce Miller, the President of CLUW, into its previously all-male Executive Council, and a number of unions have made maternity leaves, day care, and sexual harassment important policy issues.

It is mainly through their own organisations that women have been challenging the stereotypes of clerical workers as stupid, weak but useful adjuncts to men. As one woman put it, 'we don't have to be ashamed to be clerks anymore'.[17] On a larger scale, the Women's Movement has made many women no longer ashamed to be female anymore. In the United States, the radical feminist wing has probably contributed the most to women's new sense of power and worth. It has made them aware of the connection between their private feelings and public status and has taken the lead in creating theory and practice for changing both.

Radical feminists were, at first, small groups of women who separated from the New Left in 1967 and 1968. In August 1968, the first meeting of women's groups was held in Maryland. Although this led to a larger conference in Chicago later that year, no national organisation or coordination of activities resulted. In fact, there was no national women's liberation movement when the media first covered the demonstrations at the Miss America Contest in September 1968. The protesters' counterculture style of street theatre brought national media attention, but it also resulted in the unfortunate label of 'bra burners'.

'Women's liberation', which initially meant only the younger, more radical branch of the Women's Movement, soon acquired a generic meaning to include all feminists. The media trivialised the term, too, by calling it 'women's lib' and its activists 'women's libbers'. For these reasons, the radical branch of the Women's Movement will be referred to as 'radical feminism' rather than 'women's liberation'.

Terminology is a minor problem compared to the difficulty of tracing radical feminist organisations. After 1967, they began to multiply rapidly. Many quickly disappeared, while others split over political differences or spun off new groups. Some concentrated on specific issues, such as rape or health care, or were designed to meet the needs of specific sets of women – mothers, lesbians, older women, etc. Lists and even large catalogues like the impressive *The*

New Woman's Survival Sourcebook (1975) were outdated as soon as they were compiled.

Radical feminists, like participants in other social movements, were not part of the established policy-making process and needed to organise themselves for political action. Radical feminists have also served as an incipient interest group influencing policy-makers, but to a greater degree than other political activists, they emphasise personal transformation. As women become feminists, they see themselves and the world through new and different eyes. They call this change in perception, by which the 'personal' becomes 'political', 'consciousness-raising'.

Although some feminists have spoken of a moment of 'conversion' akin to a religious experience, consciousness-raising is usually a gradual process of unlearning all the external and internal aspects of the culturally prescribed female role. Along with this, there is an emotional and intellectual understanding of the ways they, as women, have been oppressed. Women then begin turning to each other, rather than men, for approval, support and assistance. They start working together in 'sisterhood' to bring about political change.

Consciousness-raising, according to Kathie Sarachild, one of its originators, was 'both a method for arriving at the truth and a means for action and organizing'. It usually occurred in small 'rap' groups which met in women's homes where women could 'share our feelings and pool them. Let's let ourselves go and see where our feelings lead us. Our feelings will lead us to ideas and then to actions.'[18]

Early feminist groups were soon experimenting with different 'CR' methods and sharing their experiences with other groups. The Redstockings, a group started by two members of New York Radical Women, is usually credited with being the first clearly to articulate the function, purpose and process of consciousness-raising. According to the Redstockings 'Manifesto' (7 July 1969), women, more than other oppressed groups, need consciousness-raising: 'Because we have lived so intimately with our oppressors, in isolation from each other, we have been kept from seeing our personal suffering as a political condition.'[19]

Sharing individual experiences is the real heart of consciousness-raising. In talking about their childhoods, sexual relationships, education, children, etc., groups of six to twelve women come to the 'understanding that many of the situations described are not personal at all, and are not based on individual inadequacies, but rather have a root in the social order'. Thus, the 'personal' becomes 'political'. And conversely, because analysis takes place only after sharing, it is 'based on a female understanding of the reality of women's condition', not on any preconceived 'male' theory.[20] Although consciousness-raising was more than individual therapy, it was not, in itself, politics. It served rather as a prerequisite for political action and as a way to reassess ongoing political activities.

Radical feminists generally point to 'patriarchy', rather than 'capitalism' or 'imperialism', as the primary cause of women's oppression. Kate Millett's *Sexual Politics* and Shulamith Firestone's *The Dialectic of Sex*, both published in 1970, were two important early works which both described the ways the 'rule by men' oppressed women and provided a framework for feminist theories of patriarchy.

Millett found examples of patriarchal power everywhere, not only in industry, the military, universities and government, but also in sexual ideologies and practices, including romantic love, literary works by men, religious philosophies and symbols, and, above all, in the family. 'Patriarchy's chief institution is the family.' Patriarchy, then, is pervasive and total. 'A referent scarcely exists with which it might be contrasted or by which it might be confuted.' It has an even more tenacious hold than class because it has passed itself off as 'nature'.[21]

Shulamith Firestone, like Millett, saw the sexual class system as 'the model for all other exploitative systems', and it 'must be eliminated first by any true revolution'. Rewording the Marxist slogan, she called for 'the revolt of the underclass (women) and the seizure of control of *reproduction*'. She also attacked the family and discussed the ways in which romantic heterosexual love is corrupted by '*an unequal balance of power*'. But whereas Millett believed that most of the distinctions between the sexes are cultural, not biological, Firestone took the position that: 'The heart of woman's oppression is her childbearing and childrearing roles.' Most feminists wanted day care facilities and legal abortion, but they did not believe that 'it was woman's reproductive biology that accounted for her original and continued oppression'. Even less popular than Firestone's premise was her 'solution' which called for reproductive

biological motherhood debate

engineering – test-tube babies and the like – to free women '*from the tyranny of their reproductive biology*'.[22]

A few years later, Adrienne Rich pointed out that female biology and reproductive capacity were not inherently oppressive. Rather, it is the *institution* of motherhood within patriarchal society which oppresses women and alienates them from their own bodies. In *Of Women Born*, Rich presented an alternative vision to Firestone's technological utopia. 'I have come to believe . . . that female biology . . . has far more radical implications than we have yet come to appreciate.' She wanted women to view their physicality as a 'resource' which could help to heal the patriarchal culture's separation of mind and body.

> In order to live a fully human life we require not only *control* of our bodies (though control is a prerequisite); we must touch the unity and resonance of our physicality, our bond with the natural order, the corporeal ground of our intelligence.

Women, Rich said, must begin 'to *think through the body*, to connect what has been so cruelly disorganized' by patriarchy.[23]

Radical feminists found they could begin with almost any phenomenon affecting women – motherhood, sexual love, rape, advertising images – and trace it to other forms of oppression. Yet this connecting process did not minimise the differences between women and men, as liberal feminists hoped, but rather sharpened them. Radical feminists criticised all aspects of 'male' culture; they did not wish to be like men or even to be accepted by men on male terms. They insisted instead that women's 'difference' did not mean 'inferiority', and they intended to prove it by creating institutions based on 'female' values.

Within their own organisations, feminists insisted on egalitarian rather than hierarchical structures. In practice, this meant 'no leaders' and often 'no structure'. 'Structurelessness' sometimes only masked the existence of informal power-wielding cliques. Women who felt left out of the inner circle resorted to 'trashing' those activists who had shown assertiveness or even competence. Charges of being an 'elitist' were enough to break the hearts of dedicated feminists such as Kate Millett. 'Trashing' was not caused by women's inability to work together, but rather by the absence of clear procedures for selecting 'leaders' who would represent, speak for and be responsible to the group.

Since radical feminist groups shared the same ideal of participatory democracy as the early New Left and the Counterculture, it is not surprising that many of them suffered from the same weaknesses. In order to 'live out' their revolutionary values, a group might focus on its internal processes at the expense of formulating any programme of action. 'Unstructured groups', one woman wrote in 1972, 'may be very effective in getting women to talk about their lives; they aren't very good for getting things done.'[24]

One major difference between radical feminist groups and those of the New Left/Counterculture was that the women's groups explicitly excluded men. Angered at their treatment in the 1960s movements, women did not believe that men were yet willing or able both to articulate an anti-patriarchal ideology and to practise it.

This 'separatism' was not a new strategy. It was practised by middle-class women's culture and the political feminist movement before 1920. But after winning the vote, much of the self-conscious female community disintegrated as women adopted male values and opted for assimilation into male institutions. It was not until the late 1960s that feminists began to argue that the strategy of integration had failed.

Separatism was not a controversial policy within the radical feminist movement. It occurred almost spontaneously and without debate, because it was a logical extension of an ideology which called men the 'class enemy' of women. Tactically, too, women knew that mixed-gender groups would only perpetuate the traditional female pattern of deferring to men, seeking their approval, and adopting their values. The presence of 'open' lesbians and an ideology of lesbian-feminism not found in the earlier women's movement also encouraged many non-lesbians to re-evaluate their relationships with men.

Although lesbianism and separatism are not identical positions, both threaten men. Radical feminists have been charged with being 'man-hating dykes'. They have responded to this in two ways: first, by saying that such an accusation is the sexist equivalent of 'red-baiting' and is designed to divide and isolate women from each other; second, by accepting the label as an accurate indicator of women's legitimate anger at a misogynous society.

Whatever the response, the essential feature of radical feminism is not man-hating, but woman-loving or sisterhood. This means 'support for all women by women'. Raising 'the estimation of women's value in women's eyes' is no small achievement in a culture which has fostered a lack of respect for women,[25] but it can take extreme forms. The Redstockings' 'pro-woman' line, for example, claimed that women were in no way responsible for their oppression and did not need to change themselves. Other radical feminists were quick to point out that this view only glorified the status quo and did not attack the patriarchy.

Another form of criticism has come from socialist-feminists, who insist on a historical dimension. Radicals often neglect to 'analyze the particular patriarchal relations that exist within each historical period within society'. Moreover, not all men benefit from patriarchy to the same degree. Patriarchy is 'a system of hierarchy, order, and control both among men and of men over women', not just a simple set of social relations which enables men to control women. Men's benefits from patriarchy depend on their different class and race positions, not only on their common sex.[26]

Although radical feminists deplore economic class and racial hierarchies, this does not stop them from attacking patriarchy in socialist as well as capitalist countries. For this reason, radical feminists look at economic systems differently from socialists. Lisa Leghorn and Katherine Parker, for example, classify the US, Cuba, the USSR and Sweden as similar 'male-defined economies' where women hold only 'token power'. In these countries women may gain rights, but not real power. These rights are given to women by male-controlled governments or for male-defined purposes and, subsequently, can be taken away.

The Women's Movement in the US has been fighting for 'negotiating power' with the male-dominated culture in order to determine vital areas of their own lives.[27] Control over their own bodies is the most basic demand. Women want to be free from both involuntary reproduction and male violence. Rape, wife battering, incest and pornography are some of the forms of male violence against which feminists have been the most active.

Before the existence of a radical feminist movement, rape was regarded primarily as a crime of 'passion' or as one involving 'stolen property'. The only 'real' rape victims were women who 'belonged to' respectable (i.e. white, middle-class) men and who had spotless reputations as virgins or monogamous wives. The battered wife was a 'symptom' of a 'dysfunctional family'. She, not the batterer, was the object of study – what had she done to 'provoke' the beating? Jokes and proverbs sanctioned both rape and wife battering. Under these conditions, they were (and still remain) under-reported crimes. Only one in ten to one in five cases come to the attention of the police. Incest was either discussed in psychoanalytic terms as a sexual taboo between mother and son or else diagnosed as a fantasy or wish on the part of the victim. Mostly there was silence, even greater than that surrounding rape and battering.

Pornography, on the other hand, has generated noisy debates. Conservatives have denounced it as sinful and immoral; liberals have praised it as healthy and sexually 'liberating'. Neither side has discussed its effects on women. Radical feminists, by placing women at the centre, see pornographic images and sexual abuse as a connected web of crimes against women. As Robin Morgan put it: 'Pornography is the theory, and rape the practice.'[28]

Rape was one of the first issues taken up by American radical feminists; the feminist analysis of wife battering, on the other hand, initially came from England, with Erin Pizzey's *Scream Quietly or the Neighbours Will Hear* (1974). Subsequently, when women began looking at incest they discovered that in approximately nine cases out of ten fathers had molested their daughters, while there were almost no cases involving mothers and sons. Sexually-abused children, like rape or battering victims, hardly ever imagined or lied about their experiences. They were more likely to keep silent, sometimes because they were promised rewards, but usually out of fear that they would not be believed. Unlike battering or rape, incest does not usually include physical force. The victim 'participates' because she trusts the male adult – a trust which he betrays. Like wife battering, incest is a repeated crime which occurs within the home. Respect for the 'sanctity' of the home is one reason why the police and helping professions are reluctant to intervene. They are also hindered by sexist assumptions and theories.

Feminists are making some progress in combating the exclusive focus on victimology as well as widespread myths about women enjoying, provoking or deserving abuse. In addition to educating and confronting the legal and helping professions, women have also taken direct action. Feminist groups run rape crisis centres and shelters for battered women and their children in almost every large and medium-sized city. These institutions provide immediate support for the victims, offer counselling and legal referral, and serve as part of a grass roots feminist political network.

The first feminist actions against pornography took place in the late 1960s and early 1970s. In 1970, for example, women demonstrated against *Playboy* and seized the offices of Grove Press. Then, activity ceased for about five years although pornography was growing into a $4 billion industry by the mid 1970s. Women were concentrating primarily on reproductive rights; they also felt intimidated by the liberal ideology of the 1970 *Report* of the Commission on Obscenity and Pornography. The Commission assumed that 'anything associated with the expression of sexuality was good'. However, as Irene Diamond has pointed out, the *Report*'s conclusion that pornography was harmless was 'not warranted on the basis of the actual data that were *available to the commission itself*'.

In 1976, women returned to the issue of pornography with *ad hoc* demonstrations around the country protesting a film called *Snuff* which purported to show the real murder of an actress. That year also marks the formation of the first feminist groups such as Women Against Violence in Pornography and Media (WAVPM) in San Francisco. The previous year Susan Brownmiller had revived Robin Morgan's argument that there was a connection between violent pornography and acts of violence. Brownmiller claimed in *Against Our Will: Men, Women and Rape* (1975) that 'Pornography is the undiluted essence of anti-female propaganda.'[29]

Since then, many feminists have come to see pornography not as explicit erotica, but as sexist propaganda. They believe it lies about women's sexual desires and needs; it teaches woman-hating by depicting women and female children as passive and controllable sex 'objects' who enjoy pain and punishment. Beginning in 1978, women have engaged in large 'Take Back the Night' marches around the country, harassed owners and customers of 'porn' establishments, and have even joined with conservatives to pass local ordinances against the 'spread' of pornography.

Not all feminists, however, accept the values, priorities and tactics of the anti-pornography movement. Critics charge that by emphasising male violence and women's need for sexual safety, anti-porn feminists 'resort to mobilizing women around their fears rather than their visions'. This not only 'recreates a very conservative sexual morality', but it also ignores other areas of women's oppression: the family, religion, the state, job discrimination and unequal pay.[30]

Although wife battering, rape, incest and the effects of violent pornography cut across class and racial lines, patriarchy alone cannot explain them or the ugly history of lynching or legally executing black men on false charges of raping white women. The murder of black men has been coupled with the refusal to believe black women who are, according to one estimate, eighteen times more likely to be rape victims than are white women.

The politics of reproduction affect women in various ways, depending upon their social positions. Abortion has been one of the most controversial issues among women. To put it simply, the early feminists, who were mainly white and middle class, concentrated on removing anti-abortion laws, while poor and especially Third World women were also concerned about involuntary sterilisation. Reproductive issues become somewhat more complex than an individual woman's 'right to choose' when we consider race and class, as Angela Davis asks us to do.

When Black and Latina women resort to abortions in such large numbers, the stories they tell are not so much about their desire to be free of their pregnancy, but rather about the miserable social conditions which dissuade them from bringing new lives into the world.[31]

Furthermore, the 'right to choose' remains within the context of a liberal ideology and its 'right' to privacy. 'Rights', argues Rosalind Pollack Petchesky, 'are by definition claims that are staked within a given order of things and relationships . . . but they do not challenge the social structure itself, the social relations of production and reproduction.'[32]

While Petchesky, like Davis, argues from a socialist-feminist perspective, others claim that 'rights' are a masculine concept which does not fully correspond to female ethics. Some recent studies by Carol Gilligan indicate that moral problems arise for women 'from conflicting responsibilities rather than from competing rights'. The moral imperative for women 'is an injunction to care', while for men it is 'an injunction to respect the rights of others'.

When a woman makes an abortion decision, she may realise that 'there is no way of acting that avoids hurt to others as well as to herself, and in this sense, no choice that is "right"'.[33]

Where radical feminists initially differed from liberals on abortion was not on ideological grounds, but in their use of stronger tactics and demands. The movement to reform abortion laws had begun prior to the feminist movement, and twelve states had reformed their laws between 1967 and 1970. But radical feminists demanded repeal of all existing state laws and confronted the legal system directly. They testified in public demonstrations about their illegal abortions and established 'self-help' clinics which provided 'underground' abortion referrals. New York, where radical feminists were strong and active, was one of the first states to repeal its abortion law in 1970.

Reformers and radicals welcomed the 1973 Supreme Court decisions (*Roe* v. *Wade* and *Doe* v. *Bolton*) which found that the 'right of privacy' precluded all state interference with abortions during the first 12 weeks of pregnancy and allowed only limited state interference in the second 12 weeks. This was not a final victory for women's reproductive freedom. First of all, as Kristin Booth Glen has pointed out, the Supreme Court 'was not upholding a *woman's* right to determine whether to bear a child. . . . Instead it was upholding a *doctor's* right to make a medical decision!' Second, and more important, this 'right', whoever held it, was turned into an empty one for poor women four years later, when the Supreme Court in 1977 ruled in three cases that the state does not have to reimburse for 'elective' abortions under Medicaid. Therefore, only women who could pay for abortions had the 'right' to them. The 1977 decisions served as a catalyst for white feminists to broaden the issue of reproductive freedom along the lines that women of colour had been urging. In Glen's words, 'we can no longer afford to separate the issues of free abortion and sterilization abuse'.[34]

Since radical feminists are also aware that reproduction is linked to the sexuality that precedes it and the motherwork that may follow, issues of sexuality and family have been central to both feminist politics and women's culture.

Sex, Love and Family Relationships

Feminists of the 1970s believed like Hippies of the 1960s that voluntary actions of consciously transformed individuals could create fundamental social change. Each group produced an alternative culture and institutions based on its distinctive values. Women in the nineteenth century had also created a culture with its own relationship patterns, institutions and methods of communication. However, much of this traditional women's culture, along with its political potential, disappeared after 1920. The revival of women's culture in the late 1960s occurred in a radically different and more politicised social context.

Female sexuality was one of the earliest feminist issues. Kate Millett opened *Sexual Politics* (1970) with a passage from one of Henry Miller's novels, which she then called 'a case of sexual politics at the fundamental level of copulation'. Instead of seeing male and female sexual behaviour as something unquestionably 'natural' or 'normal', feminists claimed that heterosexual relationships were a product of patriarchal culture and politics.

Their basic premise was that women had become alienated from their own bodies, especially their sexual desires. Instead of relating as autonomous individuals to themselves or to their partners, women responded to a world of male-created symbol and fantasy. Although the female in patriarchy did not develop the sexual symbols by which she was described, she had subscribed or succumbed to them. In the words of one feminist: 'It is a world where eroticism is defined in terms of female powerlessness, dependency, and submission. It is a world of sado-masochistic sex.'[1]

The first step out of this condition was to dispel cultural myths about female sexuality and inform women about their own sexual

138

potential. Anne Koedt, in 'The Myth of the Vaginal Orgasm' (1968), popularised the findings of Masters and Johnson on clitoral orgasm. She also argued that if women could satisfy themselves through masturbation or lesbian relationships, they 'would threaten the heterosexual *institution*' by making heterosexuality one sexual option among others.[2]

Since the male experts had been so wrong about female orgasm, then women's health care in general also deserved scrutiny. By the mid 1970s a widespread network of feminist health centres and action groups existed. From an original focus on birth control, abortion and maternity care, they expanded to include other aspects of women's health, such as nutrition and exercise. Yet reproductive issues have remained central. As feminists have pointed out, over 90 per cent of American obstetricians/gynaecologists (ob-gyns) were male and it was men who controlled reproductive politics.

The work of the women's health movement has centred on three areas: changing women's consciousness about the health care they are presently receiving, providing health services to women, and altering the established health care system. The movement emphasises self-help and institutions such as the Los Angeles Women's Health Center have sought to educate women to be better informed and more assertive consumers of health care.

The popularity of *Our Bodies, Ourselves*, written by the Boston Women's Health Collective, illustrates the movement's success in providing women with reliable and potentially consciousness-raising information. The Collective began in 1969 as a small group of women who discussed the condescending and judgmental treatment they received from their doctors. Soon they were doing their own research and sharing it with others. Eventually they decided to publish their findings, first through a small press and then with a major publishing house.

At 647 pages, the third edition, *The New Our Bodies, Ourselves* (1984), has grown to almost twice the size of the 1976 edition. Totally reorganised and less medically oriented than previous editions, it contains new chapters on body image, alcohol and drugs, alternative health care practices (including yoga and meditation), environmental and occupational health hazards, new reproductive technologies, and international health issues such as the impact of the US drug industry on women in Third World countries. There is a greater understanding of stress as a major health hazard; woman battering, sexual harassment and the sexual abuse of children have been added to the earlier concern with rape; and the health of older women is no longer centred exclusively on menopause. Like the earlier editions, *The New Our Bodies, Ourselves* is the result of many women's work, maintains a critical feminist perspective towards the established profit-oriented medical system, and provides extensive resources for further knowledge and organising.

The women's health movement has acted both as a catalyst to and a reflection of a widespread national dissatisfaction with traditional high-priced allopathic medicine. As women are becoming less accepting of the 'routine' use of episiotomies, foetal monitoring, drug-induced labour and the supine position for delivery, there have been some changes in hospital childbirth procedures. Especially important is the reintroduction of certified nurse-midwives. Their services are less expensive and more patient-centred than those of male ob-gyns. However, most midwives must practise in hospitals because the established medical profession has resisted the introduction of an adequate emergency back-up system for home births.

Feminist health clinics both provide health services at low cost and serve as model institutions in order to increase consumer pressure on the established health care system. Unlike elitist professionals, feminist health care providers aim to democratise medicine. They share skills and information so that their patients can become active participants in the healing process. At most clinics the staff structure is as non-hierarchal as possible, with far more collective decision-making than at regular medical facilities. But this also means many staff meetings and long working hours, up to 55 or more a week in some cases.

While women's clinics can point out the system's shortcomings, they are limited in whom they reach and in the services they provide. The feminist health movement still deals mainly with reproduction, that is, the areas where women's health needs differ from those of men. So far, it has not been able to make major changes in the structure of American medicine.

Love, like health, affects women's minds and bodies. Feminists have tried to demystify heterosexual romance by pointing out that love between men and women is not really reciprocal. Women are likely to fall into what Margaret Adams called 'the compassion trap', because they have been taught to 'provide the tender and compassionate components of life'.[3] Women, but not men, are socialised to nurture and foster the growth of others, even to the extent of subordinating their own individual needs. Shulamith Firestone argued that women surrender their autonomy to men because of social and economic reasons which have little to do with love. Since men are more powerful economically and socially, they are in a better 'bargaining position' in relationships. The economic dependence of women 'makes a situation of healthy love between equals impossible'.[4] Firestone concluded that men and women do not and probably cannot love in the same way and that men, not women, were deficient. What caused the discrepancy? Is it possible for men to change?

Two schools of thought have presented answers to these questions: the androgynists and the lesbians. Androgynists believe that new child-rearing practices and early school education can make women and men more compatible. Nancy Chodorow, for example, has said that 'the very fact of being mothered by a woman generates in men conflicts over masculinity, a psychology of male dominance, and a need to be superior to women.'[5] By defining masculine personality as the denial of femininity, the culture perpetuates men's emotional distance from women. She is convinced that when primary parenting is shared between women and men, the existing unequal social organisation of gender will be transformed into one which allows women and men to develop similar capacities for affection and connection to others. For the present, however, mothering by women means that women retain a closer identification with their own sex.

Misgivings about heterosexual relationships also pervade recent fiction. In her study of 37 novels written by women in the 1970s, Ann Barr Snitow found that the overall picture of male-female relationships was not a positive one. 'Instead, almost all the novelists describe sex with men as so encrusted with difficulties that only the sacrifice of self can make it work. This price now seems too high.'[6]

If heterosexual feminists have been ambivalent about their relationships with men, lesbian feminists, especially in their early writings, were angry enough to dismiss men totally. 'What is a lesbian? A lesbian is the rage of all women condensed to the point of explosion', began the Radicalesbians' influential paper, 'The Woman Identified Woman' (1970).[7] Most lesbian feminists have agreed that lesbianism is a political revolt, not only a sexual act or 'preference'. Charlotte Bunch, for example, wrote in 1972: 'Woman-identified Lesbianism is . . . a political choice. It is political because relationships between men and women are essentially political, they involve power and dominance. Since the lesbian actively rejects that relationship and chooses women, she defies the established political system.' Yet lesbians are not free from heterosexual patriarchy unless they 'become feminists and fight against woman oppression, just as feminists must become Lesbians if they hope to end male supremacy'.

The second half of Bunch's prescription, along with statements such as Jill Johnston's that 'All women are lesbians',[8] confused many women. How could heterosexual women be or become lesbians? It was unclear whether lesbian feminists were criticising heterosexuality as an institution or attacking individual women who were having heterosexual relationships.

Lesbians who wished to include heterosexual women de-emphasised or even eliminated the erotic element in same-sex relationships. Lillian Faderman, for example, in *Surpassing the Love of Men* (1981), said that 'a relationship in which two women's strongest emotions and affections are directed toward each other' is a lesbian relationship. Sexual contact need not be present.[9]

The debate over how much emphasis to place on sexual relationships plagued both lesbians and non-lesbians in the Women's Movement. In the early 1970s, some lesbians equated their own sexual relations with 'vanguard' radical feminism and used sex as a weapon against other feminists. Heterosexual feminists who were willing to risk 'lesbian-baiting' for their political work found that lesbians refused to treat them as 'sisters'. Lesbians also suffered. Heterosexual women were approaching them as sex objects and asking for a 'lesbian experience' as a sort of feminist initiation rite. Lesbians also found it difficult to deal with some women who called themselves 'politicalesbians', yet abstained from sexual relations with women while continuing to have them with men.

Women of colour, such as The Combahee River Collective, could not advocate separatism from men, because as they put it: 'Our situation as black people necessitates that we have solidarity around the fact of race.' On a more general level, the Collective also questioned the efficacy of lesbian separatism as a political strategy, 'since it so completely denies any but the sexual sources of women's oppression, negating the facts of class and race'.[10]

In addressing class and race issues, the Collective has broadened the scope of feminist sexual politics beyond that of a 'straight-lesbian' split. Another promising trend is the less polarised thinking about female sexuality found in recent writings about women's friendship and erotic desire. Adrienne Rich uses the term 'lesbian continuum' to mean 'a range – through each woman's life and throughout history – of woman-identified experience; not simply the fact that a woman has had or consciously desired genital sexual experience with another woman'. The lesbian continuum includes all forms of female 'bonding against male tyranny' and 'the giving and receiving of practical and political support' between women. Rich does not deny the existence of an erotic component in female friendships or in other close relationships such as those of mothers and daughters. Audre Lorde describes this 'erotic' not as genital sexuality, but as 'an assertion of the life force of women; of that creative energy empowered, the knowledge and use of which we are now reclaiming in our language, our history, our dancing, our loving, our work, our lives.'[11] Neither Lorde nor Rich separates the mind from the body, the spiritual from the physical.

Although the 1960s Counterculture had also wished to end the dichotomy between mind and body, it did not encourage primary erotic and emotional bonds between women. At the time no one questioned the male model of sexuality. The new female-centred view provides new definitions for 'sex', along with the possibility of a new sexual ethic. For example, Adrienne Rich has asked for a redefinition of female 'honour' so that it would no longer mean virginity, chastity and fidelity to a husband, but rather honesty among women. Lying has been one way women have survived in patriarchal cultures; Rich now hopes that women will be able to speak truthfully to each other, for 'we have a profound stake, beyond the personal, in the project of describing our reality as candidly and fully as we can'.[12]

Most recently, a more critical approach to feminist sexuality and sexual ethics has emerged, opposing some of the neo-puritan elements of the Women's Movement. Gayle Rubin, for example, argues that instead of becoming champions of greater sexual pleasure, feminists have concentrated on women's sexual victimisation and affectional preference. The Women's Movement has erected a new hierarchy of sexual value in which the egalitarian, enduring and tender lesbian relationship has replaced the monogamous, procreative heterosexual couple as the most acceptable or 'best' type. At the bottom level, however, remain women and men who engage in sado-masochism, enjoy playing masculine-feminine roles (lesbian butch-fem, for example), exchange sex for money, or choose sexual relations across generations. In other words, the feminist transformation of lesbianism has not led to an elimination of sexual hierarchy with its creation of 'outcast' and 'deviant' groups. The result of such feminist orthodoxy has been a smaller space in which women can express their sexuality. Instead of imposing limits, Amber Hollibaugh asks that feminism be 'a critical edge in the struggle to allow women more room to confront the dangers of desire. . . . We must build a movement that validates the right for a woman to say yes instead of no . . . and which reclaims an eroticism not defined by a simple political perspective or narrow vision.'[13]

In spite of their differences, all feminists oppose the Counterculture's anti-intellectual and male supremacist ideology, and emphasise women's sexual autonomy, capacity for sexual pleasure and ability to do critical and creative work.

Feminists have also envisioned and experimented with alternative household arrangements, child-rearing methods and community support systems. They have criticised the elevation of the modern nuclear family form as The Family – timeless, 'natural' and perfectly suited to fulfil its functions. They have also linked women's subordination both to the specific household arrangement of the nuclear family and to the ideology that has made this family form monolithic.

Although feminists claim that the institution of the family oppresses women, the Women's Movement did not cause the recent changes in American family life. Economic and demographic factors generated a decline in average household size, and divorce rates doubled between the mid 1960s and mid 1970s. The number of female-headed households increased 81 per cent during the 1970s. Fewer than 10 per cent of all US families now fit the ideal nuclear type: two or more children at home, father working and mother as a full-time homemaker. Despite these national trends, and because the Women's Movement furthered a new sense of women's possibilities outside marriage and motherhood, feminists have become leading scapegoats for the so-called 'breakdown' of the family.

Initially most feminists were critical of women's financial dependence on male breadwinners, the legal inequalities of married women, and the psychological and emotional discrepancies in family roles, all of which resulted in husbands/fathers accruing more power than wives/mothers. Most feminists agreed that women's unpaid or reproductive work within the home hindered them in obtaining education and paid work. Furthermore, feminists objected to the ways that families socialised children to take on traditional gender roles.

In spite of this broad agreement, distinctly different emphases and remedies came forward. Liberal feminists, inspired by Betty Friedan's *The Feminine Mystique* (1963), demanded legal and social changes which would give women the same chance to achieve individual success that middle-class men already enjoyed. Friedan's more recent book *The Second Stage* (1981) paints an optimistic picture of how both women and men can enjoy fulfilling careers and family life. Denying an 'inevitable, unbridgeable antagonism between women's equality and the family', Friedan points to greater diversity of family types and more equality within families.[14]

Most liberals recognise that a more egalitarian family structure requires social support, but they do not explain how services and programmes for economic equality can be implemented within a politically conservative system which relies on low-wage female labour. Socialists and heterosexual radical feminists join liberals in seeking ways in which women and men can work together and practise feminist principles in daily life. However, they insist that private measures, such as shared parenting, might have severe limitations.

When a woman feels ambivalent or guilty about relinquishing full-time mothering responsibilities, she realises also that her earning power and job opportunities remain less than those of her male partner. Under these circumstances, many women are strongly tempted to give up paid employment, but most women no longer have the choice to work or not work. One income per family has become inadequate, because during the 1970s the rapid gains in living standards that had prevailed since the end of the Second

World War came to a halt. Furthermore, important income differences separated American families. By the late 1970s the gap between above-average and below-average income families appeared to be widening, while the gap between male and female income was not closing. On the average, wage-earning wives contributed 38 per cent of their families' income in 1978, and that is only if they were working full-time. This share had not risen for at least 20 years.

Divorce laws, however, have changed, and divorce has even been promoted as a personal 'growth experience'. In 1970, California became the first state to develop a marital breakdown standard or a 'no-fault' divorce system. By the end of the decade, 35 states had enacted similar provisions. This has been more to men's than women's benefit.

Increasing divorce rates, widespread unwillingness of divorced fathers to support their children, and women's low earnings relative to those of men has resulted in the 'feminisation of poverty'. One study found that over a seven-year period following divorce, the economic position of the men improved by 17 per cent while that of their former wives declined by 29 per cent. In 1981 the poverty rate for all female householders was more than three times higher than that for male householders, or 34 per cent compared to a little over 10 per cent, and it was more than five times higher than husband-wife families. More than half of black and Hispanic female householders were poor, according to federal government criteria. Over 80 per cent of families receiving Aid to Families with Dependent Children (AFDC) are headed by women, but these welfare payments have not alleviated the growing poverty of women and children. Taking inflation into account, the real value of AFDC benefits declined 29 per cent between 1969 and 1981. By the early 1980s, AFDC plus foodstamps brought a household *up* to the poverty level in only three states.[15] Even within working two-parent households above the poverty level, both husbands and wives have to work harder, sacrifice leisure activities and spend less time with their children in order to maintain the family's living standard. Nonetheless, this social 'speed-up', or increase in the pace of life, falls disproportionately on women.

Socialist feminists believe that the growing numbers of 'working mothers' and 'welfare mothers' (who are often the same women) are the ones most likely to experience the ways capitalism and patriarchy both reinforce and contradict each other. Radical feminists have been particularly astute in pointing out the discrepancies between family norms and realities. They have analysed domestic violence against women, the relationship of marriage and heterosexuality, and the ideology and experience of motherhood. Furthermore, the radicals' critique of and alternatives to the family are inseparable from their concern with sexuality and sexual politics discussed above.

During the last decade and a half a battered women's movement has exposed the pervasive incidence of domestic violence. This movement has provided shelters and support for the victims and analysed the causes of this problem in new ways. Its public exposure of wife battering violates at least two taboos: the privacy of the family and the 'right' of men to control and discipline their wives. Until women themselves began to set up shelters, there was nowhere that battered women and their children could go. The Women's Movement has created a nation-wide network of shelters, but it is far from adequate. In 1981, for example, the five New York shelters were filled to capacity and had to turn away 85 out of every 100 callers asking for refuge.[16]

Even with an available shelter in the community and a sensitive, conscientious police force, many women find it difficult to leave and/or file charges against an abusive mate. A woman may still love her partner, and she is probably financially dependent on him. Feminists emphasise the economic disadvantages women face and the lack of training programmes for 'displaced' homemakers. Most battered women have children, and it is very difficult for unemployed or underemployed mothers to find affordable housing and child care. Moreover, a battered woman finds that her family and his, the priest or minister to whom she turns for help, and the couples' friends all advise her to return home and 'work' on the marriage.

Statistics may under-represent violence against women of colour and poor women of all races. Women of colour, in particular, are inhibited by their realistic fear of the police and suspicion of social welfare agencies. They also have to confront the racism and middle-class bias of the shelter workers. White shelter workers may be ignorant of the ways black women raise their children or cope with violence; they may not understand why Latinas in the shelters feel depressed and insecure when they are separated from their extended families and communities.[17] In spite of these problems, the battered women's movement has helped many women and raised the consciousness of an entire nation. Shelters themselves can provide an alternative structure, even culture, to that of the patriarchal family. Like other institutions in women's culture, such as health clinics and job centres, the shelters not only provide a needed service, but also are part of a larger political movement.

Marital rape, which may be closely linked with battering, is another form of domestic violence. Due to feminist pressure, recently a few states have made forced marital rape a crime, but most states are reluctant to do so, since even the concept of marital rape is an obvious challenge to the patriarchal dictum that a husband owns his wife's body and has the 'right' to expect sexual services from her.

Sex, whether willing or forced, is only one aspect of women's 'sex-affective' production, which also includes child-bearing, child-rearing, nurturance and affection. Although this is a historically changing process, women are still socialised to give men more attention and affection than they receive from them. The ideology of the 'private' family during the 1950s and 1960s contributed to women's inequality and isolation. Coupled with the spatial isolation of the suburbs, was the widespread diffusion of the ideal of 'companionate marriage'. Marriage was touted as the only 'normal' adult relationship. Women's loyalty to and affection for their husbands was supposed to take precedence over obligations to their families of origin, devotion to female friends or attention to their own needs. Working women are also more likely than men both to curtail their career involvement in favour of family demands and to downplay their work success out of deference to their spouses.

Some radical feminists claim that all heterosexual relationships – traditional and non-traditional – are unequal. Women can only experience true reciprocity and mutual support with other women. Although the post-war ideology of heterosexual marriage and family 'togetherness' underplayed the importance of female friendships, these relationships continued to exist. The Women's Movement and its ideology of sisterhood did not create friendships among women so much as help white middle-class women rediscover their importance. The feminist concept of sisterhood has legitimised female friendship as a serious, even primary, relationship. Sisterhood has important implications for heterosexual women, since the later age of marriage, increasing divorce rates and the midlife experience of widowhood means that women are spending less of their life spans in traditional families. The benefits of a legitimate sisterhood are even more obvious for lesbians.

Activists in the Women's Movement have formed 'fictive kinship' networks. These provide many of the advantages of an extended family without the hierarchy generally found in traditional age- and sex-graded groups. Consciousness-raising and support groups, women-run collectives and feminist service organisations provide women with security and nurturing. Women can receive from each other what they have been expected to give to men and children.

Lesbians who cannot have honest and supportive relationships with their own families especially seek out such a community. But lesbian communities, like families, are not free of tension over the degree of group unity or sameness versus individual separateness or difference. Most feminist communities are not a single household, but an overlapping series of couples, communal households, friendship circles, support groups and institutions, such as bars, coffee houses, book stores, art galleries, service organisations and newsletters. Some communities have close ties to a women's studies programme on a nearby college campus. Although this loose and varied structure may appear to permit more individual autonomy than a shared household, the bonds between members may actually be tighter than those within a nuclear family because the members are expected to share a common consciousness and ideology. Acknowledging the actual diversity of individuals can prove difficult.

Not all lesbians are feminists. Some of the non political lesbians work out the merger separation problem through strict role playing – butch and fem – and traditional couple exclusiveness. Feminists, on the other hand, eschew role playing and often question the value of monogamy in their relationships Since lesbian feminists do not view lesbianism as only a sexual preference, there may be women in the lesbian feminist community who are not, sexually speaking, lesbians.

Whether they are closeted or open, traditional or feminist, lesbians have had to rely on their friendship groups for emotional support and financial assistance. Lesbian couples break up, but the group is continuous and can be relied upon. At the same time, friendship groups or whole communities can actually undermine the formation and stability of couple relationships. An intensely romantic couple is a threat to group solidarity; both women's time, energy and money are less available for community projects. Some lesbian feminists believe that the romantic or monogamous couple is based on a heterosexual model and is, therefore, inherently regressive and limiting.

The poorest Americans also experience a conflict between the demands of a couple relationship and those of the larger community. Carol Stack found that in a poor, urban, black community the 'family' was neither nuclear nor matrifocal, but rather a network of kin and 'fictive' kin who interacted daily and provided for the survival needs of its members. In this family system the male-female couple was a far less secure arrangement than the kin network. The incompatibility between the attachments individual women and men felt towards each other and the obligations they accepted towards their kin encouraged short-lived sexual relationships, rather than enduring marriages.

While sexual preference is the most obvious difference between this black community and the lesbian ones, racism and its economic consequences are more important factors. Black women have bonded together not out of an ideology of sisterhood, but in order to cope with unemployment and welfare restrictions. Unlike middle-class feminists who choose alternatives to the nuclear family, poor people, especially poor people of colour, are prevented from achieving the ideal nuclear family because of 'tenuous resource bases'. There can be no 'private family' when goods, time and even children have to be shared among a number of households.[18]

Although black women bond together and support each other out of necessity, they are taught to define themselves in relation to men. There does not appear to be any more acceptance of same-sex relationships among black people than among white. Black men may even fear lesbianism as yet another rejection of themselves or as part of a white strategy to divide the community along gender lines.[19] Black lesbians have to contend with both the homophobia of their own communities and the racism of white women. The ideology of 'sisterhood', as it presently exists, offers no panacea for women of colour.

Radical feminists see motherhood as an institution, similar to marriage, in patriarchal society. At the same time, they believe that the mother-daughter relationship might transform patriarchy. Women have been inspired by the rediscovery of mother-daughter friendship from both historical research and utopian fiction. Feminists have questioned the popular wisdom that mother-daughter rivalry is 'natural', or that daughters inevitably rebel against their mothers. They argue instead that patriarchal devaluation of women sets mothers and daughters against each other. Instead of passing on their own strength and honesty, mothers carry out fathers' orders and even teach their daughters the passive and dependent behaviour which is supposed to attract men. On the other hand, many black and working-class mothers do not do this, or give out mixed messages about men. Black women cannot escape patriarchy, but they do teach their daughters to be strong and self-reliant. They know, from their own experience, that marriage will not bring financial or emotional security.[20]

Mothers, according to radical feminists, cannot become the strong role models their daughters need until they change their own lives. First and foremost, they need to change the institution of motherhood. One way is through shared or collective child care, so that mothers are not isolated with and wholly responsible for their children. However, feminists disagree about the role men should play in child care. Some radical feminists are distrustful of men; they do not wish to surrender their children to patriarchal conditioning. Feminist mothers of sons, in particular, do not want to raise another generation of conventional men. They find it difficult, however, to undo their own cultural conditioning that differences between the sexes are somehow 'natural' and to combat all the social conditioning that is simply beyond their control. One example is the 'homosexual threat', or the popular idea that a boy raised in a non-traditional manner will be homosexual.

Anti-feminists, in calling themselves a 'pro-family' and 'pro-life' movement, wish to deny women a language which permits choice in matters of family structure and sexual roles. Right wing spokespeople have set up a trinity of 'deviant' women: lesbian/mothers, unmarried welfare mothers, and sexually active teenage women. These women are either mothers outside heterosexual marriage or they engage in sexual activity without paying the price of compulsory motherhood. That is, each, in a different way, threatens the hegemony of the single approved type of family. For the right-wing anti-feminists, legal abortion and lesbianism subvert the patriarchal ownership of women and children, particularly the father's control over the sexuality of his

wife and teenage daughters. What the right-wing 'pro-family' forces
neglect to take into account are class and race differences, the
increased penetration of commercial norms and services into
intimate relationships, and the growth of an ideology of self-
assertiveness and selfishness.

Feminists such as Sara Ruddick counter the right-wing argument
with a plea for 'maternal thinking' based on the actual practices or
methods mothers use with children. Maternal thought 'takes issue
both with contemporary moral theory and with popular moralities
of assertiveness'. Furthermore, maternal thinking is not restricted
to mothers or to the family. It involves transforming the public
realm so that the growth and preservation of all children will be the
highest social priority.[21] This social and political dimension of
maternal thinking provides feminist culture with an ethic of caring
radically different from the right-wing reprivatisation of the family.

8. Education, Art and Spirituality

Many feminists see a close connection between their erotic empowerment and what Robin Morgan calls 'the new women's renaissance' in education and the arts. The Women's Movement is, above all, an educational endeavour. Women's centres, bookstores and art galleries, as well as health clinics and battered women's shelters, are, according to Adrienne Rich, part of 'a women's university-without-walls'.[1] An alternative or 'counter' education also exists within the walls of colleges and universities in the form of women's studies courses and programmes. Women's studies is an important measure of both the success and limits of women's culture.

From 1969–76, women's studies courses grew from 100 to over 15,000 and from two programmes to 270, operated by 8500 teachers at 1500 institutions. It was obvious by the mid 1970s that women's studies were becoming 'higher education's success story of the decade'.[2] The National Women's Studies Association was formed in 1977 to facilitate communication and enhance the development of research and teaching. It has held annual conferences since 1979.

Women's studies courses and programmes gained relatively quick success due to a combination of educational shake-ups and innovations throughout the 1960s, the large numbers of women already on campus, and the political experience women had gained from their participation in the 1960s movements.

Women's studies began as a grass-roots movement on individual campuses in 1969. After faculty members had offered a number of individual courses on women in literature, history and sociology, the next step was to create an interdisciplinary, degree-granting women's studies programme. In the beginning, these women's

153

studies programmes concentrated on white, middle-class women. Ethnic studies courses had tended to focus mainly on men. Alice Walker offered the first course on black women writers at Wellesley College in 1972, but in 1974 only 45 out of 4658 women's studies courses, or less than 1 per cent, focused on black women. Since the mid 1970s, women's studies programmes, sometimes in cooperation with ethnic studies, have added courses on women of colour. These have mainly been on black women,[3] but courses are also available on Chicana, Asian and Native American women, especially at universities where these groups comprise sizable minorities. Women's studies programmes have also made conscious efforts to recruit women of colour as teachers and students and to provide a multicultural perspective and content in all their courses. However, the curriculum remains weak in the areas of (white) working-class women and rural women.

In addition to developing new courses and research concerns, feminist educators also devised new teaching methods to break down the traditional classroom hierarchy. They borrowed from the Women's Movement the circular arrangement of seats and the use of small discussion groups as a deliberate consciousness-raising device. Instructors and students used first names with each other, students taught some of the classes, and assignments required journal keeping and 'reflection' or 'reaction' papers. In the early 1970s, especially, the trend was 'to substitute, wherever possible, groups and group processes and cooperative ("collective") projects for the individual competitive ones so familiar . . . in academe'.[4] The emphasis on collectivity extended beyond the classroom to include student participation in the governing of women's studies programmes.

Not unexpectedly, these adaptations of feminist principles soon led to controversy with administrators operating within the hierarchical structure of universities over such issues as who hires and fires women's studies teachers and whether the institution as a whole is 'healthy' for women. Women's studies practitioners scrutinised the curricula in all disciplines and asked questions about the omission of women's lives and history. They raised the issue of sexual harassment and sex discrimination in faculty hiring in nominally liberal, co-educational institutions. Although administrators and conservative faculties claim that such political activism is incongruent with accepted notions of 'dispassionate' scholarship, some of the changes women have demanded are already written into law, especially Title VII of the Civil Rights Act of 1964 and Title IX of the 1972 Education Amendments. Although women have filed both individual and class-action suits, sexism in academic employment and programmes has not been eliminated.

A more promising area has been feminist investigation into how sex discrimination may be perpetuated through the use of sex-role stereotypes in children's textbooks. Studies done in the early 1970s of elementary and high school reading, mathematics, science and foreign language texts found that females appeared far less often than males and they were featured mainly in dependent and supportive roles. Sports in all the texts were an exclusively masculine domain. Since children tend to show a greater interest in occupations portrayed by characters of their own sex, the long-range effect of these texts was to limit female vocational aspiration and achievement.[5]

The Feminist Press, founded in 1970, has been only one of the educational projects working to eliminate sex-role stereotypes in books and schools. Its Clearinghouse on Women's Studies and its Curriculum and Inservice Projects have published curricular materials, resource guides and bibliographies for women's studies at every educational level, as well as supplementary materials for high school classrooms. Women's studies courses can now be found at the high school level, mainly in history, literature and the social sciences.

These educational efforts, along with changes in the job market, may have had some impact on the courses of study women have been choosing. During the 1969–70 academic year, women earned less than 1 per cent of the engineering degrees, less than 9 per cent of those in business management and under 14 per cent of the degrees in the physical sciences. At the same time, women comprised three-quarters of those receiving BAs in education. By the 1978–79 academic year, women were still close to three-fourths of the education students, but they were earning almost 9 per cent of the engineering BAs and close to 23 per cent of the degrees in the physical sciences. Almost one-third of those receiving BAs in business were women.[6]

The question is whether women's studies will continue as a catalyst for educational and social change. In order to make the maximum impact on educational institutions, women's studies programmes may have put themselves in a precarious position. Most of their founders decided not to set up separate academic departments, but chose instead a loose 'program' structure made up of a network of feminist teachers all around the campus. Since the late 1970s, administrators, especially in public institutions, who claim they are worried about or responding to educational cutbacks have had opportunities to eliminate programmes which have made them uncomfortable.

The Women's Studies Program at California State University, Long Beach, provides a typical example of combined right-wing and administrative harassment. In the spring of 1982, conservative 'new right' women monitored and then complained about the 'lesbian emphasis' of women's studies courses, especially 'Women and Their Bodies: An Introduction to the Biology and Sexuality of Women'. The administration launched an immediate and unprecedented course review. After 'Women and Their Bodies' passed this test, Dr Betty Brooks, the instructor, was removed from teaching duties for the summer and was not allowed to teach that course in the fall. In response to similar attacks, women's studies programmes have been turning away from structural innovation and radical pedagogy. Compromising on feminist principles, they hope to survive by becoming more like traditional academic departments with adequate funding, tenured faculty and permanent curriculum.[7]

The primary vehicle for women's education and feminist community building has been neither university women's studies courses nor alternative educational institutions, but rather feminist media, especially the printed word. From the beginning, women maintained a critical, even adversary, stance towards the mainstream media and devoted considerable energy to creating their own newspapers and magazines. Many of them had had first-hand experience both with alternative media and with the ways the established media distorted the aims of the 1960s movements.

In the early days of the Women's Movement, newspapers tended to withhold information about feminist political activities. Then, as the movement grew, the press moved from a blackout to ridiculing or trivialising the movement and selecting only its more 'respectable' spokeswomen for coverage. Radical feminists, in turn, may have exacerbated an already touchy situation by denying media representatives access to their meetings and refusing interviews with male reporters.

Feminists started their own publications. Between March 1968 and August 1973, more than 560 newspapers and magazines appeared. Although many were short-lived, they provided detailed information about the Women's Movement and put women in different parts of the country in touch with each other. By the mid 1970s, women's publications had grown beyond their initial purpose of compensating for media blackout and distortion. They had become a permanent part of women's culture and ranged from general purpose political newspapers to academic, literary and spiritual journals, as well as specialised publications written by and for lesbians, women of colour and older women. The 1983 *Directory of Women's Media* listed a total of 379 women's periodicals in circulation.

The success of feminist journals can be measured by their competition: mainstream magazines designed for the 'liberated' woman. *Ms.* (1972), one of the oldest and best known, is a liberal feminist monthly. An example of 'bridge' media 'which transmit diluted feminist ideas to a broader public',[8] *Ms.* has reprinted articles from the smaller, more radical papers. It has also published articles and creative work by radical feminists, Robin Morgan, for example, and Third-World women writers, most notably black poet and novelist Alice Walker.

Like any nationally distributed commercial publication, *Ms.* depends on advertising revenue, and its ads sell products – cosmetics, stockings, alcohol, diet foods – and use images that radical feminists find harmful or demeaning. Radical and socialist feminists also find fault with *Ms.*'s liberal bias, and some deplore the magazine's presumed reduction of feminism to individual success. Actually, *Ms.* encourages women to improve existing political and social life, but not radically to change the socio-economic status quo.

In the more authentic feminist journals, both the content and the organisational structure reflect radical priorities. Unlike the early political newsletters and papers, these journals devote themselves more to celebrating women's creativity than to attacking the patriarchy. *Heresies*, for example, is a beautifully designed and lavishly illustrated large-sized quarterly, which calls itself 'an idea-oriented journal devoted to the examination of art and politics from a feminist perspective'. Each issue is devoted to a different subject – lesbian art, spirituality, music, sex, ecology – and is created by a combination of guest editors and members of the *Heresies* collective. *Chrysalis*, also a large-sized, illustrated and carefully designed periodical, was fairly typical of feminist journals in two ways: it was short-lived in spite of its high quality and it was part of an ongoing feminist network, which included *The New Woman's Survival Sourcebook* (1975) and The Los Angeles Women's Building, rather than an isolated endeavour. *Conditions*, 'a magazine of writing by women with an emphasis on writing by lesbians', is particularly noted for featuring the work of women of colour: Audre Lorde, Barbara and Beverly Smith, Pat Parker and Nelly Wong, to name a few.

Open admissions of mutual influence and sharing, along with reversals of traditional social values, are frequently found in feminist literature and art. As the perennial outsiders of the art world, women have had to re-evaluate its mythologies and practices. Along the way, they have dethroned its 'king', the artist-as-solitary-genius, in order to scrutinise the institutional and ideological barriers to female creativity.

The documentation of sexism in the arts has been ample and generally accepted, but few agree on how to eliminate it. The liberal solution of 'equal opportunity' – greater representation in museum exhibitions, a fair share of grants and teaching jobs, more serious attention by publishers, critics and collectors – does not satisfy radical feminist artists. Some of them have instead attacked the 'male' career model and the commercialisation of art. Others have criticised the very form and content of 'successful' art by arguing that women have a different sensibility from that of men. They claim that 'female' imagery and iconography cannot be judged according to the critical criteria applied to 'male' art.

Judy Chicago is one of the best known and most vocal purveyors of the concept of female imagery in visual art. As an art student, she had learned that if she wanted her work to be taken seriously, it 'should not reveal its having been made by a woman'. But by the mid 1960s, she was unhappy with her abstract and 'minimal' work despite a one-woman and several group shows. The direction she chose was to express her femaleness. She began using what she provocatively called 'cunt' forms.[9]

Chicago's most ambitious project using 'vaginal' imagery was

The Dinner Party, particularly the 39 sculptured plates, each representing a mythical or real woman in history. The viewing audiences were large and enthusiastic, but critics and museum directors resisted both the imagery and the deliberate use of traditional female crafts – needlework and china-painting.

The re-evaluation and upgrading of women's popular and domestic arts has met with greater acceptance among feminists than the issue of distinct female subject matter or imagery. Quilting, pottery-making, embroidery, china-painting, basket-making, woodcarving and so forth, move the making of art beyond the boundaries of white, male-dominated institutions and into the kitchens, parlours and gardens of 'ordinary' women. At the same time, a belated recognition can be extended to these anonymous artists. 'What did it mean for a black woman to be an artist in our grandmothers' time? In our great-grandmothers' day?' asks Alice Walker. 'It is a question with an answer cruel enough to stop the blood.' Walker's essay not only discusses the thwarted creativity of black mothers who 'handed on the creative spark, the seed of the flower they themselves never hoped to see'. She also acknowledges those who created quilts, songs or, like her own mother, a garden where 'being an artist has still been a daily part of her life'. Just as important is the role of inspirer, for as Walker says, 'no song or poem will bear my mother's name. Yet so many of the stories that I write, that we all write, are my mother's stories.'[10]

'Remembering our mothers' is a frequent theme in women's critical and creative writing. There is an intense desire to find, make and maintain connections between the past and present. A well-known case is Rita Mae Brown's *Rubyfruit Jungle* (1973), an autobiographical novel written in the tried-and-true mode of the young artist from the provinces who seeks adventure and success in the big city. But the artist is a young woman and a lesbian, who decides to return home and make her first film about her mother, Carrie, who had earlier driven Molly away. Mother and daughter achieve enough of a reconciliation near the end of the novel for Molly to say: 'And I love her. Even when I hated her, I loved her.' Cross-generational love of a different sort is the theme of June Arnold's *Sister Gin* (1975). Rather than reworking a traditional story, Arnold broke new ground by making all of the main characters middle-aged or old. After a long, tender and erotic exchange, 80-year-old Mamie Carter comforts Su, who is going through menopause, by telling her: 'The truly free is she who can be old at any age.'[11]

Most women's novels accepted by commercial publishers still emphasise either youthful or midlife heterosexual relationships. Fiction by Alix Kates Shulman, Erica Jong and even Marge Piercy falls into this category; so do Marilyn French's novels, *The Women's Room* (1977) and *The Bleeding Heart* (1980). These writers have widened the boundaries of what is considered commercially acceptable by updating the confessional or domestic drama with varying doses of 'consciousness-raising'. At the same time, the expression of resentment and anger while constructing a new identity keeps most of these novels at the level of melodrama. Dorothy Bryant's *Ella Price's Journal* (1972) is an exception. The midlife heroine tells her 'awakening' in the form of a journal in which the writing is lean and the feelings are kept close to the unfolding events. The reader is spared pleas for pity, retrospective soul-searching or political polemics.

Self-exposure has a positive side, and that is the interest in and recovery of women's letters and diaries. These neglected quilts and pots of female literature have gained the status of legitimate art forms. Anaïs Nin's diaries, which began appearing in the mid 1960s, opened the door for less polished and artfully edited work. Although one of the early anthologies, *Revelations: Diaries of Women* (1974), concentrated on the work of well-known women such as Nin, Anne Frank, Alice James, Virginia Woolf and George Eliot, more recent collections have not. *Ariadne's Thread* (1982), edited by Lyn Lifshin, features the journals of contemporary women, and Karen Payne's *Between Ourselves: Letters Between Mothers and Daughters* contains letters by both well-known historical figures and those of contemporary women, some of whom use pseudonyms.

Some feminist poets claim that their work, like that of anonymous letter-writers and diary-keepers, was done at the kitchen table, in between doing the laundry and the housework. Adrienne Rich, for example, believes that 'poetry, as much as journals and letters and diaries, has been an almost natural women's form . . . for the kinds of reasons that I wrote very short poems in the fifties – because I had to write while the children were napping, between chores.'[12] While not denying the hard work and self-discipline which goes into her poems, Rich is also claiming a connection, even a

sisterhood, with potential poets as well as with those women too
harassed and timid to write anything at all.

Many feminist writers and artists do not separate their art from
their politics. Feminist visions, they believe, can give women hope
and courage, helping them to move from being what Alice Walker
calls 'suspended women', totally victimised and oppressed by
society, to becoming 'emergent women', who can make the world
'larger for others to move in'.[13]

Walker's own work shows this transition. Her novel *The Color
Purple* (1982) won the Pulitzer Prize and the American Book Award
for fiction. The main characters, like those in her earlier short
stories, are women whose lives are beset with poverty, racial
oppression, and unloving, even violent, men. However, the majority
in her first collection, *In Love and Trouble* (1973), were 'suspended
women'. Each was caught in this cycle of oppression and violence
and could rely only on her own strength to endure what she could
not change. The stories in, as well as the title of, her second
collection, *You Can't Keep a Good Woman Down* (1981), indicate a
change of focus. Walker now raises political questions about racism,
rape, abortion and pornography – with no easy answers. For
example, 'Advancing Luna – and Ida B. Wells', deals with the
effect of an inter-racial rape. Walker's attention is not on the black
rapist and his white victim, but rather the relationship between the
white woman and her black female friend. Although a true
understanding of this particular rape must include the history of
lynching innocent black men, the healing process has to occur
between women of both races. 'Advancing Luna' is itself a
contribution towards ending a long silence on this painful subject;
The Color Purple celebrates honest communication and love among
women even in adverse circumstances.

Like art and literature, feminist spirituality manifests a variety of
expressions and viewpoints, which we will categorise simply as
liberal and radical. Liberals or reformists insist that Judaism and
Christianity should include women on an equal basis with men.
Radicals consider themselves an 'exodus' community outside
established religions, and their practices are based on 'pagan'
traditions and their own imaginations. Instead of churches, radicals
form covens or affinity groups. Feminist spirituality, especially its
radical wing, is a grass-roots movement, and the number of
adherents is impossible to determine.

Liberals insist that feminist self-development must include equal opportunity for church leadership. Their demand that women be ordained as ministers, priests and rabbis has met with some success in a number of Protestant denominations and in the reform and conservative branches of Judaism. Reformers also seek changes in Biblical interpretation, theology and liturgy in order to include women's experiences and meet women's needs. The inclusion and affirmation of women involve changes in religious language, imagery and liturgy. Ultimately, the reformers want an androgynous, instead of an androcentric, religion. Rita M. Gross, for example, wishes to transform the Jewish Father-God into a 'bisexual androgynous deity by reintroducing the image of God as female to complement the image of God as male'. Other Jewish feminists have created new Sabbath prayers for women and a feminist Passover Haggadah. Some Christian reformers believe that the restoration of the female principle and women's experience should end the one-sided development of Christian theology as 'a body-fleeing, world-negating spirituality'.[14]

Radicals would agree that a new theology or epistemology should be based on women's spiritual and physical experience; that is, a more holistic view of body and spirit. Both liberals and radicals are committed to a 'gospel' of social justice, which also includes respect for non-human life. Some, but not all, reformers even accept the radical premise that the sexism of the Christian churches is rooted in the dualistic and hierarchical nature of Judeao-Christian theology.

Radicals, however, prefer to look outside Judaism or Christianity for religious inspiration. Mary Daly's work, for example, shows a dramatic evolution from reformer to radical. In 1968, while still a 'radical Catholic', she published *The Church and the Second Sex*, in which she called for a 'reformed, democratized Church' which would face 'its responsibility to exorcise the devil of sexual prejudice'. The book almost caused her dismissal from a teaching job at a Jesuit-run college. By the time her second work, *Beyond God the Father*, appeared in 1973, Daly had come to believe that the Women's Movement, not the Church, 'has everything to do with the search for ultimate meaning and reality, which some would call God'. By 'God', she now meant a verb, rather than a noun. Instead of a static ideal of otherworldliness, of 'final' explanation and ultimate judgement, 'god' was a dynamic process of becoming.

This view of god-as-process was especially relevant to women. In addition to this radical reconception of deity, Daly predicted a 'second coming' that would ultimately benefit men as well as women.

In a more recent work, *Gyn/Ecology* (1978), Daly took a third position. No longer interested in saving men or reworking Christian terminology for post-christian ends, she created a new language and invited only women – 'Spinsters, Lesbians, Hags, Harpies, Crones, Furies' – on a 'metapatriarchal' journey out of the 'Deadly Deceptions' and 'Sado-Ritual Syndrome' of patriarchy.[15]

While Daly's transformation may be representative, her complex and creative work does not 'speak for' the feminist spirituality movement. This is not only due to her idiomatic terminology, but also because feminist spirituality is extremely diverse. It has no Bible or theology, only certain tendencies, interests and practices. These include the goddess and cultures who worshipped her, new conceptions of power and self-affirmation, and a celebration of female sexuality. These concerns are expressed through ritual, art and politics, not theological treatises or church services.

The goddess provides both historical and psychological roots. Research into ancient cultures has provided plentiful evidence of goddess worship and a possible correlation between female deity and 'matriarchy'. Merlin Stone's work on goddess-worshipping cultures indicates that women's political and economic status in the Near East declined after the invasion of the northern Indo-Europeans. Most feminists do not insist on the actual existence of a Golden Age of Matriarchy, neither do they literally worship the goddess. Rather, they use whatever evidence they find plus their own imaginations to create new symbol systems, rituals and artistic expressions, such as Donna Henes' *Spider Woman*, a series of environmental sculptures referring to the mother goddess of the Navaho Indians.

The goddess serves not as an object of worship, but rather as an 'affirmation of female power, the female body, the female will, and women's bonds and heritage'.[16] The goddess frees women from male authority and male definitions of female sexuality. Unlike the Virgin Mary who transcends carnality, the goddess is honoured by celebrating physical cycles and processes: menstruation, childbirth, menopause, old age and death.

The goddess is seen as symbolising the powers within women

and nature. These powers can be tapped by ritual, meditation, magic and political work. Starhawk equates the goddess with immanence, or the 'power-from-within', something we can do, rather than something we have, a verb rather than a noun. The goddess represents not a belief system to which one adheres, but an attitude of 'choosing to take this living world, the people and creatures on it, as the ultimate meaning and purpose of life, to see the world, the earth, and our lives as sacred.'[17] Starhawk and other 'eco-feminists', like their recent predecessors in the 1960s Counterculture, feel a sense of kinship and political solidarity with Native American peoples. They share an 'organic' and 'animistic' world view and are especially sensitive to the association between women and nature and the ways both have suffered from colonisation and rape of their resources.

Some feminists believe that witchcraft (often called 'wicca' or 'The Craft') is an appropriate way to express their earth-centred consciousness, or even that it is the religion of the goddess. Feminist witchcraft has nothing to do with Satanism or black magic. But it is not easy to define, for as Starhawk admits, it is 'a religion of poetry, not theology' and contains many variations. Small, autonomous groups of practising witches form covens in which the bonds between members may be 'closer than family'.[18] Since this usually involves an initiation process and continued commitment, only a small percentage of women interested in feminist spirituality actually join covens.

Unlike many Christian sects, witches do not proselytise. Becoming a witch is a self-selected and self-paced process. On the other hand, wiccians do not hoard their knowledge or practices; craft rituals are often shared with non-witches, especially during political demonstrations and feminist conferences. Feminist rituals release female power and involve 'magic' or *the art of changing consciousness at will*. Rituals are an expression of the feminist belief that the personal is political because they connect self-healing with social change, much as feminist consciousness-raising does. In fact, Starhawk notes the similarity between the two by saying that: 'Feminist consciousness-raising is a process based on sound magical principles.'[19]

Once again, feminists define power as 'power-within' an individual, which enables her to do, not as a power-over-others. Power-within is not solipsism, but rather a basis for relationships.

It means building a community based on reciprocity and consensus. Community structures need to remain small and 'circular', that is, non-hierarchical. Small groups can, in turn, be linked in organic, web-like – rather than pyramidal, building-block – fashion to form larger entities. It is a decentralised, essentially anarchist, vision of organisation.

Feminist spirituality is also expressed in sexual politics. Patriarchal culture has distorted sexual power into power-over games of dominance and submission. Feminist spirituality will help women reclaim their sexuality. 'The erotic can become the bridge that connects feeling with doing', says Starhawk. Therefore, sexuality 'is the realm in which the spiritual, the political, and the personal come together'.[20] Starhawk and other feminists do not mean 'genital intercourse' when they speak of sexuality, but rather the more inclusive definition of the erotic favoured by Adrienne Rich and Audre Lorde.

The principles and rituals of feminist spirituality have been directly applied in anti-pornography campaigns, environmental issues and anti-nuclear power demonstrations. In mid November 1980, over 2000 women attended the Women's Pentagon Action in Washington, DC. Their 'unity statement' stressed that 'all is connectedness. The Earth nourishes us as we with our bodies will eventually feed it. Through us, our mothers connected the human past to the human future.'[21]

Such language is a major point of difference between socialist and spiritual feminists. Socialists criticise spiritual feminists because their language and rituals appear inadequate for analysing class differences in capitalist society. Spiritual feminists find socialist terminology to be excessively 'mechanical', rational and ultimately alienating. They contend that such language only perpetuates dualistic thinking which has sanctioned the oppression of women and the exploitation of nature long before the rise of modern capitalism. While feminists in the 'womanspirit' movement contribute a necessary experiential and visionary element to the Women's Movement, they might, in turn, learn from socialists how to extend their political concerns beyond sexuality and ecology. So far, the spiritualists' analysis of class and race oppression has been a feeble one, and the 'womanspirit' movement has all but ignored women's paid and unpaid work.

The Women's Movement has succeeded in creating a feminist

counterculture consisting of woman-centred relationships, education, creative work and religion. But this women's culture is also in danger of becoming a female 'ghetto'. Currently the Women's Movement must defend its political and cultural achievements against a revival of patriarchal ideology which promulgates two contradictory but powerful myths: one, that women have already 'won' all they can collectively so that the only barriers to political and economic achievement are individual shortcomings; and two, that women are essentially different from men and can best express their peaceful and nurturing 'nature' through child-rearing. The work of some radical feminists who ascribe an inherent, almost mystical, status to 'woman' is being manipulated by conservatives to reisolate women in the home and maintain the gender hierarchy in the labour force. An essentialist emphasis on biological sex difference and female moral superiority is, in practice, not only class-biased and racist, but also a distraction from the necessary work of transforming the family, motherhood, and all other social, economic and political institutions. Feminists must reject both the capitalist promise of individual 'success' and the patriarchal reification of moral motherhood.

Even more difficult, the Women's Movement must build coalitions with men or develop a series of programmes which encourage men to become active feminists, rather than guilty, indifferent or hostile bystanders. Finally, and most important, feminist culture must extend beyond its initial white, middle-class base. This involves more than simply including the needs of working-class women and women of colour within feminist programmes and organisations. Rather, the material conditions, values, skills and cultural experiences of working-class women and women of colour must transform the nature of feminist theory and practice.

PART III: CURRENT ISSUES AND FUTURE PROSPECTS

Although most American women are not active feminists, their political consciousness and everyday circumstances have been changed by nearly two decades of feminist theory and practice. The three chapters in Part III present material on women's lives and work in the 1970s and 1980s, as well as some of the ways the Women's Movement is responding to new challenges and crises.

Chapter 9 covers some of the perspectives and experiences of racial ethnic and white working-class women, as well as recent efforts of the Women's Movement to represent more successfully a multi-cultural constituency.

The feminisation of poverty and its relationship to women's 'double day' of paid and unpaid work has become one of the most important issues of the 1970s and 1980s. Chapter 10, on women's work, is partly a continuation and update of material covered in Chapters 2 and 3, but it also analyses women's paid employment and unpaid domestic labour within the context of today's political economy and presents some new insights into old problems, most notably child care, health and environmental hazards, and sexual harassment.

Chapter 11 indicates some of the ways women are responding to the worldwide environmental crisis, increased militarism and the threat of nuclear annihilation. Not only are the concerns of American feminists becoming more diversified and less gender-specific, but they are joining other women in cross-cultural efforts to develop programmes which will both preserve the planet and enhance the lives of present and future generations.

9. Race and Class in Women's Lives

The politics and culture of the Women's Movement have mainly addressed the experiences and priorities of white middle-class women. Feminist sisterhood emphasises shared conditions based on gender, but the identities and political priorities of racial ethnic[1] and white working-class women must also include race and class. Black women, for example, have practised 'sisterhood' in their churches, clubs and extended family networks, but as Bonnie Thornton Dill notes, 'we have not used it as the anvil to forge our political identities'. Rather, the 'political identities of Afro-American women have largely been formed around issues of race'.[2]

It is not racial differences in themselves, but the personal and institutional politics of racism that have divided the Women's Movement much as they have the larger society. Racism not only creates false differences among women, it also obscures real ones based on culture, or a group's shared values and beliefs, and on structure, that is, the ways in which peoples' experiences and opportunities are shaped by the social relations and status arrangements of American society. Sex discrimination must be located not only in racial ethnic cultures, but also in the broader dimensions of political, economic and social organisation.

Class and race overlap, but one category does not wholly encompass the other. Although racial ethnic women in the US are disproportionately poor when compared to white women, 'colour-blind' theorists of class ignore the non-economic ways that whites oppress people of colour and overlook important cultural and structural variations among both racial and white ethnic groups. Liberals, on the other hand, have tended to equate class and race by viewing poverty as a particular problem of 'non-whites'. This not only reinforces racist stereotypes and ignores gender differences

169

within racial ethnic groups, it also hides the fact that all women face economic vulnerability when they lose access to male wages or salaries. This 'feminisation of poverty' is a problem facing increasing numbers of formerly middle-class women.

We shall first describe how the perceptions and priorities of women of colour evolve in relation to both their race and their gender. Next, we will present some of their views and experiences with regard to feminism, sexuality and reproduction, male dominance, work and family relations. Finally, we shall discuss the feminisation of poverty as an issue and reality in women's lives which, to some extent, transcends both ethnicity and traditional concepts of class.

Out of a total female population of 120,267,000 in 1983, racial ethnic women numbered 18,049,000, or approximately one woman in five. However, overall figures are misleading because racial ethnic people are not evenly distributed throughout the US. Blacks have become the majority population, or close to it, in some of the Northeastern cities as well as retaining their strong presence in the rural and urban South. Over half of Hispanics live in either California or Texas. Although Asians comprise only 1.5 per cent of the US population, they are concentrated along the West Coast. According to 1980 Census figures, black women are the most numerous at 13,975,836. Hispanics come next with 7,328,842 women; 60 per cent of Hispanics are Chicanas (Mexican-American women). The total number of Asian women (Japanese, Chinese, Filipino, Korean, Vietnamese and Indian) is 1,686,295, with Native Americans plus Eskimos numbering 711,153.

Women of colour experience doubled or divided political loyalties because they must confront both racism and sexism. Although black women preceded white women in recognising and reacting to sexism in the Civil Rights Movement, many would not join a separate women's movement. The survival of black people has depended on women and men working together, even as women confront men over sexist practices on a personal level and within black organisations. In 1968, Frances Beal wrote 'Double Jeopardy: to be Black & Female', as a staff position paper for SNCC, by then an all-black organisation. 'Any white group', she said, 'that does not have an anti-imperialist and anti-racist ideology has absolutely nothing in common with the black woman's struggle.' Beal's questions about the new women's liberation movement were to be echoed by many women of colour: 'Are white women asking to be equal to white men in their pernicious treatment of third world peoples? What assurance have black women that white women will be any less racist and exploitative if they had the power and were in a position to do so?' At the same time, she criticised black men for accepting the myth of Black Matriarchy, for it was not black women who have 'castrated' black men, but a system of racist capitalism which 'proceeded to do so without signing any agreements with black women'.[3]

On the other hand, Chicanas, other Hispanic women and, to some extent, Asian women, have been characterised as overly submissive and dependent on male authority, in comparison to Anglo women. This simplistic view presents Chicanas as victims of 'machismo', and it overlooks sexism among whites, variations among Chicano men and women, structural factors responsible for gender differences and, most important, the history and perceptions of Chicanas themselves.

A long history of labour militancy has made Chicanas aware both of the parallels between Anglo racism and male chauvinism and of women's contributions in unpaid and paid work towards family and community survival. *Salt of the Earth* (1954), a film made by blacklisted leftists unable to find work in the Hollywood studios, was based on an actual strike by Mexican-American zinc miners in New Mexico. Only after Ramon, one of the strikers, has to do the family wash does he understand his wife's work in the home. When he balks at Esperanza's new leadership role in the strike, she retorts with: 'The Anglo bosses look down on you, and you hate them for it. "Stay in your place, you dirty Mexican" – that's what they tell you. But why must you say to me, "Stay in *your* place"? Do you feel better having someone lower than you?'[4]

In the 1960s and 1970s, Chicanas participated in farmworkers' strikes and helped win union contracts from growers so as to obtain parity with industrial workers under the National Labor Relations Act (1935) from which farmworkers had been excluded. Jessie Lopez De La Cruz, a migrant farmworker since childhood, made it her special mission to get other women involved in the union. 'Men gave us the most trouble', she recalled. 'They were for the union, but they were not taking orders from women'.[5] However, after the first contract was won, she suggested that women be elected to the local committee and the men agreed. Chicana labour activism in the 1970s also included the pecan shellers in Texas who went on strike in 1973 because they were paid less than male workers and the Farah strike from 1972–4, involving some 4000 workers, mainly Chicanas, who organised national opposition to the garment company until its owner recognised the union. Sensitive to the legacy of Anglo colonisation of Mexican land in the nineteenth century and the last seventy years of racial discrimination and class conflict, Chicanas remain wary about making common cause with white women. They prefer to address such women's issues as welfare, birth control, abortion and employment within the context of their own communities.

Poor women of colour have had to place family and community survival before individual aspirations for fulfilment and self-expression. Chicanas and Native American women have been the primary preservers of their peoples' histories, traditions and languages. Some of the cultural values of Native Americans, Hispanics and Asians appear to be more 'feminine' than those of Anglo Protestants because they emphasise cooperation over competitiveness, modesty rather than self-assertiveness, and devotion to kin more than individual mobility. Such group-centred behaviour conflicts with the way material success and prestige are accrued in the educational and economic systems of the dominant culture.

This is not to say that racial ethnic cultures are sexually egalitarian. Movements for racial and national liberation have tended mainly to address and benefit men, yet male leaders urged women to support these movements rather than align with white feminists on gender issues. The Chicana, for example, 'was warned by her Raza brothers to stay away from the women's movement because of its destructive effect on the Chicano culture and family. But she began to feel the damage this same family and culture had done to her.'[6] Asian cultures have likewise provided little support for the independent woman. Younger Chinese and Japanese women who espouse either feminist personal politics or mainstream individualism risk conflict with their parents and estrangement from their communities.

White, middle-class women can generally choose gender as the predominant source for their identity. Racial ethnic women must adopt a 'multiple identity' which includes race, gender and often class; the interaction of all three contributes to the personal and social identities of black, Chicana, Native American and Asian women. To some extent, this is also true for such white ethnic women as Jews and Italians, as well as white Protestant Appalachian (or 'Hillbilly') women.

Race, gender and class are themselves oversimplifications of a more complex reality which includes a variety of cultures within each racial category. Native Americans are the most obvious example, for they were originally several hundred different cultures. Although some of these are either extinct or radically altered, today's Lakotas (Sioux) are still more dissimilar from Hopis than Greeks are from Germans. Among Chinese and Chicanos, important distinctions exist between old and recent immigrants, rural and urban dwellers, and older and younger generations. Economic class differences between and within racial ethnic groups are almost as wide as those in American society generally. Finally, within each ethnic community there exist lesbians and other sexual minorities.

For individual women of colour, 'multiple identity' often leads to a combination of external difficulties and internalised conflicts. Audre Lorde, a black lesbian feminist, finds that: 'I am constantly being encouraged to pluck out some one aspect of myself and present this as the meaningful whole, eclipsing or denying the other parts of self.' Black organisations expect her to repress her lesbianism, and white feminists do not appreciate her disavowal of gender separatism or her anger at racism.

Merle Woo, in 'Letter to Ma', acknowledges that her Korean mother gave her a legacy which combined strength with self-effacement, but American racism and sexism led only to self-hatred. 'For deeply ingrained in me, Ma, there has been that strong, compulsive force to sink into self-contempt, passivity, and despair.' Like many women of colour, Woo would rather educate traditional Asian women about feminism and lesbianism than assume the thankless role of 'instant resource for information on Asian American women' to groups of white women who 'usually leave to never continue their education about us on their own'.

Barbara Cameron, a Lakota, points out how difficult it is for her people to maintain a balance between white and Indian worlds – 'Native Americans have a very high suicide rate' – and also describes a 'complex set of "racisms"' within the Indian community itself and among racial ethnic groups. 'We form alliances loosely based on the fact that we have a common oppressor, yet we do not have a commitment to talk about our own fears and misconceptions about each other.' Cameron has found that at conferences 'third world means black people only', and issues affecting Asians and Native Americans receive inadequate attention.[7]

Women of colour thus have to struggle against both general and specific forms of racism, sexism and homophobia found within and outside their own communities. Since the Women's Movement reflects the race and class divisions of the larger society, it is useful to see how these have surfaced and some of the ways they are being addressed.

Women of colour, as well as white ethnic and working-class women, have felt excluded from the Women's Movement. Even though they support many feminist objectives, their priorities differ. As Donna Redmond, a white 'Hillbilly' from the Appalachia region, put it: 'Middle-class women's lib is a trend; working women's liberation is a necessity.'[8] Racial ethnic women find that whites ignore the histories and cultures of people of colour; feminist history, literary criticism and women's studies courses omit the work of racial ethnic women; feminist art works, such as Judy Chicago's *The Dinner Party*, give only token, stereotyped representation to women of colour. Exclusion sometimes extends to denying real differences among women in the interest of 'sisterhood', as well as reactions of guilt and defensiveness when racist behaviour is pointed out. According to Cherríe Moraga, the typical response by white feminist groups has been:

> 'Well, we're open to *all* women; why don't they (women of color) come?' .... But there is seldom any analysis of how the very nature and structure of the group itself may be founded on racist or classist assumptions. More importantly, so often the women seem to feel no loss, no lack, no absence when women of colour are not involved.[9]

Jewish women, too, have encountered a lack of sisterly understanding in the Women's Movement. Anti-semitism, like other forms of racism, has led to invisibility or omission, insult, and internalised oppression or self-hatred. One of the most sensitive areas has been black-Jewish relationships. Although obvious parallels exist between Jews and blacks because both have suffered more for their race than their sex, the two groups have also been competitors against each other for housing and jobs. Nevertheless, some honest and constructive dialogue is also occurring between American Jewish and black women. Elly Bulkin, for example, has cautioned her Jewish sisters that although they may feel a painful sense of betrayal at the anti-semitism of non-Jewish women of colour, they should not forget that the anti-semitism of non-Jewish whites has 'immeasurably more power' to harm them. Alice Walker asks that Jews 'understand people of color's hatred of imperialism and colonialism', and that blacks reject anti-semitism. Women, she adds, should note that, 'The brotherhood of Moslem men – all colors – may exist. . ., but part of the glue that holds it together is the thorough suppression of women.'[10]

Guilt feelings are, at best, a hindrance to such dialogue and, as Adrienne Rich warns, can even 'become a form of solipsism, a preoccupation with our own feelings which prevents us from ever connecting with the experience of others'. The 'strength of women', says Audre Lorde, lies not in guilt, but 'in recognizing differences between us as creative, and in standing to those distortions which we inherited without blame, but which are now ours to alter.' One of these 'distortions' is the unequal struggle for survival. 'You fear your children will grow up to join the patriarchy and testify against you, we fear our children will be dragged from a car and shot down in the street, and you will turn your backs upon the reasons they are dying.'[11]

If women's oppression cannot be attributed solely to men, then middle-class white women share some of the responsibility for oppressing other women. An essential step out of this situation is to free 'difference' from a hierarchical context of 'superior' and 'inferior'. Only when difference does not mean that one must be the inferior can it become a creative force for change. Separatism, on the other hand, is an extreme but not constructive solution. 'What I really feel is radical', says Barbara Smith, 'is trying to make coalitions with people who are different from you.' In order to make such coalitions viable, women are calling for multicultural and mutliclass perspectives. Judit Moschkovich, a Jewish immigrant from Argentina, believes that if the 'new feminist or women's culture' remains 'within an Anglo-American cultural framework', it 'would still be just as racist and ethnocentric as patriarchal American culture'. In an open letter to Mary Daly, Audre Lorde

pointed out that *Gyn/Ecology* distorted black women's heritage both
by ignoring African goddesses and warriors and by including black
women only as victims of African genital mutilation.[12]

A problem similar to that of expecting women to educate men
out of their sexist ways has been some white women's view that
racism can only be solved by women of colour. By claiming, for
example, that only black women can teach black history, culture
and literature, they forget that women have already surmounted
the difficulty of understanding and teaching the works of men. A
racist feminist culture is a contradiction in terms, for it means that
'a part of ourselves will remain forever unknown to us'.[13]

One of these 'unknowns' is anger and its uses. White women
have been taught that anger is 'unfeminine' and destructive, or else
they equate it with male violence and brute force. But people of
colour have found anger to be an appropriate weapon against
physical and psychological annihilation. 'My anger', remarks Audre
Lorde, 'has meant pain to me but it has also meant survival.'
Lorde believes that anger between peers is different from the
systematic and institutionalised hatred of oppressors. If anger is
both honestly expressed and attentively heard, it can be aimed
vertically at the real oppressors, instead of horizontally at one's
sisters. But, first, the fear of disagreement and difference must be
individually transmuted. At the Second Sex Conference in 1979,
Lorde asked her audience for more than 'mere tolerance of
difference.'

> *I urge each one of us here to reach down into that deep place of knowledge
> inside herself and touch that terror and loathing of any difference that lives
> there. See whose face it wears.* Then the personal as the political can
> begin to illuminate all our choices.[14]

Such a strategy will allow racial ethnic women to draw strength
from cultural diversity. Models can be found in the relatively
egalitarian relationships between black women and men, the
emphasis on generosity and consensus decision-making among
many Native American cultures, or the ability to speak and
understand a language other than or in addition to English. They
can also take pride in histories which include both individual
resistance and collective struggle. Many whites, however, do not
believe they have a distinctive culture or heritage. Usually they

have forgotten or denied their ethnic backgrounds or unique religious and class perspectives. According to Ricky Sherover-Marcuse, unlearning racism cannot be achieved without recovering accurate information about one's own ethnicity and cultural heritage. In her workshops she encourages white participants to recognise that they come from traditions which have a history of resistance to injustice. Each person also has an individual history of defying racist and sexist conditioning, as a child, for example, who asked an adult (at least once) that forbidden question, or who has exclaimed (even to her or himself), 'That's not fair!'

Although women of colour welcome the active work and support of white women in the struggle against sexism and homophobia, they demand the right to set their own terms and priorities. For this reason, Alice Walker prefers to call strong black women who love other women 'womanists' rather than 'feminists' or 'lesbians'. 'Womanist', she explains, is from 'womanish', a 'black folk expression of mothers to female children' who display 'outrageous, audacious, courageous or *willful* behavior' and who want to know and do 'grown-up' things. Black feminists and lesbians – or 'womanists' – to be consistent with black cultural values, have had to affirm 'connectedness to the entire community and the world, rather than separation, *regardless* of who worked and slept with whom'.[15]

Nevertheless, black and other lesbians of colour experience difficulties within their own communities. Racial ethnic groups not only emulate the dominant culture's homophobia, but also label any despised or feared behaviour as a 'white' problem or disease. Men of colour who did not want to lose women's support in political struggles against racism initially reacted to feminism with hostile lesbian-baiting. Black feminists and/or lesbians, for example, found themselves accused of undermining 'Black nationhood' by consorting with the white enemy. In the midst of such accusations not only were lesbian mothers omitted, but also the connection between homophobia and misogyny. As feminists of colour have pointed out, woman-hating only diminishes the strength and unity of ethnic communities.

It also ignores some of the traditions of these cultures. Some Native American peoples, for example, prior to the inroads of Christianity, had a tolerant and even reverential attitude towards homosexuals. Many Native Americans continue to worship female deities and regard Mother Earth as sacred. Traditionally in such different cultures as the Southwestern Hopis and the Eastern tribes of the Iroquois Confederacy, tribal lands were passed through the female line. Black women, out of necessity, have had to be 'strong' and combine family care with wage-earning. This was a respected model of womanhood among many blacks until the 1960s and 1970s when white policy-makers claimed that the 'female-headed' family (rather than racial discrimination) was responsible for black male unemployment. Some black men, too, demanded their 'manhood' without questioning white patriarchal models.

Sexual conservatism within racial and white ethnic cultures is, in part, a survival reaction to a history of genocidal strategies and contemporary 'population control' schemes. Yet cultures as diverse as black Protestants, Hispanic and Italian Catholics, and Ashkenazi Jews all share a belief in male supremacy coupled with religious strictures against homosexuality. According to Gloria Joseph, blacks think that lesbians are 'unnatural' because they seem to act like men, and 'there is a prohibition against usurping the prerogatives or the appearance of the male'. Although lesbian relationships have been openly mentioned in the lyrics of female blues singers, lesbianism in the sexual socialisation of black women 'is a story with silences and denials as its most salient features'.

In Hispanic cultures the silence has been almost total. Oliva M. Espín, a practising psychotherapist, found that: 'Although emotional and physical closeness among women is encouraged. . ., overt acknowledgment of lesbianism is even more restricted than in mainstream American society.'[16] Frequent contact with and dependence upon family members are important in these cultures, and Hispanic lesbians fear that 'coming out' will deprive them of these essential relationships. While most work by and about Chicanas, including the collected articles in *Twice A Minority: Mexican American Women* (1980), treat their subjects almost exclusively within a familial and heterosexual context, recently a few lesbians, such as Cherríe Moraga and Gloria Anzaldúa in their anthology *This Bridge Called My Back* (1981) are finally breaking the silence about Chicana lesbianism.

Since cultural views of homosexuality are closely linked to those of sexuality generally, it is not surprising that racial ethnic, like white, cultures attempt to restrict female sexual expression to a marital, procreative model. Women of colour have to contend not only with the norms of their own cultures, but also with white stereotypes, slanders and violence. Black slave women were systematically violated by the white master in order to increase the size of the plantation's labour force. It was common for Anglo conquerers to rape Chicanas and Native American women. Later, these women were restricted to domestic service jobs, where they were coerced into sexual liaisons with their white employers. As a result of their sexual exploitation, black, Chicana and Native American women have been stigmatised as 'natural' sluts and whores. This image persists in spite of cultural imperatives about pre-marital chastity, vigilant policing by mothers to ensure their daughters' virginity and, especially among Hispanic Catholics, the Virgin Mary as a role model of asexual motherhood. The stereotype of the 'excessive' sexuality of dark-skinned women accounts for some of the reactive 'macho' behaviour by men of colour. They have been unable either to prevent white male rape of their wives, sisters, mothers and daughters or to exercise the patriarchal 'right' of exclusive ownership over 'their' women. According to Bell Hooks, black women have not learned clearly to distinguish between racist and sexist behaviours.

Since they perceived white male sexual overtures as racist, they could not understand that the sexism motivating these acts was not that different from the sexism motivating aggressive sexual overtures of black men.

In spite of negative stereotypes and cruel treatment, black women value sexual relationships with men. Hooks found that the 'great majority' of her black subjects felt 'that the most important aspect of a woman's life was her relationship with a man'.[17] Yet, as a result of cultural experience and economic hardship, women of colour and white working-class women often develop a more complex, ambivalent and realistic set of expectations and practices than do middle-class women. Affection and pleasure are tempered by sexual bargaining and criticism of male behaviour. As the authors of one of the first major works on Chicanas state: 'Chicana attitudes toward the Chicano decidedly contradict the long honored stereotype of the woman as passive and the male as dominant.'[18] Short stories and poems by Bernice Zamora, Caroline Castillo and Sylvia Delgado have criticised the sexual double standard by which the female alone is blamed for pre-marital sexuality and pregnancy. Woman-bonding and revenge against the tyrannical male were the themes of Estela Portillo Trambley's story 'If It Weren't for the Honeysuckle' (1975), while Angela de Hoyos' poem 'Words Unspoken' (1977) took a more compassionate view of the vulnerable, desperate man underneath the brave 'machismo'.

The sexual norms of Hispanic cultures, as well as racial oppression, are responsible for the ambivalence surrounding heterosexual relationships. Some women 'express pride at their own lack of sexual pleasure or desire', and there exists 'a widespread belief among Latin women of all social classes that most men are undependable and are not to be trusted'. Yet they will endure a man's infidelities and abuses because 'having a man around is an important source of a woman's sense of self-worth'.

Although Afro-American sexual norms appear to be less repressive than those of Hispanic cultures, many black women also view men as untrustworthy and feel the necessity to bargain with them. If men seek gratification in sexual conquest, women need verbal and material signs that they are 'respected'. As one woman expressed it: 'if I don't get something for it, he'd probably think I'd give it to anybody free. I don't want him to think that. . . . So I just collect a little rent and get me some threads now and then.'[19]

Black women worry about a shortage of eligible men. Some of the perceived scarcity is due to undercounting black men for the Population Census, but black women are less likely to live with a husband than either whites or Hispanics. In 1981 over 47 per cent of black families with children present were headed by women, a rise from 31 per cent in 1970. There is a definite connection between income level and family structure. While only 18 per cent of the black children in families with incomes under $4000 lived with both parents, 90 per cent of those with incomes over $15,000 did. Yet since Chicanos have a much lower rate of female-headed families and only a slightly better economic profile, cultural differences must be taken into account. Black women have had not only higher rates of labour force participation, but also lower fertility rates than Chicanas. Gender roles are more flexible, and blacks have been more accepting of children born of single women than have either whites or Hispanics.

Although motherhood is expected of all women, it is central in those cultures where women have been subjected to involuntary sterilisation and other forms of population control. Motherhood transforms socially devalued sexuality into a respected 'womanly' role. The equation of womanhood with motherhood has been strong among low-income black women. Joyce Ladner found that motherhood was the 'standard for becoming a woman that was accepted by the majority of people in the community'. Chicanos also consider motherhood 'to be the fulfillment of womanhood. . . . Mexican American women are expected to be mothers, first and foremost.'[20] Even among many white working-class people, adulthood is achieved through marriage and parenthood. In Lillian Rubin's study of working-class families, the birth of the first child occurred less than a year after marriage, and the couples' economic situation did not allow for 'adult only' leisure time. Parental roles and responsibilities quickly took precedence over the marriage relationship.

Motherhood is especially important when economic conditions permit few other life choices. A black welfare mother explained that pregnancy was one of the few times she felt 'good' – 'At least then I am . . . making something grow.' Chicanas emigrating from rural Mexico have few alternatives to be 'una mujer' except through motherhood. Their husbands regard large families as evidence of their masculinity. In a study of ten Chicanas who were the victims of non-consenting sterilisations, eight of the marriages suffered irreparable damage. Each woman's sense of self-worth was shattered, and she felt excluded from a community whose celebrations centred around baptism, confirmation, communion and marriage.[21]

As we saw in Chapter 6, 'reproductive rights' present different issues for white middle-class women and poor women, especially women of colour. Although women of all races and classes seek and have abortions, their reasons for doing so and the type of medical services available vary according to class, race and age. During the 1970s, rising college attendance and employment, later marriage and higher abortion rates were all found among middle-class and working-class women, both black and white – but not among the very poor. In a poll taken by *Life* magazine in 1981, 80 per cent of the women of colour, compared to 67 per cent of white women, said that women should have the legal right to obtain abortions. Black women, however, tend to have abortions at a somewhat later age than white women and generally after they have given birth to at least one child. A study done in the early 1970s of pregnant unmarried adolescents in California found that the women who took their pregnancies to term 'were more likely to be younger, Mexican-American, and from working-class families'. Later studies confirm that white teenagers have consistently higher abortion rates than do blacks or Chicanas, and those from higher socioeconomic classes choose to get abortions at twice the rate of those living in poverty areas.[22]

After adolescence, however, abortion rates change dramatically. During the 1970s, Medicaid-eligible women (who are poor and disproportionately from racial ethnic groups) had an abortion rate three times higher than those of white, unmarried middle- or working-class women. Women who can pursue advanced education and professional careers seek abortions in order to postpone the responsibilities of motherhood. Poor women are driven by immediate economic necessity to terminate their pregnancies. In some cases, then, low-income women are denied the 'reproductive right' to bear a wanted child. Since they have little choice of medical services, poor women have been either pressured by physicians in public hospitals to have abortions or denied this option in Catholic hospitals.

In 1977 Congress passed the Hyde Amendment, the first of an increasingly restrictive series of measures prohibiting federal Medicaid funding for abortion. The Supreme Court upheld this legislation in 1981 (*Harris* v. *McRae*). Although some individual states still provide revenues for abortion services, the cut off of federal funding, along with an overall decrease in welfare spending, has increasingly forced poor women to choose between uncontrolled child-bearing, abstinence from sexual intercourse, medically unsafe abortions or sterilisation. Under such conditions, sterilisation cannot be called a free choice.

Women of colour have been the primary targets of involuntary sterilisation. The ten Chicanas mentioned earlier were pressured into signing consent forms during the intensive stage of labour and/or were misinformed about the operation. Four of the women were unaware they had been sterilised until they sought birth control devices. Similar cases involving black women include eleven teenagers in Montgomery, Alabama, and Nial Ruth Cox of North Carolina who at the age of 18 'consented' to sterilisation after officials threatened to discontinue her family's welfare payments.

She was assured that her infertility would be temporary. As recently as 1970, sterilisation rates for racial ethnic women were double those for whites. By 1975, however, overall sterilisation rates between whites and non-whites had become roughly identical. It appears, however, that sterilised white women are generally in their early thirties and close to 90 per cent are married; racial ethnic women tend to be younger and unmarried. Sterilisation rates also vary among racial ethnic groups. In the late 1970s, it was estimated that at least 24 per cent of all Native American women of child-bearing age, over 35 per cent of Puerto Rican women, and approximately 20 per cent of Chicanas and black women had been sterilised. A Native American publication at the end of the decade claimed that as many as 42 per cent of Indian women of child-bearing age and 10 per cent of the men had undergone sterilisation.

The apparent convergence of white and racial ethnic sterilisation rates since the mid 1970s does not mean that racial differences have disappeared. Rather, they have been subsumed under income level and welfare status. Poor women of all races have higher sterilisation rates than middle-class women. Unlike abortion, sterilisation remains federally funded, and 97 per cent of the doctors in public hospitals favour the procedure for welfare mothers with illegitimate children. Depending on the geographical region, Medicaid recipients are two to four times more likely to be sterilised than women not dependent on public assistance. Women on welfare with three or more children are 67 per cent more likely to be sterilised than non-welfare women with the same number of children.[23]

Poor white and racial ethnic women want to choose among birth control methods, instead of being coerced into permanent infertility. Pro-natalist cultural values may be less of a hindrance in controlling reproduction than economics, education and bureaucratic insensitivity. This is particularly true for Chicanas who have the highest birthrate of any ethnic population in the US. While Chicanas in professional occupations bear almost exactly the same average number of children as similarly educated white women, Chicanas on the whole are the most poorly educated population in the country. Less than a quarter have completed high school. Chicana mothers are less likely to be in the labour force than are black mothers, and Chicanas who work full-time, year round, earn less than black women do. The findings of seven recent studies indicate a high verbal acceptance of birth control among Chicanas, but low income and educational levels, plus racial/linguistic discrimination by the middle-class Anglo-dominated health care system hinder effective use of contraceptive devices.[24]

Poor women cannot afford the regular services of an obstetrician or paediatrician. Deprived of continuous and preventive health care, maternal and infant mortality rates remain higher among racial ethnic than white populations. In 1979, as in 1959, black infants were twice as likely to die than were white infants. Women of colour have reason to resent the way birth control is promoted in their communities while their families lack more essential, general health services. Moreover, since 1980, federal programmes supplying poor women and children with funds for health and nutrition have been cut back.

White and racial ethnic working-class and poor women cannot take their families' health and security for granted. Given the tenuous nature of family stability, they treasure kinship ties and traditional roles more than white, middle-class women do. Motherhood provides working-class and poor women with self-esteem and community approval; it even compensates for the lack of authority and autonomy in their poorly paid service and clerical jobs.

Family relationships are shaped by many social and personal variables. Among the most important are economic: the overall amount of resources available, the sources from which they are derived, and the way they are distributed among family members. Distribution is, in turn, related to the gender division of labour within the household and in paid employment. While women of all classes do the major portion of unpaid household labour, working-class women also take paid jobs primarily to sustain their families, rather than enhance or 'express' themselves. Even if men's control of women's labour forms the material base for patriarchy, as feminists contend, women experience and evaluate this control differently when it is exercised by individual men to whom they are devoted, rather than by impersonal corporate or state agencies.

Family life among the working class and poor is certainly not free of age- and gender-based conflict, but several reasons make the feminist critiques of the nuclear family irrelevant to many racial ethnic and white working-class women. In the face of economic hardship and racial oppression, family unity and pooling of resources are essential for survival. Intra-family gender conflicts do not surface as conscious political issues. The working-class 'patriarch' has little power outside his family; within it, he usually has to share the 'breadwinner' position with other family members or the state. Both male and female wage-earners in low-income families are likely to work in non-unionised service jobs or as unskilled manual labourers. Because many working-class and poor women, in contrast to middle-class women, do not envy their husbands' work, they also do not find their own domestic roles oppressive.

Despite media and even feminist stereotypes, the gender division of labour is not rigidly maintained in all working-class families. In interviews with four generations of New Mexico Chicanas, both older and younger women described how domestic tasks were shared with their husbands and children. 'We've been married thirty-five years', recalled Esperanza Salcido, 'and I can honestly say he's done the dishes all the time. . . . When I was working, we even shared the ironing, until the kids were old enough to do their own. Then everyone ironed – the girls and the boys both.' Emma Gonzales, who holds a local political office, also spoke of her husband's encouragement and help, and she expressed an opinion shared by many working women: 'I still feel my family comes first. It's not worth it to sacrifice the happiness of your husband and your family for your job.'[25]

Since most women work because of economic necessity, they do not regard paid employment as a form of 'liberation'. Donna Redmond, a receptionist from Atlanta, Georgia, works to support her two children. 'If being able to work like a horse for a living is being liberated for a woman, I'd just as soon be dependent.' Redmond is white, but like many women of colour she knows that marriage is not an economic panacea. 'Even if you've got a man, it's not easy. The women have to work too, cause they're mostly low-income families.' Two out of three working women are single, widowed, divorced, separated or have husbands who earn less than $15,000 a year. For this female majority 'the superwoman who knits marriage, career, and motherhood into a satisfying life without dropping a stitch is as oppressive a role model as the airbrushed Bunny in the Playboy centerfold or That Cosmopolitan Girl.'[26]

Overwork, unemployment, stress and economic hardship all contribute to the vicissitudes of marital love. Neither has the nation's welfare system made it easy for women to live with men and obtain state assistance. In a study of a low-income black community, Bettylou Valentine found that the female-headed household was not a common form except on official papers. If her sample is typical, statistics on female-headed households, especially in black communities, would have to be regarded as somewhat exaggerated.

Contrary to popular myths, welfare does not provide the sole income for poor families, and welfare recipients are not a permanent 'underclass'. The Panel Study of Income Dynamics (PSID), a longitudinal study using a national sample, found that both poverty and welfare use have been widespread. Between 1969 and 1978, one-fourth of the nation's population lived in families that received welfare income at some point. Yet only one-third of the recipients relied on it for more than half the family income and only 1 per cent of the population could be defined as permanently poor, or dependent on welfare for all ten years. Usually families mixed work and welfare or alternated between them. In 'Blackston', the community Valentine studied, women, men and even children not only supplemented welfare with sporadic, low-paid employment but they also engaged in 'hustling', or a variety of informal non-market work and illegal activities. These ghetto residents regarded police and fire protection, as well as garbage collection, as legal, white forms of 'hustling' directed against them. While the white workers who held these jobs earned three times the legal minimum wage paid to many blacks, the community received only repression, damage and neglect from these agencies.[27]

The lack of basic social services and protection, plus discrimination by professional care-givers such as teachers, social workers and physicians, has taught many poor people to rely on their own kin and friendship networks. Women play a major role in nourishing and maintaining their families. They engage in barter, such as babysitting in return for the use of a car, and in frequent borrowing back and forth of groceries, household appliances and food stamps. Kin and friendship networks also support strategies which resist the values and institutions of the dominant culture, especially in racial ethnic communities. For example, Maxine Hong Kingston's China-born parents taught her the following maxims for defying 'white ghosts':

Lie to Americans. . . . Don't report crimes; tell them we have no crimes and no poverty. Give a new name every time you get arrested; the ghosts won't recognize you. Pay the new immigrants twenty-five cents an hour and say we have no unemployment. And, of course, tell them we're against Communism.[28]

Depending on the circumstances, extended families and other non-nuclear arrangements, various subterfuges with welfare departments, acceptance of extra-legal sources of income, and even the attempt to maintain some semblance of traditional gender roles can all be ways to survive and resist.

In this milieu, women of colour cannot easily defy or criticise their cultures' emphasis on marriage and motherhood. Chicana feminists, for example, wish to transcend some of the conventional limitations placed on women, yet they simultaneously work to enhance the solidarity of family and community. The importance of 'familial politics', or the family unit as a participant in political organisations and struggles, is one reason why ideologies that advocate the liberation of women apart from that of men are disdained. As long as the family serves 'vital psychological protective functions for colonized groups', women of colour will require that their traditional family roles be supported, valued, and 'opened up', rather than rejected.[29]

Economic factors reinforce traditional gender roles for white women, too. Many working women find that their economic security depends less on their jobs than on the presence of an employed male partner. The feminisation of poverty includes not only women whose poverty status is rooted in race and age discrimination, but also the 'new' poor – nominally middle-class women who experience serious economic loss after a divorce or death of a spouse. Unmarried or no longer married women find that they cannot earn enough to support themselves and their children.

One reason why women earn less than men is that the working-class struggle for the 'family wage' excluded women. The policies both of labour unions and of government agencies predicated that male workers should support wives and children at home. Although the family wage provided an adequate income for some segments of the working class, it has been neither widespread nor long-lived enough to benefit most families. More important, the 'man-sized' wage kept women's wages low.

As we have seen in earlier chapters, one of the greatest changes in the post-war economy has been the increased labour force participation of married women with children. This second family income did contribute significantly to higher living standards, especially during the 1960s when the median income for all American families rose 36 per cent. However, from 1969 to 1978, the overall rise in median income was only 5 per cent, and incomes of families with only one earner fell about 7 per cent behind the cost of living. The wages of married women have become necessary to maintain, rather than enhance, their families' well-being.

Currently, dual wage-earner families are experiencing a general decline in both their future prospects and their present quality of life. Women and men are working harder, sacrificing leisure time and family life, increasing their burden of indebtedness and saving less. Rising housing costs provide one measure of this new 'immiseration'. The Department of Housing and Urban Development estimated that in 1970 half of the American people could afford to buy a median-priced new home; by 1979, only 13 per cent could afford new-home ownership. By the end of the 1970s, American families were spending almost 36 per cent of their disposable income for housing, double the average ten years earlier.[30] Renters, too, are overspending for shelter. In the 1970s rents rose by 123 per cent while the median income of renters increased by only 70 per cent. The lower the income, the higher the percentage paid for housing. Very low-income people pay up to 60 per cent of their income in rent.

Women and children have been the hardest hit by the 'stagflation' (recessions plus inflation) of the middle and late 1970s and by the national government's redirection of tax revenues from social services to increased military spending. Two out of three adults in poverty are women, and the feminisation of poverty accounted for virtually all the growth in the official poverty rolls during the 1970s. Between 1970 and 1980, the number of poor families headed by women rose by one-third, while poor male-headed families decreased by 18 per cent. In 1981, the poverty rate for all female householders was more than three times higher than for male householders and more than five times that for husband-wife families.

Although unmarried women have generally had high rates of poverty, during the 1970s the divorce rate more than doubled, thus increasing the number of female-headed households. Also over the same period, families headed by never-married women climbed to 3.4 million, an increase of 356 per cent. 'The result of divorce, in an overwhelming number of cases, is that men become singles and women become single mothers.'[31] Divorced women with children tend to be poorer than their ex-husbands. In California, where half of all marriages end in divorce, a man's standard of living increases by 49 per cent on the average, while his ex-wife's falls by 74 per cent. Half of the divorced mothers in California do not receive the full child support payments ordered by the courts, and over half of the women and children receiving welfare in that state have ex-husbands and fathers who earn more than $15,000 a year, but who contribute little or nothing to support their children.

While marital disruption significantly increases white women's chances for being poor, it virtually ensures economic hardship for women of colour, especially black women whose divorce rates are higher than those of whites or Hispanics. Remarriage, on the other hand, improves the economic status of women, but it is far more common for divorced men than divorced women to remarry and more frequent for white women than for black women. Although not all women are equally poor, their economic position depends to a large extent on their relationship with a man or their lack of it.

The political conservatism of the late 1970s and 1980s has coincided with a growing tendency to attribute the poverty of women and children exclusively to the 'breakdown' of the nuclear family, and to claim that women's economic insecurity is caused by high rates of divorce and single motherhood. The New Right, for example, believes that the solution to both 'sexual immorality' and women's poverty is to reinstate the traditional 'Christian' family and remove any alternatives, such as welfare and abortion might provide. The most extreme view is one that would return women to exclusively domestic roles and re-establish the father as the family's sole wage-earner. Critics point out that since both the welfare state and the wage-earning mother actually developed out of prior changes in industrial capitalism and the dissolution of the traditional patriarchal family, restoration of this sort is unlikely. For this reason, the views of neo-conservatives have been more influential than those of the New Right. Instead of emphasising the family, neo-conservatives favour a dismantling of programmes such as affirmative action, which have benefited white women and people of colour, so that 'market forces' in the private sector can operate more freely. The end result for women economically will remain the same; working women 'on their own' will still have to rely on the higher wages of men.

A somewhat different, but still conservative, argument has come from such 'revisionist' feminists as Betty Friedan and Jean Elshtain. They contend that radical feminists have alienated potential supporters by their anti-family and anti-motherhood views. Unlike the radicals, these revisionists are not interested in issues of sexual politics and do not subscribe to the feminist dictum that the 'personal is political'. Instead of analysing the 'private' family as a political institution based on unequal power relationships, they support it as the most viable and even 'natural' arrangement for the care and socialisation of children. The underlying assumption of all three approaches is that only heterosexual marriage offers women both emotional intimacy and economic security. Although a husband's wages or salary certainly contribute to an individual woman's material well-being, this does not eliminate the economic vulnerability of women as a sex class or the economic differentiation of women and men.

Rather than seeing the source of women's poverty as radical feminists or the welfare state, Barbara Ehrenreich puts much of the blame on an earlier 'male revolt' against the breadwinner role. She traces the rejection of marriage and family responsibilities to such anti-family publications as *Playboy* (which began in 1953) and the male 'Beats' of the 1950s, who formed permanent attachments only with each other. Popular science, too, lent legitimacy to the male rebellion by emphasising the connection between heart disease and the stress of the breadwinner role. The 'parasitic, spendthrift wife' was indicted as a major killer of men. 'The long-term effect of the coronary scare was to undermine women's claims to a share of the husband's wage.'[32] If Ehrenreich is correct, then even if all men today had an opportunity to earn wages sufficient to support families, there is no guarantee that they would do so. The inadequate contributions that divorced men make towards child support lend weight to the argument that many fathers have not formed lasting attachments to or a sense of responsibility for their children.

Although the feminisation of poverty puts all women at risk, black and Hispanic women who head households have higher poverty rates than white women. In 1981, close to 40 per cent of white female heads with two children under 18 years of age lived in poverty, while over 60 per cent of similarly situated black and Hispanic women did. The PSID showed that 70 per cent of black children, compared to 30 per cent of white children, were poor at some time during the 1970s; 30 per cent of the black children, but only 2 per cent of the white children, were poor for at least six out of the ten years.[33] Despite political movements and legislation against racial discrimination, the economic gap between white and racial ethnic people has not been eliminated.

The distinct character of women's poverty lies not in the increase of female-headed households or in the persistence of racism, but in women's unpaid family work and underpaid jobs in a sex-segregated labour market. Women are 'paid for' housework and child care either out of the wages of an employed male or by the state in the form of welfare. In both cases they are under patriarchal rule. Women who are 'free' from the private patriarchy of an individual man often require the public support and professional care-taking services of the male-dominated state. Welfare is one form of public patriarchy.

The United States maintains a two-tier welfare system, and not all recipients of public funds are poor. In 1982, for example, 38 per cent of Americans received benefits from one or more of six programmes: Social Security, veterans benefits, unemployment compensation, Supplementary Security Income, Aid to Families of Dependent Children (AFDC) and food stamps. The first three are designed for 'legitimate' insurance beneficiaries who are eligible for payments by 'right', that is, by virtue of their own or their employers' prior contributions to the programme. The last three are means-tested. Targeted for the poor, their recipients face the severe social stigma associated with official public dependency.

Women constitute a larger proportion of those who receive income from means-tested programmes than from insurance programmes. They are 81 per cent of AFDC recipients and only 41 per cent of unemployment compensation beneficiaries.[34] Although the requirements differ among the means-tested programmes, AFDC recipients are usually eligible for food stamps, medical care (Medicaid) and child care. AFDC is the core of the government's programme for single mothers and their children. Unlike Sweden, the Federal Republic of Germany, France, the United Kingdom, Canada or Australia, the US does not offer any universal family or child allowances which are *not* income-tested. Therefore, Americans who claim public assistance in order to support children must be not only poor, but also they must maintain themselves and their dependents on inadequate AFDC funds.

The real value of AFDC declined 29 per cent between 1969 and 1981 due to inflation. At the beginning of this decade, AFDC plus food stamps brought a household up to the poverty level in only three American states. Then, the Reagan administration's Omnibus Budget Reconciliation Act of 1981 (OBRA) penalised the working poor by raising the tax rate on the earned income of welfare recipients and by establishing lower and more restrictive income limits. Mothers who had worked at low-income jobs in order to supplement AFDC payments found that their employment disqualified them for welfare. However, 40 per cent of those who have had to leave the AFDC programme continue to earn incomes below the poverty level. Working women removed from the welfare rolls are either ineligible for such ancillary programmes as food stamps, Medicaid and child care, or they are not informed of their possible continued eligibility. The average monthly income of nearly 300 women in six Michigan counties who had lost AFDC in 1982 dropped from $822 to $771. This lower amount added up to an annual income below the poverty level of $9862 for a non-farm family of four. Only 29 per cent received some coverage for medical expenses through their employment and one in five continued to have Medicaid. Nearly 40 per cent did not have health insurance for their whole family.[35]

OBRA was intended not only to cut welfare costs, but also to prevent the psychological harm supposedly caused by long-term welfare dependency. The non-material rewards of joining the work force have to compensate for lowered incomes. In over half the American states, a family of three in 1983 would have had a larger disposable income if none of its members worked. In California, for example, a three-member family with no earners would have received an income equal to 95 per cent of the poverty level, but if one member worked full-time at the legal minimum wage, the family's total disposable income would have amounted to 81 per cent of the poverty level. The 1981 poverty level for a family of three (the average-sized female-headed household) was set at

$7250, yet one out of three women working full-time that year earned under $7000. Two out of three minimum-wage workers are women.

Working mothers find that child care expenses can cut their salaries almost in half. The full-time female worker in 1980 earned an average of $11,197, while the average cost of day care for two children was $5000. Under the Reagan administration, the maximum child care allowance for women on AFDC is $160 a month per child, which comes to $3840 a year for two children. In California, less than one-third of the children with working mothers find care in licensed, affordable child care homes or centres; nationally, 11 million children under the age of 11 have no care while their parents are working.

As women age, especially if they are women of colour, the likelihood of poverty increases. Women make up close to 60 per cent of the population over 65, but they number three-fourths of the elderly poor. The poverty rate for women over 65 is double that of men; for older black women, it is double that of white women. Almost 23 per cent of white widows and one-half of widowed blacks over 65 were living below the official poverty level in 1980. The median income for single older women in 1979 was $3097, and only 5 per cent had annual incomes of more than $5000. Four out of five women of colour over 65 were living on individual incomes below $2000 a year.

Since there are nine potential brides for every bridegroom over the age of 65, few older women compared to men will remarry. Over half the women aged 65 and older are widows, while 75 per cent of the men in this age group are married and living with their spouses. Three out of five older women rely on Social Security as their sole source of income. Only 20 per cent of retirement-age women can supplement Social Security benefits with pensions based on their own or their husbands' employment records. Women are often employed in those industries and jobs where there is no pension coverage, and many older women have either not held paid jobs or they alternated employment with homemaking. The situation of the older homemaker clearly illustrates the relationship between women's poverty and their unpaid work. Years of child care and housework are not counted towards pensions or Social Security benefits. Older, once-married women are eligible for Social Security through their husbands' retirement benefits, but the most

a widow can collect is half of her husband's payment, and she has
to wait until she is 60 to receive any of it.

The Reagan administration has cut federal funding for means-
tested programmes and other vital support services, such as low-
income housing, subsidised legal services and inexpensive public
transportation. The military budget, however, has increased 25 per
cent since 1981. The $7.2 billion budgeted in 1983 for the MX
missile and the B-1 bomber programmes could have funded the
entire AFDC programme; the military increase in 1984 would have
more than paid for Medicaid programmes for the disabled and
elderly.

As the poor face destitution, middle-class government workers
are losing their jobs. The expansion of government-sponsored social
services in the 1960s created employment opportunities for educated
white women and people of colour. In 1976, close to half of the
female professionals worked in government agencies. Black men
and women were, in 1980, over 50 per cent more likely to find
employment in the public sector than were similarly qualified
whites. Since the initiation of cuts, racial ethnic federal employees
have been laid off at a rate 50 per cent greater than white
employees, and the lay-off rate for female administrators has been
150 per cent higher than for males. Since private industry's record
of hiring professional black and white women or black men has
been poor, the partial dismantling of the welfare state is eliminating
the recent gains of this 'new' middle class. Military spending
creates less employment, especially for women, than the same
amount spent in the civilian sector. For example, 1 billion dollars
creates 76,000 jobs in defence and 139,000 jobs in health care.

The recent reductions in what was already an inadequate welfare
system demonstrate both the low social value placed on women's
unpaid work and the connection between such work and the
feminisation of poverty. As will be shown in the next chapter, paid
work provides some women with new opportunities, but it also
contributes to women's economic vulnerability. The number of
poor families could be cut in half if working women earned the
same as similarly qualified men.

10. Paid and Unpaid Work: the 1970s and 1980s

Since the late 1960s the Women's Movement has been encouraging women to enter non-traditional professional, managerial and skilled blue-collar occupations. Feminists have made the public more aware of gender-based differences in wages, the need for child care services, equality in training and promotion, and an end to sexual harassment at the workplace. They insist that housework and child care be shared equally between women and men and call for increased social services to enable both sexes to engage in paid employment and family life.

These and other issues have become increasingly important as growing numbers of women enter the labour force. Most women workers are married and most have children. Employment issues and family needs can no longer be separated, especially as employed women do almost all the unpaid housework and child care. The 'double day' has become the most salient reality of women's everyday lives, and it underlies many of the issues to be covered in this chapter: sex segregation in the labour market, differences in women's and men's employment opportunities, discrepancies in female and male earnings, technological deskilling of occupations dominated by women, and the transfer of jobs to low-wage female workers within and outside the United States.

In 1984, 50 million women were in the labour force, compared to 32 million in 1971. Women contributed more than 62 per cent of the total growth in the civilian workforce from 1975 through 1984. In 1960, 37.7 per cent of women 16 years of age and over were in the labour force; ten years later, 43 per cent were either working or seeking employment. By 1984, 54 per cent of all women

195

were in the labour force, with 70 per cent of those between the ages of 25 and 54 either employed or looking for work. In 1970, women made up 38 per cent of the civilian workforce; by 1984, they were close to 44 per cent.

White women no longer leave paid employment at the onset of motherhood and return to work when their youngest child begins school. Their workforce participation, like that of black women, has become almost continuous, or closer to the white male pattern. The most dramatic change since 1960 has occurred in the employment rates of women 24–34 years of age, the peak child-bearing years. In 1960, 36 per cent of the women in this age group were in the labour force, compared to 51 per cent of the 18 and 19 year olds and 49 per cent of the 45–54 year-old women. Age-group differences were declining by 1970, with 53.6 per cent of the 18 and 19 year-old women, 45 per cent of those between 25 and 34, and 54.4 per cent of women 45–54 years old in the workforce. By 1981, workforce participation had become *highest* among women aged 25 to 34. Almost 67 per cent were in the labour force, compared to 61 per cent of the 18 and 19 year olds and 61 per cent of the mid-life women. In 1970, one-third of all mothers with children under 6 years of age held or sought jobs; by 1984, a majority (52.1 per cent) of these mothers had joined the workforce. Close to 48 per cent of mothers with a child under 3 are currently employed, with 65 per cent of them working full-time. Women with children over the age of 6 have a labour force participation rate of almost 70 per cent. In spite of the increase in the number of female-headed households, the most striking gain in employment over the last decade has occurred among married mothers whose participation rate rose from 45 per cent in 1975 to 59 per cent in 1984.

Although the Women's Movement has addressed the needs of women workers, it is not responsible for the increased percentage of mothers in the labour force or the growing convergence of women's and men's employment patterns. The present high rates of female employment are the result of economic need and the continued growth in clerical and service jobs which have traditionally employed women. The corporate search for increased profits and lower labour costs has led to growing numbers of low-wage and part-time jobs. These are filled mainly by women, young people and men of colour. At least 80 per cent of employed women are working in female-dominated occupations. They are also concentrated in employment sectors where new technology is reorganising the work process, generally making it less skilled and more stressful.

The majority of women work because of economic need. In addition to single, divorced and widowed women, nearly 20 per cent of the female labour force are married women whose husbands earned less than $15,000 in 1983. Although most women cannot earn enough to support families, their wages have become increasingly necessary. Less than one-fourth of American families in the early 1980s were being supported by the husband's earnings alone, while close to 52 per cent depended on the salaries of both husband and wife.[1] At the same time, continued sexism, acceptance of capitalist values and entrenched business practices have prevented any radical change in employment opportunities and workplace conditions.

Women not only face inequities in the labour market, but also their socially-assigned family responsibilities often preclude total commitment to their jobs. In the absence of corporate and government support for family needs, women are at a disadvantage, compared to men, in competing for high-status managerial, professional and technical positions. Employed women spend, on the average, 3.8 hours a day performing unpaid household work, while their husbands devote only 1.6 hours. However, the reasons why women's unpaid work time is triple that of men vary according to economic class and are based on different perceptions of women's paid employment and traditional gender roles.

Financial need is not the only incentive for a working-class woman to seek employment, but it may be in her interest to emphasise material concerns rather than social and psychological needs. If members of her family regard her job as an essential monetary contribution to their well-being, she possesses a certain leverage to negotiate some redistribution of household tasks. However, working-class men perceive housework as demeaning and unmasculine, and they are supported in this view not only by other men, but also by their wives. Therefore, both women and men tend to hide whatever housework men may perform. As one study pointed out: 'Complaining about how little a husband does at home seems to be a more acceptable topic of conversation among women than "bragging" about how much housework he takes on.' In middle-class households, the ideal is that employed husbands and wives should share housework, and women 'present an exaggerated picture of their husbands' actual involvement'.[2] Egalitarian appearances are belied by the middle-class view that a woman enters the labour force mainly for psychological enhancement rather than because of financial necessity. The husband and other family members believe they are making a sacrifice by allowing her to work and in return she owes them undiminished care and service.

Economic class continues to play a determining role in women's employment opportunities. While college-educated, middle-class women can now aspire to professional and managerial careers, working-class women with high school diplomas continue to seek clerical, service and factory jobs. However, some long-standing racial differences among working women are diminishing. The influx of women into the workforce during the 1970s has resulted in nearly equal labour force participation rates. In 1982, 53 per cent of black women, 52 per cent of white women, and 48 per cent of Hispanic women were either employed or actively seeking work. White mothers are almost as likely to be in the workforce as black mothers. Almost 63 per cent of black mothers of children under 18 were in the labour force in 1984 compared to 60 per cent of white mothers. Over the last generation the gap in educational level between white and black women has been closing. In 1962 there were almost two years difference in education, but by 1983 the median years of schooling for black women workers was only one-fifth of a year less than that of white women.

Income differences among women have also declined. In 1964, the median income for black women who worked full-time, year-round was 69 per cent of the white female income; by 1981, it reached 90 per cent. Black women in 1983 who worked year-round, full-time were approaching income parity with their white counterparts – $13,000 compared to white women's $14,677. This rise in black women's wages relative to those of white women is partly due to increasing numbers of black women entering professional, technical, clerical and skilled blue-collar occupations, along with their continuous movement out of private household work. Almost 16 per cent of employed women of colour were professional and technical workers in 1982, compared to 18 per cent of white women; over 35 per cent of white female workers and close to 30 per cent of non-white women held clerical jobs.

However, women of colour are still over-represented as factory workers – 13.5 per cent compared to 8.2 per cent of white women – and almost 30 per cent of women of colour are service workers compared to 18 per cent of employed white women.

Although black women earn almost the same median income as white women, they are far more likely to experience economic deprivation. First of all, black men earned only 71 per cent of the median income of white men in 1981. This is an improvement over the 66 per cent they earned in 1964, but it means that black families continue to have less income than white ones. In 1983, the average income for a black family was $14,506, considerably less than the $25,757 for white families. The gap is smaller but still significant when only two-earner, married-couple families are considered: $26,389 for blacks and $32,569 for whites. The poverty rate for black married-couple families in 1983 was 15.5 per cent, more than double the rate for whites. In the last chapter we noted that far more black than white women are heads of households, and that black women who head families have almost twice the poverty rates of similarly situated whites.

Along with women's low earnings relative to those of men and continuing racial inequality in wages and occupations, unemployment rates are much higher for blacks of both sexes than for whites, especially among teenagers. These official rates understate the problem. Only those actively seeking work are counted, not women and men who are too discouraged to initiate a job search or who have been unemployed for so long that they are ineligible for unemployment insurance.

TABLE 10.1   Unemployment rates 1984

Teenagers (aged 16–19)	Rate	Adults (aged 20 and over)	Rate
Black men	42.7	Black men	14.3
Black women	42.6	Black women	13.5
White men	16.8	White men	5.7
White women	15.2	White women	5.8

SOURCE: Women's Bureau, US Department of Labor, 'Black Women in the Labor Force' (Washington, DC: Fact Sheet No. 85–6, July 1985).

The major difference between white and black women today lies not in their own jobs and income, but in the better chances married white women have to share the resources of the highest income earners – white men. As Phyllis Marynick Palmer points out, 'it is a fallacy when white women claim that they are only slightly better off than black women. Most white women do not *in reality* live on what they earn.' Yet the fact remains 'that for most women, economic well-being means attachment to a male wage earner', and few working women can attain economic security on their own.[3]

NON-TRADITIONAL WORK: PROMISES, PIONEERS AND PROBLEMS

One way that women can earn more is to enter occupations numerically dominated by men, since these generally pay considerably more than traditionally female jobs. During the last twenty years, women's occupational choices have expanded. Laws which prohibit excluding women and training programmes to help them acquire new skills have opened up non-traditional professional and technical work, as well as skilled blue-collar trades. However, women's continued success in these employment sectors is contingent upon the attitudes of employers and co-workers, the elimination of sexual harassment and health hazards, and the provision of child care facilities and other forms of relief from household responsibilities.

The legal framework for eliminating sex discrimination in employment consists of national, state and local laws and enforcement agencies, including the courts. Since national or federal policies are the most influential, we will confine our examples to this level. Three important laws were passed in the 1960s. The Equal Pay Act of 1963 prohibits employers from paying different wages, because of sex, to women and men employed in the same establishment and doing substantially the same work. Title VII of the 1964 Civil Rights Act makes it unlawful for employers to 'refuse to hire or to discharge any individual' or to 'discriminate against any individual with respect to . . . compensation, terms, conditions, or privileges of employment, because of such individual's race, color, religion, sex, or national origin.' Title VII also forbids employers from segregating or classifying employees or applicants for employment on the basis of race, sex, etc., in ways that would deprive them of employment opportunities. Age discrimination, a major problem for women re-entering the labour force after a period of full-time family work, is covered by the Age Discrimination in Employment Act (1968) which prohibits employers, employment agencies and labour unions from discriminating against persons 40–70 years of age.

With the passage of the Equal Employment Opportunity Act in 1972, Congress extended Title VII to include public employees. Title IX of the Education Amendments of 1972 prohibits sex discrimination in all federally assisted education programmes and covers employment, education, counselling, facilities and extra-curricular activities in elementary and secondary schools, as well as colleges, universities and vocational education programmes. Two other laws beneficial to working women are the Equal Credit Opportunity Act of 1974 prohibiting creditors from discriminating on the basis of sex or marital status, and the 1978 Pregnancy Discrimination Act which makes it illegal to discriminate in employment on the basis of pregnancy.

Executive Orders – No. 11246 issued by President Lyndon Johnson in 1965 and amended by Nos 11375 (1968) and 11478 (1969) – have potentially more power to benefit women than anti-discrimination laws, for they not only prohibit firms which do business with the government from discriminating in employment, but also require most federal contractors and agencies to take 'affirmative action' to correct practices and overcome special barriers to employment for minorities and women. Theoretically, employment qualifications or practices which appear to be sex-neutral could be declared discriminatory if they have a disparate effect on women.

Unfortunately, the federal government has not made enforcement of anti-discrimination laws or implementation of affirmative action policies a high priority. Federal agencies, according to Joan Abramson's study, had poor enforcement records during the 1970s. For example, the Equal Employment Opportunity Commission (EEOC), responsible for enforcing the Civil Rights Act of 1964, was burdened both with a huge backlog of cases and its own weak enforcement powers. The Office of Civil Rights within the Department of Health, Education and Welfare, responsible for

Title IX of the Education Amendments of 1972, accepted false or misleading statistics from educational institutions which were attempting to block affirmative action. Even when discrimination was proven in federal court cases, the 'winning' plaintiffs received little or no redress, and they continued to report workplace discrimination and harassment.

Sex discrimination has been widespread within the federal government itself, including the anti-discrimination agencies and the Department of Justice. During the 1970s, over three-fourths of women employees worked in the four lowest grade levels and less than 3 per cent of the top-paying federal jobs were held by women. Federal courts have not treated sex discrimination as seriously as they have race discrimination. Rather than applying the principle of 'strict scrutiny' which would make classifications based on sex 'inherently suspect', the courts have generally used a 'reasonableness' test which makes it difficult to prove that treating women and men differently constitutes discrimination. What appeared to be a promising trend towards 'strict scrutiny' in *Reed* v. *Reed* (1971) and *Frontiero* v. *Richardson* (1973) has not continued. Instead, in *Board of Curators of the University of Missouri* v. *Horowitz* (1978), the Supreme Court upheld the dismissal of a female medical student on 'academic grounds' even though the complaints of Horowitz's professors focused on her personal appearance, not her excellent academic record.[4]

Since the mid 1970s the liberal commitment to modify those aspects of the economic system which have handicapped women and people of colour has weakened, and conservatives have gained support by blaming disadvantaged people for asking 'too much' of the government or demanding 'special treatment'. Affirmative action programmes, in particular, have become increasingly controversial, as the economy does not appear to be growing fast enough to employ all those who seek work.

The Reagan administration has argued since January 1981 that any set of goals and timetables for increasing minority or women's employment both 'discriminates' against white males and hinders individual incentive by promising equality of results rather than equality of opportunity. Although the Supreme Court upheld the constitutionality of affirmative action in 1986, the administration had already weakened wage-discrimination and sex-segregation guidelines. By 1983, the enforcement staff in the Office of Federal

Contract Compliance Programs (OFCCP) was only half the size it had been in 1979, and the agency's budget had been cut by one-third in real dollars. On the one hand, Reagan's administration recognises the female wage-earner only as an individual, rather than as a member of a sex class. On the other hand, Reagan and his advisers emphasise that women's lack of employment opportunity and advancement is rooted in 'natural' differences between women and men which the state cannot and should not attempt to alter.

Behind these contradictory views is the administration's alliance with corporate ideology and its reluctance to use government power to 'interfere' with 'standard business practices' even when these perpetuate gender or racial discrimination. Ronald Reagan's re-election in 1984 and the defeat of the Equal Rights Amendment (ERA), which would have given women a constitutional claim to legal equality with men, are not promising indicators for any immediate shift in government policy.

In spite of this inauspicious political climate, women who have grown up within a context of feminist ideas and activity have different work expectations from the previous generation. It is no longer unusual for women to define themselves in terms of their occupations, not only by their unpaid family roles, and to prepare themselves for continuous rather than intermittent employment. The presence of women in non-traditional medical, legal, managerial and skilled craft occupations has provided younger women with new role models. Although actual employment gains have been modest, younger women are permitted and occasionally even encouraged to train for a wider variety of occupations.

Women and men still tend to study different subjects in college, but there is less segregation than formerly. In 1971, less than 3 per cent of college-educated women earned bachelor's degrees in business and management, compared to 22 per cent of the men. Ten years later, close to 16 per cent of college women and 27 per cent of men majored in business. In 1980–81, three times as many women than men earned BAs in education, the same ratio as in 1971. However, while 36 per cent of college women had majored in education in 1971, only 17.5 per cent did in 1981. Although men were nine times more likely to study engineering than were women in the early 1980s, this represented an improvement over 1971 when only one-tenth of 1 per cent of women took their bachelor's degrees in engineering while over 10 per cent of the men did.

In 1960, women had earned only 3 per cent of all professional degrees, and the proportion grew slowly until the 1970s, when women began to make striking gains in medical, legal and other professional fields. By 1979, they were earning 24 per cent of all professional degrees. Sex-discrimination legislation helped women to more than triple their enrolment in medical schools, from 7.7 per cent in 1964–65 to 26.5 per cent in 1980–81. Title IX of the Education Amendments also played a key role in eliminating discrimination in law school admissions, and female law students increased from only 4 per cent in the mid 1960s to over one-third in 1980.

The proportion of doctorates earned by women has grown from 14 per cent in 1970 to 28 per cent in 1980. However, sex differences prevail in graduate students' choice of subjects. In 1981, nearly half of women's doctorates were in education or psychology. Over 10 per cent of men's doctorates, but only 1 per cent of women's, were in engineering, and three times as many men earned doctorates in the physical sciences than did women. The concentration of doctorates in traditionally female fields has been even more marked among women of colour than among white women; 40 per cent of the PhDs awarded to black women and half of those earned by Hispanic women in the early 1980s were in education. Most women students, especially doctoral candidates, are still earning degrees in female-dominated fields, which are also presently glutted with applicants, while men's degrees are distributed among a larger number of the more lucrative and growing employment areas.[5]

As Table 10.2 indicates, women have increased their representation in some male-dominated occupations, most notably engineering, law, medicine, and finance, but the sex composition in traditionally female jobs has remained stable. Almost all nurses, secretaries, garment makers and private household workers were women both in 1970 and in 1981, and the proportion of female service workers, especially in the health industry, has not changed significantly. Since most of the increases have occurred in professional and technical fields, employment prospects appear to have improved more for educated, middle-class women than they have for working-class women. Although women have made some gains in the skilled trades, particularly printing, men continue to hold a disproportionate share of the better-paying jobs. Only 16 per cent of women blue-collar workers were craft and kindred

TABLE 10.2   Women as percentage of all workers in selected
occupations

	1970	1981
Professional-technical	40.0	44.7
Accountants	25.3	38.5
Computer specialists	19.6	27.1
Engineers	1.6	4.3
Lawyers-judges	4.7	14.0
Physicians-osteopaths	8.9	13.8
Registered nurses	97.4	96.8
Teachers, except college and university	70.4	70.6
Teachers, college and university	28.3	35.3
Managerial-administrative, except farm	16.6	27.4
Bank officials-financial managers	17.6	37.4
Buyers-purchasing agents	20.8	35.0
Food service	33.7	40.5
Sales managers-department heads, retail	24.1	40.4
Sales workers	39.4	45.4
Sales clerks, retail	64.8	71.3
Clerical	73.6	80.5
Bank tellers	86.1	93.7
Bookkeepers	82.1	91.2
Cashiers	84.0	86.4
Office machine operators	73.5	73.7
Secretaries-typists	96.6	98.6
Shipping-receiving clerks	14.3	22.5
Craft	4.9	6.3
Carpenters	1.3	1.9
Mechanics, including automotive	2.0	1.9
Printing	14.8	25.0
Operatives, except transport	38.4	39.8
Assemblers	48.7	52.3
Laundry and dry-cleaning operatives	62.9	66.1
Sewers and stitchers	93.8	96.0
Transport equipment operatives	4.5	8.9
Bus drivers	28.5	47.3
Truckdrivers	1.5	2.7
Service workers	60.5	62.2
Private household	96.9	96.5
Food service	68.8	66.5
Cooks	62.5	51.9
Health service	88.0	89.3
Personal service	66.5	76.1
Protective service	6.2	10.1

SOURCE: Bureau of Labor Statistics, US Department of Labor, *The Female-Male Earnings Gap: A Review of Employment and Earnings Issues* (Washington, DC: US Government Printing Office, Report 673, September 1982) p. 8.

workers in 1982, while 47 per cent of the men in the blue-collar category were in the skilled crafts.

Working women still remain concentrated in a small number of occupations. Half of them are employed in just 17 out of 400 occupations listed by the Bureau of the Census, while half of the male workforce is distributed among 63 occupations. One-quarter of all employed women are found in five occupations: secretary, bookkeeper, elementary school teacher, waitress and retail sales clerk. Over 34 per cent of all employed women were working in clerical jobs in 1982, compared to less than 7 per cent of working men.

The modest increase of women in male-dominated professions and trades has coincided with changes towards routinisation and deskilling in these occupations, as well as loss of power by professional organisations and labour unions. Professional and managerial occupations have developed both a finely graded hierarchy and a split between highly prestigious jobs with good pay and opportunities for advancement and a new class of more routinised, poorly paid jobs which lack promotion ladders. As one study pointed out, women's gains have been mainly confined to this newer sector where 'professional barriers restricting entry have been weakened by some manifestation of the concentration and centralization of capital, and the consequent loss of power by professional associations'.[6]

Women college teachers, for example, are concentrated in institutions where teaching loads are heavy and there is little time to write and publish. Most of them are either in the lower ranks or hold positions which do not lead to tenure. In 1980–81, women were only 10 per cent of full professors, but over one-half of the low-ranking instructors and lecturers. Part-time employment grew dramatically in the 1970s, as universities cut their instructional budgets. Women hold a disproportionate number of these appointments which rarely carry fringe benefits, offer no security or chance to earn tenure, and never provide paid leaves or sabbaticals.

The American Medical Association (AMA), which had traditionally maintained the high income and prestige of doctors by restrictive entry policies, has lost power to both industry and government. An increasing number of medical practitioners have become salaried hospital employees rather than self-employed professionals. The increasing number of women physicians is in part due to this reorganisation of the profession. At the same time, competition for the more prestigious specialties has intensified in the medical, legal and academic fields. Newcomers face longer hours of work, increased pressure, higher standards of performance, relatively lower entry-level salaries, and prolonged periods of employment insecurity.

For these reasons professional women are concentrated in the less pre-eminent specialities and workplaces. Female attorneys, for example, tend to cluster in family law, trusts and estates, and public interest or poverty law. They are also more likely to work in legal clinics where working conditions and opportunities for advancement are inferior to those in law firms.

Women's entry into corporate management has been partly facilitated by specialisation, routinisation and rationalisation of management functions. The increasing use of 'objective criteria' for evaluating employee performance reduces the likelihood of merely reproducing the social characteristics (including gender) of those already in the occupation. Women's apparent progress in computer programming is also the result of a greater division of labour and growth in less skilled jobs.

Women have entered skilled craft jobs just at the time when trades are being deskilled or even eliminated by automation. For example, under the 1973 affirmative action agreement that American Telephone and Telegraph (AT&T) signed with the federal government, the conglomerate had to give many of its female clericals and telephone operators the opportunity to enter non-traditional craft jobs. However, electronic switching equipment has caused a drastic reduction in the number of central office technicians, and computers have reduced the number of employees needed to test lines and equipment. Technological displacement at AT&T during the 1970s also eliminated many traditional female jobs, primarily lower-level clericals, their immediate supervisors, and telephone operators. Between 1972 and 1975, men as a group gained 13,767 jobs while women lost over 22,000. In other words, planned technological change eliminated more jobs for women at AT&T than affirmative action provided.[7]

While the 'sensational breakthroughs' of female 'pioneers' have generated an inordinate amount of publicity, far less attention has been paid to the conditions these women actually face in their new occupations, the barriers which hinder additional numbers of women from choosing similar work, and the reasons why entry-level women find it more difficult than men to earn promotions. Women in non-traditional work often encounter entrenched male prejudice against them, as well as a male-defined workplace culture. Institutional mores and practices designed to test and reward men often conflict with women's socially learned values and priorities. Most important, women's responsibility for unpaid housework and child care decreases their chances for success in demanding careers.

The qualities most frequently cited for success and mobility in managerial and professional work are aggressiveness, decisiveness, competitiveness and risk-taking, which are normally expected of men but not women. Characteristics customarily associated with women – tenderness, submissiveness, nurturance and emotionality – are less socially valued and do not match what the sociological literature calls 'the managerial behavioral model'. Even when women do not behave in 'typically feminine' ways, they are perceived to be less competent in the workplace than men. Since professional and managerial careers have been designed for men free of child-bearing and child-rearing, women aspiring to professional success either become anomalies as females by not embracing family roles or they find themselves penalised for the time and energy they devote to motherwork and housework. A recent study of 600 women senior managers of large corporations found that over half were not married and 61 per cent had no children. More than half of the divorced executives cited their careers as a cause of their marital break-ups.[8]

While marriage and motherhood do not curtail women from most forms of political participation, running for political office remains largely a male activity. Officeholders must work long and unusual hours, especially during election campaigns, and politicians fear that female candidates may be exposed to criticism as inadequate wives and neglectful mothers. On the other hand, women are entering the legal profession in greater numbers, and law has traditionally served as a training ground for American politicians. In 1975, the percentage of offices held by women nationwide was 4 per cent; by 1980, it had risen to 12 per cent, a three-fold gain in just five years.

Women have shown the greatest success in entering state

legislatures. Before the 1972 election, there were 344 women legislators; in 1976, the number had climbed to 685, or 9.1 per cent of the total; and by 1983, women had risen to 13.3 per cent of state legislators, or 991 out of 7435. Between 1974 and 1983, three women were elected governors of states in their own right, rather than coming to the office largely or entirely in their capacity as wives. Although the number of women in the national House of Representatives and Senate has shown no clear growth pattern from 1947 to 1984, the 98th Congress (1983–84) did have the highest number of women ever in the House: 22 out of 435 members, or 5 per cent. That same Congress was the first time two women out of 100 members served in the Senate simultaneously without inheriting the office from a deceased spouse. Largely because of family responsibilities, women begin serving in Congress at an older age than men, and most do not acquire the seniority needed to exercise power.

While Sandra Day O'Connor broke 190 years of tradition by becoming the first woman justice of the US Supreme Court, Ronald Reagan's overall appointment record has been poorer than that of his predecessor. Over 15 per cent of Jimmy Carter's judicial appointments, but only 8 per cent of Reagan's, have been awarded to women. In 1984, Geraldine Ferraro became the first woman picked by a major political party to run for Vice-President on the Democratic ticket. To date, neither the Democrats nor Republicans have considered a female presidential candidate.[9]

Women who succeed in politics and other male-dominated occupations usually adopt the work patterns and priorities of men. In Wall Street law firms, for example, Cynthia Fuchs Epstein found that: 'Everyone agrees that women who expect to make it must play by men's rules.' Not only is overtime work expected, but some women in the New York firms claimed they worked harder than their male colleagues in order to 'prove' themselves. Rosabeth Moss Kanter's study of a large corporation emphasised that the incentives were all centred on mobility and advancement. 'It was hard to raise the issue of alternative definitions of success.'[10]

Therefore the successful woman, like her male counterpart, must be willing to work evenings and weekends, travel to conferences and meetings, and engage in 'leisure' activities with colleagues which often require athletic skill. She must not only be task-oriented and competitive, but she must also become an accepted member of the 'team'. She adapts to these established patterns in order to achieve material success and prestige and to avoid invidious sex-role stereotyping and sexual harassment. Like Jews, men of colour and other historical 'outsiders', women find they have to perform according to the established criteria. They lack both the time and the numerical support to change the rules.

Even when successful women accept corporate values and show more ambition than their role counterparts, they become 'stuck' about two-thirds up the corporate ladder. The majority of them acknowledge that a variety of sexual barriers exists at the top executive level. These include difficulties in convincing men of their ability, exclusion from the leisure activities of the male-dominated 'inner circle', and the persistence of certain aspects of their own female socialisation, especially lack of confidence.

Working-class women enter blue-collar occupations not as an expression of feminist principles, but in order to earn wages that are often three times higher than those paid in clerical and service jobs. Their new workplaces, however, have a strong, even exaggerated, masculine culture. On construction sites, apprentice carpenter Lisa deCaprio found: 'There's a constant level of humiliation. It's like the army. You have to learn it's not personal. The men just accept it.' But as jobs become scarcer and affirmative action rules weaker, blue-collar women are facing more overt male resentment. Many of the industries where women made gains in the 1970s are those in which recent layoffs have been high – automobiles, steel and construction. In 1981, there were 1366 women in skilled steel mill jobs, up from only 154 women craft workers in 1970. But by 1983, with one-half of steelworkers laid off, few skilled women remained in the mills.[11]

In all non-traditional occupations, women become 'tokens' if they are few in number among their male co-workers. Issues stemming from tokenism include not only the pressures of having to work 'twice as hard' mentioned earlier, but also psychological and social stresses. Tokens often feel lonely and isolated. They must hide their individuality behind carefully constructed public personae that can distort their sense of self. Since they find that true disclosure to peers is not possible, occasions when co-workers are relaxing around after-dinner drinks or at sports events are particularly stressful. Token women who are successful in their work roles also face pressures and inducements to dissociate themselves both from women's interests in general and from female co-workers who have not won peer acceptance or demonstrated extraordinary competence.

For these reasons, the mere presence of a few courageous and ambitious 'pioneers' in medicine, law, corporate management, politics, skilled trades and protective services does not necessarily lead to the recruitment of less extraordinary women or to the transformation of the workplace environment.

Women experience different employment prospects and problems from men because of the closer connection between their work and family lives. A central concern of employed mothers and potential mothers is child care. Child care encompasses not only day-care programmes, but also tax credits, paid and unpaid child-care leaves for parents, flexible work schedules, and various cash allowances for child-rearing. In the US, only tax credits are available in the form of deductions for dependent children and, since 1976, for child-care expenses. As shown in Chapter 9, the US is one of the few industrialised nations which does not provide a family or child allowance other than means-tested welfare programmes.

Historically, public day care was a social welfare or charity service for 'troubled' families. During the 1930s Depression, some federal and state funds became available for child care in order to provide jobs for unemployed teachers and other school personnel under the Works Progress Administration (WPA). The federal government also allocated funds for day care during the Second World War to reduce the absenteeism of mothers working in vital war industries. Understaffed and relatively few in number, the wartime centres admitted only one out of ten children who needed care. After the war federally-funded care was quickly eliminated.

In 1964, a new pre-school programme called Headstart provided comprehensive rather than merely custodial care and resembled the nursery schools of the middle class. Congress significantly expanded federal appropriations for day care as part of the 1967 Social Security Amendments. Although the goal was to reduce the public welfare burden by encouraging poor mothers to seek work, the generous funding and flexible eligibility requirements allowed working-class and middle-class mothers, as well as welfare recipients, to benefit from the increased number of day-care facilities. Since 1967, there has been no further legislation providing directly for an expanded programme of child care. In 1971, President Richard Nixon vetoed the Comprehensive Child Development Act and restigmatised day care by arguing that child care arrangements outside the family would 'sovietize' America. Nixon's veto also reinforced two related traditional attitudes: first, that the nuclear family is 'natural' and 'private', not an institution amenable to government intervention, and second, that child-rearing is primarily a mother's responsibility.

The 1976 child-care tax credit does acknowledge the increased number of employed women by providing indirect child-care aid. Working parents can recover part of the cost of care for children under 15, but the tax credit does nothing to make day-care services more abundant. By the early 1980s, more than 32 million children under 18 had working mothers, and more than 8 million of these children were under 6. Even before the child-care budget cuts made by the Reagan administration, less than a million and a half of these children were enrolled in either Headstart or government funded day-care programmes. Other licensed centres had places for less than one-eighth of the children under 6 with working mothers. A government study published in 1982 indicated that 20 per cent of the pre-school children whose mothers worked full-time were cared for in their own homes, most often by a father or another relative, and another 8 per cent stayed with their mothers at work. The largest group, 47 per cent, were placed in someone else's home, usually not that of a relative. In these informal arrangements, parents generally cannot claim the child-care tax credit since unlicensed babysitters do not wish their small income reported for tax or social security purposes.

It is impossible to determine the number of children left without care of any kind, but one government study estimated that 32,000 pre-schoolers are caring for themselves and 2 million school-age children between 7 and 13 are unsupervised 'latch-key' children. Although 52.1 per cent of mothers with children under 6 were in the labour force in 1984, approximately 20 per cent more would be looking for work if child care were available.

Out of 6 million employers, some 2000 are now underwriting some form of child-care assistance, usually through indirect methods which stop short of building and operating day-care centres. The most common programmes involve unpaid maternity and paternity leaves, part-time work, job sharing and sick-child time off. A few corporations either offer vouchers and discounts for child care or allow employees to choose child care from a menu of optional benefits.

Unlike many European countries, paid maternity and child-care leaves are not granted as a matter of social right. Since 1978, employers have had to treat pregnancy like any other temporary disability, but they are not required by federal law to provide disability benefits. Five states do require such benefits, and 95 per cent of the country's 384 largest corporations offer disability benefits for pregnancy, with at least some pay. Some public sector employees have won the right through union agreements to unpaid maternity and child-care (or sick-child) leave without loss of seniority. This still leaves approximately 60 per cent of working women in the US unprotected by disability insurance during pregnancy, and at least one-third are not guaranteed the same or a comparable job when they return to work. Although 37 per cent of the major corporations offer paternity leave in order to avoid sex discrimination suits, they actually discourage men from taking them. New mothers who choose the option of returning to work on a part-time basis do not advance as quickly as their full-time colleagues.[12]

WORKING WOMEN IN THE CURRENT LABOUR MARKET

While it appears that motherhood is the primary reason why women either do not enter male-dominated occupations at all or else do not expect to advance as quickly as their male counterparts, it is not actually motherhood itself which limits women's employment options. The American economic system neither provides substantial relief from family responsibilities nor designs work to accommodate family needs. One of the greatest obstacles to change is that corporations profit by paying women lower wages in overcrowded female occupations.

Four-fifths of employed women work in occupations numerically dominated by their own sex; women are also more likely to be found in the 'secondary labour market', where firms are highly competitive and labour-intensive. These businesses save money on labour costs by paying low wages and by not providing sick leave, paid vacations, opportunities for promotion or even job security.

Estimates vary as to how many women would have to change jobs in order to match the occupational distribution of men. The US Commission on Civil Rights reported in 1978 that nearly three-fourths of women workers would have to switch occupations, while another, more recent study by the Department of Commerce found that the 'index of segregation' in 1981 was 61.7, a decline of 6.6 percentage points since 1972. Although this indicates that women have begun to enter traditionally male occupations, the magnitude of employment segregation by sex remains substantial.

Industries which employ the greatest proportion of women also pay the lowest hourly earnings. Out of 52 industries, Table 10.3 lists the 10 which employ the highest proportion of women and the

TABLE 10.3   Women's employment and average hourly earnings by industry

Industry	Women Workers (%)	Rank of average hourly earnings from 1 to 52
Apparel and other textile products	81.9	50
Health services	81.3	36
Banking	70.8	46
Apparel and accessory stores	70.0	51
Credit agencies other than banks	69.7	43
Legal services	69.3	21
General merchandise stores	66.0	47
Insurance carriers	60.6	30
Leather and leather products	60.2	49
Eating and drinking places	56.3	52
Petroleum and coal products	15.3	2
Lumber and wood products	14.5	32
Trucking and warehousing	12.7	12
General building contractors	11.7	10
Primary metal industries	11.6	6
Metal mining	9.7	3
Special trade contractors	9.1	4
Non-metallic minerals, except fuels	8.0	18
Heavy construction contracting	7.2	5
Bituminous coal and lignite mining	5.1	1

SOURCE: Bureau of Labor Statistics, US Department of Labor, *The Female-Male Earnings Gap: A Review of Employment and Earnings Issues* (Washington, DC: US Government Printing Office, Report 673, September 1982) p. 7.

10 which employ the lowest, along with average hourly earnings ranked from 1 to 52. With only a few exceptions, a clear inverse relationship exists between well-paying industries and the proportion of women workers. Also, within each industry, women tend to be concentrated in the lower-paying occupations. They are, for example, clerical and para-legal workers rather than attorneys in legal services.

As shown earlier in Table 10.2, almost all clerical workers are women, as are registered nurses and health care workers, private household workers, and sewers and stitchers. Clerical work, which employs over one-third of all working women, is absolutely and proportionately the largest scale female occupation, and, as Evelyn Nakano Glenn and Roslyn L. Feldberg argue, it 'represents the prototypical female employment experience'.[13] For this reason, we shall concentrate on the recent changes in clerical jobs, many of which are also occurring in other types of women's work.

The skills required of clerical workers are undervalued or unrecognised, while at the same time, clerical work is being deskilled. Although undervaluation and deskilling reinforce sexual and racial hierarchies in the workplace, women of colour are finding that office automation has facilitated their entry into clerical work. This accounts for some of the growing similarity of women's work across racial lines, even though women of colour are still over-represented in the older forms of low-wage, labour-intensive service and factory work.

Two models of clerical work currently exist: the older office 'marriage', found mainly among secretaries and characterised by loyalty to an individual employer; and the increasingly widespread office 'factory', in which external and quantitative controls are used to motivate workers and monitor their productivity.

The office 'marriage', according to Rosabeth Moss Kanter, is the result of short promotion ladders for secretaries which depend upon their relationships with individual bosses. Secretaries, therefore, tend to personalise situations and 'learn the *boss* rather than the organization'. They employ the classical strategies of dependent wives to get what they want from more powerful 'husbands': assumed helplessness, emotional manipulation and gossip. Furthermore, secretaries become accustomed, even 'addicted', to praise and flattery, instead of expecting more concrete and tangible rewards. These character traits are not innately female, but rather represent strategies employed by people to achieve some recognition and control within the constraints imposed 'by the social organization of their job'.[14] That is, the job of secretary, not the gender of the person filling it, tends to encourage timidity, praise-addiction and emotionality. However, since almost all secretaries are women, their behaviour reinforces traditional gender stereotypes, and the secretarial image is extended to all working women.

Conversely, since the human interaction skills of secretaries and other clerical workers are considered expressions of the feminine personality, they are either devalued or rendered invisible as occupational skills. Attentive listening, character assessment, diplomacy and persuasiveness are recognised and rewarded at the predominantly male managerial levels, but not in the clerical ranks. For example, administrators in a Southern hospital saw the black ward secretaries as coordinators and organisers of medical records, not as intermediaries between patients and medical specialists. Only when those underpaid women walked off their jobs did their teaching and other human interaction skills cease being 'invisible' work.[15]

Women tend to carry out responsible work while occupying low clerical grades. Designation of a job as 'clerical' rather than 'administrative' depends more on the gender of the employee than on the nature of the work. In industry too, 'skilled' or 'craft' work tends to be the jobs done mainly by men. Not only have women been traditionally excluded from 'skilled' work, but more recently there has also developed a gender-based segregation between labour-intensive (female) and capital-intensive (male) operations. Two California researchers were told that assembly jobs in the Silicon Valley electronics industry were 'easy' and 'unskilled'. 'The only skill one needed . . . was manual dexterity, which women had anyway, particularly Asian women, who had as well a high tolerance for tedious work.'[16]

In addition to employment segregation by sex and the ways in which job classifications and descriptions are used to devalue or deny women's skills, automation is changing many jobs. Some, such as telephone operators and stenographers, are becoming obsolete; others are undergoing deskilling and depersonalising. Clerical work provides an excellent example of how increases in capital investment do not necessarily improve women's skills and salaries.

Although the 'typing pool' was an early form of office 'factory', the introduction of computers intensifies office depersonalisation and also eliminates many of the skills once necessary to produce attractive, accurate documents. Word-processing technologies introduce a greater division of labour into office work, tie the human word-processor more closely to her machine, and reduce the human interaction skills needed in clerical work. In most offices, word processing eliminates work variety and decision-making. Since the machine can precisely monitor and measure productivity and accuracy, managers are able to exercise more control over their clerical staff. Word-processing operators generally work under intense speed-ups, and the job is a highly stressful one.

Working face-to-face with a TV screen all day long reduces both the social fabric of offices and the paternalistic supervisor-worker relationship. As workers' responsibilities become narrower in scope and their tasks are more closely monitored, their job satisfaction also diminishes. The turnover rate reaches as high as 100 per cent a year in some word-processing centres. As a result, managers look even more to the centralised and computerised office to increase short-range profitability, despite the harm both to worker morale and to long-range productivity. Under these circumstances, clerical workers are less likely to identify their interests with those of management.

The argument that computers eliminate the repetitiveness of many clerical tasks, upgrade the work and allow for more creativity is true only for high-level positions, mainly held by men. In 1980, for example, women were 22 per cent of all systems analysts, but over 95 per cent of keypunch operators, the least skilled and most routine of computer jobs.

The effects of computerisation are not limited to clerical work. In retail sales, where women have traditionally been assigned to the less remunerative specialities, mergers and computerisation have increased job insecurity for saleswomen and eroded their selling skills. The automation of library work is leading to a decrease in the number of professional librarians, relative to non-professional staff. While close to 85 per cent of all librarians are women, few of them have yet entered the emerging field of information-systems management.

Technological change has brought only limited benefits to women partly because they are not employed in high-technology occupations: engineers, life and physical scientists, mathematical specialists, engineering and science technicians, and computer specialists. Although women are beginning to enter these scientific and engineering fields, they are still vastly outnumbered by men. Furthermore, 'high-tech' industries have not contributed much to total employment growth; government estimates range from 5 to 15 per cent for the 1972–82 period, and all high-tech occupations together constituted less than 4 per cent of total employment in 1982.

Employment opportunities for women have been mainly in the expanding service sector, including clerical work, where low wages, high turnover and part-time employment are common. We find a close relationship between the growth of the service sector, women's increasing labour force participation, and the feminisation of poverty.

Service industries have come to dominate the American economy. Between 1970 and 1980, they absorbed close to 86 per cent of all private sector employment growth, while goods-producing industries showed a 13.6 per cent decline in employment. Service-producing industries are more labour-intensive and lower-waged than goods-producing industries, and between 1970 and 1980 the wage differential widened dramatically. In 1970, workers in retail trade earned 62 cents for every dollar earned by manufacturing employees; by 1980 sales workers were earning only 52 cents. During the same period, relative wage rates in the financial sector declined from 84 to 72 cents for every dollar paid in weekly manufacturing wages. Employees in the service sector have twice the turnover rate of those in manufacturing and a substantially higher rate of part-time employment. While 17 per cent of manufacturing employees worked part-time in 1977, over 29 per cent of service workers did. In short, as Joan Smith points out, 'the contemporary economy has moved to center stage a labor force that must be continually endowed with marginal characteristics'.

Most of this labour force is female. Between 1970 and 1980 women contributed over three-quarters of the increase in financial, real estate and insurance firms and more than 60 per cent in both the service-producing and retail food store industries. Most of these new jobs also yield the lowest wages. Between 1970 and 1980 close to 90 per cent of the women entering the labour force found jobs in establishments which paid 63 cents for every dollar paid elsewhere in the private sector. It appears that women's poverty is no longer the result of their relative exclusion from the labour force, but rather is built into the very conditions under which they are actively incorporated into paid work.[17]

Most of these women's jobs are not unionised, because until recently the American labour movement did little to organise the predominantly female clerical and service sectors. Male union leaders focused on a narrow range of workplace issues, such as maintaining the 'family wage' for male workers, and claimed that women were only 'temporary' workers. These traditional views are beginning to change because of women's growing visibility as permanent workers and their increased presence in the labour movement through such organisations as the Coalition of Labor Union Women (CLUW).

The decline of the unionised manufacturing sector means that the survival of the labour movement depends on its organising white-collar and service workers, the majority of whom are women. The fastest growing unions are those in the public and health care sectors. Women account for half of the increase in union membership over the past twenty years, and currently make up close to one-third of all unionised workers. However, only about 16 per cent of all employed women are labour union members, and women's workplace organising often occurs outside established union structures.

As noted in Chapter 6, clerical workers during the 1970s started their own labour organisations. As more and more women begin to view themselves as long-term workers, they too will seek for ways to improve their job conditions and earning power. The deskilling and depersonalising of clerical occupations has encouraged women to develop a 'worker consciousness' distinct from managerial priorities. The traditional white-collar identification with management is no longer a major impediment to union organising.

Clerical workers, however, are not all working-class women. Due to limited job opportunities, women with a variety of backgrounds, education levels and qualifications find themselves in the same occupation. The educational attainment of clerical workers ranges from less than high school to postgraduate college degrees. Of all married female clerical workers in 1981, 50 per cent had white-collar/professional husbands and 43 per cent, blue-collar husbands, including semi-skilled and unskilled workers.[18]

Despite the absence of a traditional working-class situation, there has been an increase in workplace activity among clerical and other women workers, especially at the grass-roots level. Kinship and friendship networks play an important role both in building a women's workplace culture and in sustaining collective protest actions. The ward secretaries who staged the effective walkout at a Southern hospital had a history of bringing family members and friends into the hospital as new employees and creating friendships and family-like relations with co-workers. Secretaries who trained new employees also passed on to them a secretarial rather than a managerial view of the job. Sewers in a New England clothing factory, many of whom were recent immigrants from Portugal and Latin America, developed solidarity across ethnic lines despite the absence of union support. These women had engaged in daily resistance struggles with management and created an informal work culture which socialised new employees into an informal set of rules designed to alleviate some of the competition of the piece-rate system.

While women's work culture and day-to-day struggles indicate that working women are neither passive nor pro-management, the effectiveness of such informal strategies depends on management response, the nature of an industry and the state of the local and national economy.[19] Labour union support can transform spontaneous actions, such as work stoppages, into more sustained resistance. Through contracts and grievance procedures, unions can also provide an institutionalised structure for maintaining wage levels and benefits.

In 1981, 9 to 5, a national working women's group, joined forces with the Service Employees International Union (SEIU) and established District 925. The District's national organising drive has emphasised that unionised clerical workers earn 30 per cent more than their non-unionised counterparts. Other unions, such as the American Federation of State, County, and Municipal Employees (AFSCME), the Office and Professional Employees International Union, and the Teamsters, have also been organising the clerical workforce. In 1982, the Coalition of Labor Union Women (CLUW) mounted a joint campaign with unions in the Washington, DC-Baltimore area, the first time that CLUW has worked directly with international unions to organise the unorganised.

CLUW has also shown its independence from organised labour by endorsing several measures in 1984 which were at odds with established AFL-CIO policy: support for the nuclear freeze, a call for the transfer of public funds from the military budget to social programmes, and opposition to US intervention in Central America and military aid to El Salvador. Its High Technology task force is analysing the anti-union potential of computer homework or 'out-work' and the shift of clerical and manufacturing work to overseas sites. Progressive unions, such as the United Auto Workers (UAW), SEIU, and AFSCME, have made child care and maternity benefits prominent items on their bargaining agendas. Comparable worth (equal pay for work of equal value) is another issue supported by unions with high female membership.

Nevertheless, women are still fighting for recognition as union leaders. CLUW president Joyce Miller, the first woman appointed to the AFL-CIO Executive Council in 1979, was joined in 1981 by Barbara Hutchinson of the American Federation of Government Employees. With these two exceptions, women have yet to reach the highest levels and hold only 12 per cent of all leadership posts. Although both the exclusionary practices of male-dominated unions and women's own lack of confidence contribute to this scarcity, no single factor is more important than housework and child care. Women simply lack the time to become involved. Like many workers, Linda Phillips, a shop steward at a New Jersey Revlon plant, believes that: 'You can't deal with women in unions without dealing with family and children.'[20]

CHANGES AND CONTINUITIES IN WOMEN'S UNPAID WORK

Although the later age of marriage, falling birthrates, rising divorce rates and the erosion of the male-earned 'family wage', have caused growing numbers of women to seek employment, their inadequate 'female wages' have kept most of them economically dependent on either individual men or the state. Most women work a double day consisting of paid employment and unpaid domestic labour, and many women's jobs are commercialised extensions of the work they perform at home – preparing food, sewing clothes, providing emotional support, and nursing the ill. Women both work in the fast-food and child-care industries and purchase their products or services. In order to pay for essential services and/or dishwashers, home computers and other 'labour-saving' devices, they must continue to earn wages. Chapter 3 discussed how household technology has eliminated some forms of household drudgery while also creating new work, especially by raising the standards of cleanliness. It should be added that kitchen appliances such as microwave ovens, self-defrosting freezers and multiple-speed blenders waste natural resources and present health hazards to their users, as do many home-cleaning products and detergents. Self-service stores have depersonalised shopping and require that customers, rather than sales clerks, be informed about products and where to locate them.

The fast-food industry, in particular, has not only changed food preparation but it has also transformed the eating habits of millions of Americans. The daily family dinner at home is becoming, like lunch and breakfast before it, a dying institution. When family members go to a McDonald's or other fast-food establishment together, they know exactly what they will eat, what they will pay, and how the restaurant will look. This standardised ritual, as described by Susan Strasser,

> requires no responsibility other than ordering (with as few words as possible) and paying; nobody has to set or clear the table, wash the dishes, or compliment the cook on her cuisine, the traditional responsibilities of husbands and children at the family dinner.[21]

Since fast-food chains are either large companies or subsidiaries of still larger firms (such as Pillsbury, General Foods and Ralston Purina), they represent an important and pervasive example of corporate intrusion into daily life.

They are also a distortion of the early twentieth-century feminist vision of socialised housework, popularised by Charlotte Perkins Gilman and others, which included 'kitchenless homes', community dining rooms and cooked food services, as well as collective laundries and child-care centres. Instead of cooperative or socialised housework, some household tasks have been transformed into commercial endeavours, where profitability is the motivating factor. Like other occupations, housework has been both deskilled and removed from workers' control, as corporate executives exert their influence over what families will eat and wear, what games they will play and even what values they will share.

Commercialised household services and products employ women, but not all female workers can afford to buy the products they produce, patronise restaurants and laundries, or call a weekly cleaning service. It appears that some women are partially 'liberated' from arduous, time-consuming chores by transferring them to other less affluent women, people of colour and teenagers.

Even those women fortunate enough to enjoy some of the 'conveniences' of commercialised services and products have not actually been freed from domestic responsibilities. Employed women generally cut their housework time in half – from 52 to 26 hours a week – but they are still left with a longer working day than that of most men. Feminists demand either a more equal division of household and family responsibilities, or wages and social security benefits for housewives. The 'wages for housework' movement has uncovered the hidden economic value of women's unpaid work, but it has not wholly destroyed the notion that certain jobs are 'women's work'.

Sharing housework and parenting across gender lines, on the other hand, appears more radical because it would break down the distinction between women's and men's 'spheres', rather than simply recognise and upgrade work women are already doing. But sharing, as already shown, is difficult to put into practice. Male resistance to it is one major obstacle. Another is that the length of the standard work day and week allows relatively few hours of discretionary time. The middle-class career model, for example, assumes that aspiring managers and professionals will be totally committed to their work. Women often postpone motherhood beyond their optimum child-bearing years, and then find that neither their workplaces nor their work hours are designed to accommodate the needs of young children or the school schedules of older ones.

The burden of housework increases substantially when there are young children or many children in the household, and it is the mother's, not the father's, work week which expands to meet these family needs. Furthermore, single or divorced mothers with the same size families spend approximately eight hours a week less time on housework than married women. It appears that a husband requires additional housework, since married women are expected to provide their husbands with sex, affection and attention. Conversation might even be included as one of women's unpaid jobs. Pamela M. Fishman found that among white professional couples, purported to have the most egalitarian marriages, women laboured at the work of interaction, while men controlled conversations either by introducing topics or by failing to respond to subjects suggested by their wives. 'Women ask more questions and use attention beginnings. They do support work while men are talking and generally do active maintenance and continuation work in conversations.' Women are expected to be both 'good listeners' when men are talking and to fill silences and keep a conversation moving. Conversely, women who dominate conversations are derided as 'castrating bitches' who 'start arguments'.

Overall, then, most studies have shown that about 70 per cent of the time spent on housework falls to women, with men and children dividing the remainder, and that husbands of employed women spend very little more time on housework than those whose wives are not employed. Employed women spend less time doing housework because the changing boundaries between home and market have increasingly shifted housework to commercial sites. But a woman's work day is longer now than when she served as a full-time housewife.

According to architect Dolores Hayden, reducing housework and reorganising it more equitably between women and men is difficult because of the spatial designs of 'private' homes. The isolated domestic workplace, even when filled with labour-saving appliances, requires an inordinate amount of time and energy to maintain. Therefore women might do well both to analyse the 'private home as a spatial component of their economic oppression' and to envision alternatives to housework other than the existing profit-making enterprises.[22] Labour unions and other workers' organisations must also realise that women's economic opportunities and political commitments are circumscribed both by the time and energy they devote to unpaid work and by the image of women as unpaid workers.

NEW APPROACHES TO OLD ISSUES: HEALTH HAZARDS, SEXUAL HARASSMENT AND LOW WAGES

Traditionally, safeguarding the health of workers meant excluding women of child-bearing age from jobs where exposure to chemical substances might cause reproductive difficulties or foetal abnormalities. Although the 1970 Occupational Safety and Health Act (OSHA, which is also the acronym for the federal regulatory agency) promised uniform safety and health protection for workers of both sexes, the older practice of excluding women from certain non-traditional jobs has not disappeared. No one, however, has proposed that women be removed from traditionally female jobs which also pose reproductive dangers. Health workers in hospital operating rooms experience a higher rate of miscarriage and birth malformations in their offspring from their work with aneasthetic gases; elementary school teachers are exposed to 'German measles', a well known teratogenic agent; video display terminals (VDTs) used by clerical workers may be linked to birth problems; and houseworkers rely on cleaning agents and appliances which contain harmful chemicals and pollutants.

Men are also at risk from reproductive hazards. Chemicals suspected as carcinogens can affect an unborn child through a mutagenic response of the male's reproductive cells. Reproductive problems, therefore, are not confined to pregnant women and infants born with birth defects, but also include damage to adult germ cells or sexual organs, reductions in potency and fertility, and childhood morbidity and malignancies beyond early infancy.

The practice of removing some workers from a hazardous environment or restricting their work options tends to place the burden of reproductive health on individual workers rather than putting pressure on employers to provide safe and healthy workplaces. Pregnant workers, in particular, suffer from this lack of public responsibility. The Pregnancy Discrimination Act (PDA) of 1978 guarantees female workers the same rights as males, but men are never pregnant or breast-feeding. Feminists who lobbied for this legislation did not want to imperil women's newly-gained jobs by calling attention to pregnancy-related needs. Instead, they accepted a model which held that women are no different from men. Since pregnant or breast-feeding women do not fit the male 'norm', they may be denied time off for pre-natal care appointments, or else these absences are assessed negatively in employment evaluations. No accommodations are made for breast-feeding workers to pump their breasts and refrigerate the milk. Under PDA, pregnancy is viewed as a 'temporary disability', but pre-natal care does not fit clearly into this medical model since it is preventive, not curative. Breast-feeding workers are neither ill nor orarily disabled. Because PDA does not insist on a minimal set of benefits, even those women fortunate enough to be granted maternity leaves receive only enough time to recuperate from the physical stress of delivery, not for nurturing the new baby or recovering from exhaustion. As Wendy Chavkin points out, these and other problems arise 'from the deeply held conviction that reproduction is a private, not a social, phenomenon, and one for which society is not responsible'.[23]

At the same time, the reproductive rights of working women are threatened by the crusade against abortion and by coerced sterilisations. In 1983, Congress passed the Smith amendment prohibiting coverage for abortion in any federal employee benefit plan. Since PDA exempts abortions from obligatory health care coverage, many private employer health plans also exclude elective abortions. Yet American Cyanamid, General Motors, B.F. Goodrich, Allied Chemical and Olin, to name a few, ban women from certain work locations unless they can prove they are sterile. Some women employed in these companies have 'chosen' to be sterilised in order to keep their jobs.

Neither of these 'foetus protection' policies takes into account the reproductive and other health risks that chemical substances pose to adult workers of both sexes. Furthermore, substances considered too dangerous for pregnant women to handle do not remain at the workplace, but spread into workers' homes, the air and the community's water supply.

Since the mid 1970s, women's organisations, environmentalists and labour unions have been working together to educate the public and pressure government agencies about these hazards. Two such groups are the Electronics Committee on Safety and Health in California's Silicon Valley and the Coalition for the Reproductive Rights of Workers (CRROW). Among the problems addressed by Women of All Red Nations (WARN), a multi-issue organisation founded by Native American women in 1978, have been land use for energy development, political repression of Native American activists, sterilisation abuse and a plethora of environmental hazards, including pesticides and radioactivity in the drinking water at the Pine Ridge Reservation in South Dakota.

A significant reduction in workplace health hazards and environmental pollution depends not only on citizen awareness and activity, but also on corporate and government support. Although there is an obvious need for more research on the synergistic or combined effects of chemicals, corporate and government leaders have not shown a marked interest in funding such research. OSHA has set standards of 'Threshold Limit Values' on only a small percentage of the new chemicals used in industry and has delayed implementing regulations. The understaffed and underbudgeted agency has had a poor record both in investigating workplace complaints and in levying penalties against culpable employers. Neither corporations nor government are taking an active role in educating workers and consumers about toxic chemicals or encouraging the efforts of citizens' groups. Instead, the anti-labour and anti-regulatory policies of the Reagan administration have almost devastated OSHA and other federal agencies designated to protect the workplace and environment. Farmworkers, electronics assembly workers and clerical workers are only some who are experiencing the results of this negligence.

In 1984, after an eleven-year court battle with the government, farmworkers appeared finally to have won the right to have toilets, drinking water and handwashing facilities in the field. But OSHA has continued to delay issuing the necessary regulations, even though its own study reported that only one-fourth of the country's agricultural employers provided sanitary facilities. Agriculture is the nation's third most dangerous type of employment, after mining and construction. Unlike those high-wage, male-dominated industries, farmwork is done by poorly paid adults and children. Over half are people of colour, mainly Hispanic, and many are migratory workers. Farmworkers are exposed not only to excessive heat and sun, but also to pesticides which they inhale, ingest with their food and absorb through their skins. The lack of basic sanitation facilities causes kidney diseases and urinary tract infections and spreads dysentery and typhoid

Although the electronics industry promotes itself as the 'clean' and 'healthy' industry of the future, it uses hundreds of potentially dangerous substances to produce microchips. Up to 90 per cent of the assembly workforce are women, which may explain why the industry complains about 'hysteria-prone' worker charges of chemical sensitisation and other health problems, when it might instead make a commitment to improve environmental monitoring and controls.

In addition to older office health problems caused by excessive sitting or standing, fluorescent lighting, and ozone from copying machines, clerical workers are exposed to new hazards from computers and office design. Working with VDTs causes eye strain, muscular fatigue and stress. Despite safeguards, some VDTs also emit radiation. 'Closed' office buildings, where windows do not open and central air conditioning systems recirculate filtered air, are leading to a variety of health problems ranging from chronic eye, nose and throat irritations; headaches, fatigue, and reduced ability to concentrate; to allergies and even lung impairment. Out of 130 occupations, the National Institute for Occupational Safety and Health found that secretaries were second only to labourers in the incidence of stress-related diseases, and that people who work on VDTs experience more stress than any other occupational group, including air traffic controllers. Women clerical workers develop coronary heart disease at almost twice the rate of other working women, including housewives. Those most at risk are married to blue-collar husbands and have children to care for at home.

Housework contains the same sources of stress found in many types of women's waged work: lack of participation in decision-making, low job satisfaction, no opportunity to learn new skills, a work pace which is too slow or too fast, confinement to the work area, devaluation of the work, lack of job security, and abuse. Some of these stress-producing conditions are also present at comparable types of men's work, but most women have two such jobs and experience sexual abuse at both far more often than men do. At home, women are battered and raped; at the workplace, they are sexually harassed. In addition to the physical danger and psychological damage common to all forms of abuse, sexual harassment on the job has economically devastating consequences.

Sexual harassment is unwanted attention or demands of a sexual nature within the context of an employment or educational situation. It generally involves a relationship which is unequal in terms of gender and economic power. Typically, a male supervisor or professor demands sexual favours from a female worker or student. Sexual harassment is an expression of an ideology which permits male sexual dominance of women and employers' control over workers. It reinforces women's traditionally inferior role in the labour force. In Catharine MacKinnon's words: 'Economic power is to sexual harassment as physical force is to rape.'[24]

Yet unlike rape, the major... involve physical assault. Se... harassment or abuse, unwanted... 'date', sexist remarks about wo... touching of or brushing against... important, the request for sexual favo... or overt threats concerning one's job, g... promotion. According to the Equal Em... Commission (EEOC) guidelines adopted... sexual advances constitute sexual harassment... discrimination – when: (i) submission to such... either explicitly or implicitly a term or condition o... admission to an academic programme; (ii) submissio... of such conduct is used as a basis for decisions... individual's employment status or academic standing; or... conduct has the purpose or effect of substantially interferi... an individual's job or classroom performance, or creati... intimidating, hostile or offensive work or study environment.

Sexual harassment is not a new problem, but it was unnam... and unrecognised until the mid 1970s. In a pioneering survey o... 9000 women published by *Redbook* magazine in 1976, 88 per cent reported some form of unwanted sexual attention in their work lives. Since then, sexual harassment has become publicly acknowledged and officially defined by legislatures and courts. Grass-roots organisations such as the Alliance Against Sexual Coercion in Cambridge, Massachusetts, the Coalition Against Sexual Harassment (Minneapolis), and Women's Alliance for Job Equality (Philadelphia) have been acting as educational and advocacy agencies and/or providing counselling and referral services. Studies conducted by the Working Women's Institute based in New York indicate that sexual harassment is not restricted to a particular dyad, but can be 'atmospheric' or 'endemic' to an entire workplace. It may take the form of humiliating women by requiring that they dress in sexually revealing clothing or by a public display of derogatory images of women.

Whatever its forms and context, sexual harassment leads to one or more of the following economic and psychological consequences for its victims: stress, decreased productivity, absenteeism and job loss. Although statistics vary widely, all of the studies conducted so far indicate that sexual harassment is a prevalent and serious

...ent workers
...their jobs,
...employees
...elephone-
...workers ...d that 36
...sexual ...ssment;
...been ...xually
...workers ...rking
...more
...d of ...lt of
...ent were ...to
...of
...r
...their tasks and
...women began to ...in
...career choices.

...ty of sexual harassment cases do not
...ual harassment includes verbal
...sexual attention or pressure to
...en's appearance, unnecessary
woman's body and, most
...s accompanied by implied
...rades or possibilities for
...ployment Opportunity
...in 1980, unwelcome
...— and therefore sex
...conduct is made
...employment or
...n or rejection
...ffecting an
(iii) such
...g with
...g an

...economic effects, sexual harassment ...as
...for women's mental and physical health. Over
...of the women in the Working Women's Institute survey
...general psychological stress symptoms. Tension, anger,
...depression, embarrassment, sleeplessness and guilt pervaded
...and damaged relationships with co-workers, family
...friends. The 1980 government survey in Illinois also
...that sexual harassment had adverse effects on the victims'
emotional and physical health, as well as their job performance.
Furthermore, sexual harassment cost taxpayers $189 million over a
two-year period due to job turnover, absenteeism and increased use
of health benefits.[25]

Although sexual harassment has been reported in every type of
work setting, there are differences between fields that are
traditionally female and those where women are entering
occupations formerly held only by men. The Working Women's
Institute found that harassment in traditional occupations –
secretaries, nurses, waitresses, etc. – appears to be an expression
and reinforcement of already existing gender roles and power
differences. In non-traditional occupations, sexual comments, jokes
and leers are actually hostile ways to let the 'outsider' know she is
not wanted on the work site and to force her to leave. Sexual
harassment is not a display of entrenched male authority, as it is in
more traditional work settings, but rather 'a form of retaliation

against the women for invading a male sphere and threatening male economic and social status'.

Many women in non-traditional occupations, especially skilled trades and police work, try to deny or minimise the harassment by telling themselves that it is part of the ritual hazing all new workers must endure. They hope that by acting 'cool' and 'tough' they will eventually win the acceptance of their co-workers. Women in traditional jobs also attempt to cope with the problem individually, but they often feel guilty (as well as angry) and blame themselves for the incidents. A sense of futility may also be present, based on their own relatively powerless position within the organisation against that of a 'valued' and 'respected' supervisor or professor.[26]

For these reasons, the most common response is to 'go along' with the sexual harasser by appearing either to 'ignore' his behaviour or even to act 'flattered' by it. The victim hopes that she can satisfy his ego and his unwanted attentions will cease. Unfortunately, many men have learned to interpret both subtle rejections and more overt expressions of resistance as encouraging signs. Socialised to view women primarily as sex objects, they 'sexualise' women at workplaces and in classrooms and expect sexual compliance from them as one of the compensations for an otherwise boring or mechanised workplace existence. Catharine MacKinnon suggests that 'male sexual desire itself may be aroused by female vulnerability'. Since economic and physical inequality is built into social conceptions of 'sexiness' and heterosexual attractiveness, a woman in an economically subordinate position becomes sexually 'enticing'.[27]

We can therefore expect that women's perceptions of sexual harassment and other forms of sexual abuse will differ from those of men. A study conducted of the entire University of Rhode Island community showed that men considered sexually related behaviour on the job and at school 'more natural, more to be expected, and less problematic and serious' than did women. However, both women and men shared the view that women 'must expect to be sexually approached, teased, or insulted'. Younger, undergraduate women, in particular, not only accepted such behaviour by men as 'part of life', but also that women had the primary responsibility for avoiding sexual abuse. Older women, on the other hand, showed noticeably less tolerance of this 'normal' male behaviour and more willingness to challenge it.[28]

The leaders in resisting sexual harassment and initiating law suits have been black women. As the most economically and sexually at risk, they stand to lose the most by sexual harassment, yet they may also see themselves as having the least to lose by a struggle against it. More sensitive than white women to the operation of racism on an individual/sexual level, black women are less likely to be confused and mystified by the 'attentions' of white male supervisors.

Women have gained important legal leverage through Title VII of the 1964 Civil Rights Act which prohibits sex discrimination and especially by the 1980 EEOC guidelines mentioned earlier which define sexual harassment as a form of sex discrimination. Although court decisions on sexual harassment cases have been generally favourable, litigation requires considerable time, money and perseverance, as well as the risk of being counter-sued for defamation of character or slander. More promising are some of the educational and organising efforts made by labour unions such as the American Federation of State, County, and Municipal Employees (AFSCME), American Federation of Government Employees (AFGE) and the United Auto Workers (UAW). UAW has sexual harassment clauses in its contracts with Chrysler and Ford; District 65, Distributive Workers of America, has also inserted a sexual harassment clause in its contract with Boston University. Corporate managers, concerned about legal consequences and decreased productivity, have developed training sessions and grievance procedures and distributed policy statements prohibiting sexual harassment.

While employers treat sexual harassment as a production problem caused by 'deviant' employees, it is inextricably connected to and one of the consequences of a sex-segregated labour market in which women's jobs are undervalued and underpaid.

The difference between women's and men's annual earnings has not diminished in the last two decades. Full-time, year-round female workers earned 60.8 per cent of male annual earnings in 1960, 59.4 per cent in 1970, and 59.2 per cent in 1981. Women's low wages are the primary reason why female-headed households are generally poor households.

As discussed earlier, a strong correlation exists between predominantly female occupations and low wages. It is not simply that women are clustered in the poorly-paying sectors of the economy or even in occupational categories which pay low wages. Women also earn less than men within the same major occupational groups, as indicated in Table 10.4 below. Women are found in the lower-paying specialities within each occupational group and have fewer opportunities for promotion and advancement. The gender gap is so wide that female executives and administrators are paid less than male clerical workers; the weekly earnings of skilled craftswomen are lower than those of male labourers.

One explanation of these gender differences looks at workers' personal characteristics. Men earn more because they have a

TABLE 10.4   Median weekly earnings of full-time workers in 1984[a]

Occupation	Men ($)	Women ($)	Ratio female/male
Total	400	259	64.8
Managerial and professional	553	378	68.4
Executive, administrative and managerial	568	358	63.0
Professional	534	394	73.8
Technical, sales and administrative support	404	256	63.4
Technicians and related support	451	312	69.2
Sales occupations	403	212	52.6
Administrative support, including clerical	380	257	67.6
Service occupations	259	180	69.5
Private household	208	130	62.5
Protective service	370	288	76.2
Other service occupations	224	182	81.3
Precision production, craft and repair	401	254	63.3
Operators, fabricators and labourers	321	209	65.1
Machine operators, assemblers and inspectors	331	208	62.8
Transportation and material moving	354	253	71.5
Handlers, equipment cleaners, helpers and labourers	258	207	80.2
Farming, forestry and fishing	205	177	86.3

[a]It should be noted that the earnings gap in usual weekly earnings is generally smaller than that of annual income/earnings.
SOURCE: Women's Bureau and Bureau of Labor Statistics, US Department of Labor, 'Facts on U.S. Working Women', Fact Sheet No. 85–7 (Washington, DC: US Government Printing Office, July 1985) p. 3.

greater stock of 'human capital' in the form of education and training, work experience and continuity, commitment to their jobs, and better health records. The problem with the 'human capital' approach is that women get a lower rate of return on their education and work experience than men do. For example, women with four or more years of college had a median income of $9928 in 1979, compared to $21,538 earned by college-educated men. Men without a high school diploma earned more than women with BAs, while the wages of female high school graduates were less than those of men with fewer than eight years of schooling. Recent studies show that from one-half to two-thirds of the earnings gap can be attributed to various forms of discrimination. These range from excluding or discouraging women from entering or advancing in the more lucrative employment areas to systematically underpaying certain jobs because they are held mainly by women.[29]

Comparable worth is one way of correcting the underpayment of women rooted in the gender division of labour without a massive shift of women into non-traditional occupations. Existing jobs are evaluated according to educational prerequisites, skills, effort, responsibilities and working conditions, in order to arrive at a quantitative basis for determining equal wages for work of 'equal value'. Such analyses challenge both prevailing standards of job evaluation and existing wage structures, for they find that wages are not determined by impersonal 'market forces', but are set within a system of segmented labour markets which 'connect the worth of different kinds of work with ideas about the inherent worth of workers'. No relationship exists between the skills involved in women's work and the wages paid.[30] Instead, female positions are underpaid relative to comparable jobs held by men. For example, in Minnesota the predominantly female occupation of typing pool supervisor received more job points than the predominantly male position of painter, yet the women were paid $334 less per month. In the state of Washington, the work of licensed practical nurses (women) and correctional officers (men) were rated as equal, but the nurses earned over $400 less per month than the officers, and in San Jose, California, senior carpenters (male) earned almost $400 more a month than equally rated senior legal secretaries.

Although these job evaluations have been conducted only within individual firms or in public agencies, a sizable number of workers can be affected when the employer is a state or a city. As a result of a class action suit filed by AFSCME against the state of Washington, a federal district court ruled in 1983 that Washington was guilty of sex discrimination for failing to raise women's salaries to the levels called for by the state's own evaluation of civil service jobs. AFSCME Local 101's strike against the city of San Jose over pay inequities led to a settlement that included upgrading job classifications held mostly by women. The International United Electrical Workers (IUE) and the Communications Workers of America (CWA), as well as the American Nurses Association and the National Education Association, have made pay equity a bargaining issue.

However, due to the costs involved in increasing women's salaries and the Reagan administration's opposition to pay equity, comparable worth has had only limited success. A federal court of appeals in 1985 overturned AFSCME's 1983 victory in Washington state, and California Governor George Deukemejian vetoed an appropriation which would have increased wages for female state workers. Although California is one of thirty states which either have comparable worth laws or have begun to introduce them, without adequate funding such legislation means little to working women.

Business associations such as the US Chamber of Commerce and the National Association of Manufacturers oppose comparable worth, not only because of its cost, but also on the grounds that it would interfere with 'an employer's inalienable right to set pay strategies'. These include paying non-unionised workers less than those with union contracts and setting wages in the South lower than those for identical jobs at the same company in the North.[31]

While business and government resist comparable worth, radicals are quick to point out its limitations. Comparable worth argues for gender equality within the existing wage system, but it does not attack the principle of a hierarchy of wages and occupations. It questions social values and priorities only in so far as they have led to undervaluing traditionally female occupations such as child-care workers, nursery school teachers and practical nurses. Comparable worth will not lessen racial divisions between women which are related to different occupational specialties. Registered nurses, for example, tend to be white women, while lower-paid licensed practical nurses and nurses' aides are predominantly women of colour.

Furthermore, existing marketplace values may make it impossible to measure and reward women's unpaid work adequately. As Clair Brown points out, women's household labour 'focuses on individual and family well-being, and its personalized care and nurturing cannot be given a price tag'. Family work and volunteer work in social, religious and political organisations are part of a 'noncompetitive economy' based on cooperation, mutual aid and service to others, while the market economy is individualistic and competitive.[32] Only a radical, non-quantitative definition of 'socially valuable work' can hope to include women's family and volunteer labour.

Comparable worth also has serious geographical limitations. Attempts to raise wages in traditionally low-paying fields within the US may simply increase the exportation of these jobs to Third World countries. The gender division of labour is an international phenomenon. California electronics firms, for example, have shifted their labour-intensive jobs to Asian and Latin workers – 80–90 per cent of whom are women – while American workers perform the initial stages and final assembly. Asian 'free trade' or 'export processing' zones and the *maquiladoras* across the border in Mexico allow US-based corporations to escape paying higher American wages, as well as more stringent health and safety standards. American Airlines processes its tickets in Barbados because data entry operators there are paid between $1.75 and $3 per hour, while those in the US earn from $5 to $7. This Barbados-based operation is one result of the decade-long effort to organise and upgrade white-collar workers in the United States.

Multinational corporations prefer to employ young, single women and pay them less than their male counterparts. These women are viewed as a docile labour force willing to perform boring, repetitive tasks, even though in Guatemala, the Philippines, Dominican Republic and South Korea, to name a few, female 'docility' has had to be reinforced by bans on labour unions and police action against strikes and other organising attempts.

The wages and working conditions of American clerical and factory women are directly affected not only by this corporate 'preference' for low-paid, foreign labour, but also by the exploitation of immigrant women living in the US. Sweatshops in the garment industry operate illegally on the fringes of the economy in order to avoid unemployment insurance, minimum wage rates, child labour laws and overtime pay regulations. Sweatshop workers are 90 per cent women, and the majority are immigrants from the Caribbean, Central America and Asia. Since a large proportion are also 'undocumented', that is, without proper immigration papers, they are especially vulnerable and exploited. In the electronics industry, 40 per cent of the assembly line workers are immigrant women: Filipinas, Thais, Samoans, Mexicans and Vietnamese. While wages for semiconductor assembly in the US are superior to those overseas, they are among the lowest in all of US industry.[33]

It appears that women in many countries are becoming a 'reserve army' of labour for multinational corporations. American women can no longer gain job security and improved working conditions for themselves without developing a global perspective which addresses the paid and unpaid work of women all over the world.

In the 1980s, women are organising beyond national boundaries in anti-nuclear, peace and environmental movements, while simultaneously introducing feminist perspectives into these movements. International conferences and publications have become forums for women to share their experiences and critically compare corporate and governmental priorities and policies. The next chapter will discuss some of the ways women are creating a new agenda in order to address problems of sex discrimination from a global perspective of connection, cooperation, preservation and social transformation.

11. Problems, Prospects and the Feminist Future

The Women's Movement in the United States appears to be declining in numbers and political influence while, at the same time, becoming part of an international movement with expanded, less gender-specific programmes. In publications, conferences, demonstrations and peace camps, women are sharing new visions for achieving global security without military conflict and nuclear threats. They are creating new perspectives on international development which not only include and benefit women, but also avoid cultural disruption and environmental devastation.

At the same time, religious, economic and political conservatives in the US and other countries are retarding progress towards gender equality, perpetuating racial and class inequities and heightening global tensions. Along with the defeat of the Equal Rights Amendment in June 1982, the Reagan administration's increased 'defence' budgets, offensive military operations in Central America and the Middle East, and strident 'anti-terrorist' rhetoric are inhibiting progressive political thought and action. The American Women's Movement has also been facing organised anti-feminist campaigns, especially against reproductive choice and gay rights, an apparent lack of interest by young women in radical feminist politics, and conservative tendencies within its own ranks.

Although the 'New Right' has led crusades against abortion and the ERA, it is not a unified anti-feminist movement. Evangelical or 'fundamentalist' women, in particular, generally show a lack of interest in political and social issues. While many echo the male-defined Evangelical point of view on national defence, sexuality, the family and feminism, Carol Virginia Pohli found that a quarter to a third do not. Over one-fourth of the white Evangelical women she interviewed want black people to receive more employment opportunities, do not condone the segregated conditions of their churches and disapprove of increased federal spending for defence. One-third admitted wishing they had been men during times of crisis or frustration in their lives and, contrary to Evangelical teachings, 27 per cent believed that masculinity and femininity were optional human variations, not innate traits. Close to half of the women favoured the ERA. Pohli attributes these dissenting opinions both to the Protestant tradition of individualism which encourages independent thinking and to the influence of the Women's Movement even among these conservative, apolitical Christians.[1]

Unfortunately, some liberal feminists have reacted to New Right rhetoric by becoming more conservative themselves. Betty Friedan, for example, has recently claimed that the Women's Movement alienated potential supporters by appealing to women only as 'individualists', and not as wives and mothers. The ERA, abortion and child care would have gained more support had they been presented as necessary 'for the very survival of the family'.[2] What Friedan calls 'second-stage feminism' simply revives the notion of woman-as-compassionate-mother and reiterates her long-standing distaste for the sexual politics of radical feminists, especially lesbians. By insisting that sex should be a private, even 'closeted', subject, Friedan ignores both the threat of sexual regulation by conservatives and the success the Women's Movement has had in making women conscious of the connection between their private lives and public affairs.

Rather than ignoring sexuality or reifying the nuclear family, feminists need further to explore desire and love. According to Judith Stacey, the Women's Movement has 'done a better job of criticizing heterosexuality as institution and practice ... than studying its history or appreciating its complexity and continued vitality, even for feminists'.[3]

The absence of feminist perspectives on heterosexual romance may be one reason why young women are not attracted to the Women's Movement. Unlike earlier feminists, adolescents do not face the 'confinement' of the nuclear family, but rather the realities of female economic independence. Close to 40 per cent of the children born in the 1968–69 cohort have experienced a family

break-up by the age of 13. Sharon Thompson found that white
heterosexual working-class girls expected to work, but they do not
expect emotional satisfaction from their jobs. Sex and romance,
therefore, form the 'fundamental projects' and adventures of their
lives. Relationships are not sought primarily for sexual pleasure,
but to achieve 'true, monogamous, permanent, one-man, one-
woman couple love'. Despite changed material and social conditions
which make female independence almost 'inescapable', young
women still attempt to bargain their sexuality for male love and
commitment.

Consequently, many of them are having sexual experience before
their desire for it is aroused, but they are not really having 'too
much, too soon', as conservatives lament. Rather, as Thompson
points out: 'They have too little – too little pleasure, too few
options, not enough sexual power.'[4] These problems are shared, to
some extent, even by middle-class professional women. Feeling
emotionally undernourished by their careers, they seek personal
fulfilment through marriage and motherhood.

Women need more understanding of gender politics and male
sexual decision-making, as well as a positive integration of love and
work. Feminists can help construct a better future not only by
addressing issues of heterosexual romance, including intimacy,
surrender, pleasure and power, but also by strengthening the
connection between the personal and the political.

The 'personal is political' is essential to a feminist perspective
because it assumes that individual problems and opportunities are
not separate from institutional practices and changes. Feminists
should not demand that individual women be admitted to positions
of power, but rather that power needs to be redefined and
institutions fundamentally changed. As Charlotte Bunch points
out, feminism is not only about 'women's issues', but 'a political
perspective . . . . based on women's experiences that questions
patriarchal modes of domination in all areas of life'.[5] All issues are
potentially 'women's issues'. There is a relationship between
violence in the home and a nation's growing military budget; the
sexual harassment of underpaid women workers is connected to
industrial 'rape' of the environment and capital investments in
apartheid South Africa.

In the last decade, two examples of this feminist 'connectedness'
have been the recommendations of the 'National Plan of Action',

adopted at the National Women's Conference in November and the 'gender gap' in voting patterns and political prioriti women and men. The National Women's Conference, held in Houston, Texas, was an outgrowth of the United Nations Decade for Women. Supported by federal law to make policy recommendations to the President and Congress, its 'National Plan of Action' included 'women's issues' which prior to the feminist movement had not been conceptualised as 'political', as well as political issues not generally considered as 'women's issues'. The Plan called for an end to child abuse, support for women's reproductive freedom and sexual preference, and programmes to help battered, disabled, older, rural and racial minority women. It recommended that the national government enact a comparable worth law and enforce already existing anti-discrimination laws related to women's employment. Federal and state governments were asked to treat welfare and poverty 'as major women's issues' and increase funding for Social Security, Aid to Families with Dependent Children, and other income transfer programmes. The 'National Plan of Action' also expanded feminist concerns by demanding women's participation 'in the formulation and execution of all aspects of United States foreign policy', and urging that the United States 'take the lead' in nuclear disarmament and develop 'initiatives to advance the cause of world peace'. It recommended that US development agencies 'promote the involvement' of women in the developing world 'in determining their own needs and priorities in programs intended for their benefit'.[6]

This increasing concern by liberal feminists over economic allocations and foreign policy led to a conflict with the Carter administration Bella B. Abzug, appointed by Jimmy Carter as a co-chair of the National Advisory Committee on Women, was dismissed from that position for overstepping the bounds of 'legitimate' criticism. Among other things, Abzug had questioned the administration's large expenditures for military and defence requirements and criticised Carter's anti-inflation programme because it imposed disproportionate economic burdens on women. It can be argued that Carter's firing of Abzug, along with his anti-abortion stand and lukewarm support for the ERA, laid the foundation for Reagan's anti-feminist election platform in 1980. As Zillah Eisentein points out: 'The major fear the Carter administration had was that women were beginning to connect the relationship in their lives between economic exploitation and sexual subordination. This is what Carter had to stop.[7]

Although Reagan gives no support to 'women's issues' – whether broadly or narrowly construed – women themselves have spoken out on economic policy issues, defence spending and Third World development as being part of their 'sphere'. A significant difference has also appeared between female and male voters.

In the 1980 presidential election and the 1982 congressional elections, women's votes diverged from men's by approximately ten percentage points in favour of the Democrats. During his first term as President 10 per cent fewer women than men approved of Ronald Reagan's performance. Opinion polls have shown that women tend to be more pacifist than men, more concerned about the environment and more supportive of government social welfare programmes. Although the Grenada invasion in October 1983 raised Reagan's rating among women from 47 to 49 per cent, men's approval climbed from 59 to 67 per cent. A CBS news poll in April 1984 found that while 34 per cent of men approved of the Reagan administration's policy in Latin America, only 25 per cent of the women did.[8] Even though this difference was not wide enough to prevent Reagan's re-election in 1984, it has caused peace, social welfare and environmental issues to be described as 'gender gap' or even 'women's' issues.

Feminism, Barbara Ehrenreich suggests, may have moved women 'to the left of men'. Relatively privileged women have become alienated 'from the pro-business, pro-Cold War interests of the men of their class'. While 58 per cent of male college graduates chose Reagan in 1980, 41 per cent of similarly educated women did. In the absence of a socialist or labour party, the American Women's Movement 'has been a major carrier of social democratic values throughout the '70s and '80s'. Women's greater support for a social welfare state can be partly attributed both to the persistence of traditional female values, such as compassion and caring, and to the similarities between the feminist movement and social welfare programmes, both of which have challenged the separation of family and state, private and public life. Another more obvious reason is that Reagan's economic policies have affected women more adversely than they have men. In 1981, 42 per cent of the men polled, but only 27 per cent of women, said they were 'better off' economically under Reagan.[9] While wage-earning and low-income women have been the hardest hit and most critical of 'Reaganomics', the dismantling of the welfare state has also, as shown in Chapter 9, reversed the gains made by white professional women and black people employed in the public sector.

Soaring defence budgets and cutbacks in social services have made both the connection between Reagan's foreign and domestic policies and the contradictions of Reaganism much clearer to women. Although it is a recent expression of expansive capitalist patriarchy, Reaganism is primarily an ideology of nostalgia. Its foreign policy is based on a 'strong' America unchallenged in the world, while its economic philosophy glorifies individual selfishness and turns the inequities of American society into a positive virtue.[10] As a counterpoise to the military and the market, Reaganism favours a revival of the traditional nuclear family, including the nineteenth-century ideal of the 'moral mother'.

However, as shown in the last chapter, most women work both in the market and at home. They are treated as 'secondary' earners and continue to do a disproportionate share of unpaid domestic labour. Although women have to transcend the liberal capitalist dichotomy of family and market in their daily lives, they remain oppressed by it. Feminists, therefore, should continue to address the issue of women's double day and the connections between compulsory heterosexuality, women's status in marriage, unpaid family work and exploitation as wage-earners.

In order to develop creative alternatives to Reaganism, a global perspective is essential. Analyses of women's employment issues, for example, must include an understanding of how multinational corporations are able to exploit female poverty and discourage unionisation by shifting labour-intensive jobs to Third World countries. Educational efforts must simultaneously address women's personal experiences and encourage respect for cultural diversity As Charlotte Bunch points out, the limitation of the 'personal is political' has been that.

Each of our personal perceptions of women's needs and reality have been so shaped by the racism, anti-semitism, classism, etc. of our cultures that we cannot depend on our perceptions alone as the basis for analysis and action. We need to learn from other women's lives and views as well.

Through international conferences, transnational networks and multilingual publications, women have been communicating both their shared experiences and their cultural differences in an effort to learn how 'to be global in consciousness while taking action locally'.[11] Both official and informal activities have contributed to this process. The United Nations International Women's Year (1975) followed by the World Decade for Women (1976–85) sponsored three world conferences: Mexico City (1975), Copenhagen (1980) and Nairobi, Kenya (1985). At each, there were actually two conferences: one consisting of official delegates who represented their governments and a parallel forum of non-governmental organisations (NGOs). Since the NGO representatives were less conservative and not restrained by national priorities, they exchanged information more freely, struggled over political and cultural differences, and envisioned more radical, long-term programmes to implement the Decade's goals of equality, development and peace.

The UN decade catalysed not only the women who attended the conferences or supported UN efforts, but also those who initially regarded it as a 'co-optation' of feminism. Among the dissenters were the organisers of the International Tribunal on Crimes Against Women, held in Brussels in March 1976. Over 2000 women from 40 countries participated in what was essentially an international 'speak out' against crimes of violence, especially rape and wife battering, as well as crimes of sexual oppression, including compulsory heterosexuality, forced motherhood, pornography and prostitution. Testimony on war and militarism was limited to the experiences of female political prisoners; economic issues, especially the 'double oppression' of Third World, immigrant and religious minority women, were addressed as additional patriarchal 'crimes' against women. Although the Tribunal was an international forum, it concentrated mainly on issues of 'sexual politics'.[12] In retrospect, it represents a transitional step in the development of global feminism, just prior to the emergence of peace, development and the environment as central concerns.

Environmental issues have been typically expressed through women's community organising around local concerns. Women's workplace, community health and spirituality groups have been active in local campaigns against specific health hazards: toxic chemicals, pesticide spraying, exposure to nuclear radiation and asbestos in school buildings. These grass-roots organisations have changed the environmental movement from its earlier focus on wildlife protection, forest conservation and overpopulation to a movement addressing the effects of industrial pollution on human health.

Women are more likely than men to hold leadership positions in community environmental groups, and their primary reason for doing so is concern over their children and future generations. According to a study by Nicholas Freudenberg and Ellen Zaltzberg, women perceive 'their involvement in enviromental action as an extension of traditional female roles rather than as a challenge to these roles'.[13] While there is nothing inherently progressive about women's attempts to safeguard their families, environmental activism does present an opportunity to integrate personal concerns with knowledge about corporate- and government-caused health threats. Most community activists do not develop thoroughly radical or anti-capitalist perspectives, but they do become critical of the corporations which are making them sick and the government officials who lie to them.

Women's activism has also contributed to greater organisational flexibility and innovative non-violent tactics. At Love Canal, for example, a Mothers Day rally in front of the Hooker Chemical Company creatively politicised both a traditional annual celebration and a revered image. Decision-making by consensus, rotating leadership, and little or no organisational hierarchy draw upon processes developed by the early Women's Movement.

Some female environmental activists are building coalitions with labour organisations around workplace health issues and seeking labour support for women's reproductive rights, including access to safe abortions, protection against dangerous contraceptives and the elimination of involuntary or coerced sterilisations. Eco-feminists, on the other hand, are contributing to 'deep ecology' by combining 'post-patriarchal' spirituality with a reverence for Mother Earth. Unlike traditional resource management or conservation, deep ecology calls for a change in consciousness corresponding to the paradigm shift in the physical sciences – from a mechanistic, quantifiable, dualistic world view to 'a view of the world as inherently alive, dynamic, and relational – valued in and of itself'. Political protest can express this 'relational' consciousness. In opposing a new nuclear power plant, comments Starhawk, 'we are confronting something real, and our transformation of consciousness is integrated with our transformation of the reality that surrounds us'.[14]

Some American eco-feminists have recently become active in Green politics, a movement which began in the Federal Republic of Germany a decade ago. Charlene Spretnak, editor of *The Politics of Feminist Spirituality* (1982), believes that Green values – ecological wisdom, non-violence, cooperative and community-based economics, and respect for cultural diversity – are similar to her earth-centred feminist spirituality. Spretnak has co-authored *Green Politics: The Global Promise* with physicist Fritjof Capra, whose previous work includes *The Tao of Physics* and *The Turning Point*. The Elmwood Institute (Berkeley, California), organised by Capra in 1983, serves as an intellectual resource base for the American Green movement.

Although the Greens are not yet as numerous or influential in the US as they are in Europe, their combination of politics, ecology and spirituality coincides with a growing awareness that the political programmes of socialists and capitalists have not preserved the environment or distributed the world's resources equitably. The development models of both the US and the Soviet Union assume that complex technology and industrial growth will 'modernise' the world's 'underdeveloped' regions. They do not question whether capital accumulation, increasing production and expanding trade are the best ways to measure economic 'growth', or even conceive that 'growth' may be other than material. Although their ideologies differ, both Soviet and American planners have been responsible for environmental disasters and major disruptions in indigenous patterns of agriculture, household production and family structure. Neither 'superpower' has paid much attention to workers' basic material needs and spiritual aspirations, or to gender differences, even though development has had a different impact on women's work from that it has had on men's.

In the shift from subsistence to market-oriented agriculture or from handicraft to factory production, women often lose effective control over productive resources. Increasing numbers of them become low-wage workers either in 'export processing zones' located in their own countries or as immigrants to First World countries. The use of immigrant labour has had a long history in the US, but export-processing industries, or 'runaway shops', represent a new strategy. Instead of importing workers, corporations export jobs. Runaway shops 'link the concerns of women workers in advanced industrial nations and developing countries, since the increase of jobs in the Third World generally implies a decrease elsewhere'. For example, employment in the New York City garment industry, especially its unionised sector, is declining. The industry has not only been moving abroad, but has also gone 'underground', employing undocumented immigrants at below the legal minimum wage.[15]

The entry of Third World women into export-oriented industrial labour is often accompanied by high levels of male unemployment and a growing number of economically vulnerable female-headed households. Industries which mainly employ men, on the other hand, leave women both with heavier workloads at home and with the loss of traditional income-producing activities which formerly allowed them some autonomy and status. In some cases, development simply reinforces those traditional values and conditions which have oppressed women; in others, it weakens traditional forms of patriarchal control while introducing new ones. In Singapore and Malaysia, for example, employed women have gained some degree of economic autonomy from their patriarchal families, but they are exposed to capitalist exploitation and state control. In Mexico, the US strawberry companies reinforce patriarchal values by paying women low wages and employing them intermittently. According to Lourdes Arizpe and Josefina Aranda, 'the companies take advantage of the traditional idea that any income earned by a daughter, wife, or mother is an "extra" over and above the main income of the father, husband, or son'.[16]

Development has not raised women's status because most female workers earn low wages and are employed in low-status jobs. Employed women continue to bear the major burden of household chores, child care and other unpaid reproductive work. Although Third World women experience a far greater degree of economic exploitation than do First World women, the 'double day' has become a cross-cultural phenomenon. Not only do women perform 90 per cent of the world's unpaid work, but they are universally regarded as less valuable employees. As Aline K. Wong points out: 'As long as sexual segregation characterizes the occupational world and women are bound by domestic responsibilties, they will remain a peripheral work force.'[17]

Some feminists have proposed integrating women's unpaid work into the market economy by paying wages to individual mothers and household maintainers and/or by socialising domestic work through publicly or privately funded programmes. Others, including Hilda Scott, Hazel Henderson, Lisa Leghorn, Katherine Parker, Barbara Ehrenreich and Deirdre English, suggest a radically different approach in which the 'use values' of caring, humanising activities would become central to economic planning. The 'growth' model would be replaced by a 'basic needs approach', emphasising food, shelter, health care, education and rest. Child care, for example, would not be dismissed as each woman's individual problem; rather, the nurturing of children would become 'a transcendent public priority'. Market values, Ehrenreich and English insist, 'must be pushed back to the margins. And the "womanly" values of community and caring must rise to the center as the only *human* principles.'[18] These 'womanly values' include adequate social services, a livable environment and reduced military spending.

The early Women's Movement expanded 'politics' to include the 'personal'. Today's feminists want to transform economics, not only by incorporating the experiences, needs and values of women, but also convincing men that these 'female-centred' values will enhance their lives and those of future generations.

Feminist peace activists, in particular, argue that much of the 'defence' budget could be converted to producing life-sustaining goods and services. Many of them also believe that psycho-spiritual changes are necessary in order to transform personal, social and global values and relationships. They see themselves as members of an international movement and maintain close ties with women's peace groups in Europe and Asia.

Since the late 1940s, national 'security' has involved nuclear weapons, permanent military alliances such as the North Atlantic Treaty Organization (NATO), and the close partnership of government, industry and science. It has become increasingly difficult to separate military from civilian life or to distinguish between war-related and 'peacetime' production. The growth of electronics and nuclear power illustrates not only private industries' increasing dependence on government subsidies and sponsorship but also a general militarisation of society.

Militarism refers not only to relationships between nations, but also to each country's internal politics, economics and culture.

Hierarchy, discipline, obedience and organised violence are not confined to members of the armed forces, but extend into 'civilian' social and political life. Quintessentially patriarchal, these values and practices reinforce gender and racial hierarchies and perpetuate traditional gender roles.

For these reasons, there is a growing awareness in various national women's movements that militarism is a feminist issue. As victims of violence on a personal level, women are more likely to be critical of organised, state-controlled violence. Many feminists also question the ways women have been employed and manipulated by the armed forces, yet are ambivalent about the expanded roles promised to new female enlistees. They see a close relationship between US military expenditures and the nation's current social and economic problems.

After deducting interest on the national debt and other fixed expenses, nearly half of the 'disposable' US federal budget is spent on the military. The portion allocated to new weapons has increased from 37.2 per cent of the defence budget in 1980 to 48.6 per cent in 1984. Many of these weapons are designed for nuclear deterrence or for use in a 'limited' nuclear war. Feminists recognise that every dollar spent on the military is a dollar not available for social programmes, and they are arguing on a weapon-by-weapon basis for a transfer of spending.

According to Sheila Tobias' calculations, the entire national child abuse programme costs one F-14 fighter plane; the price of 56 MX missiles could restore the cuts and increase funding for the national food stamps programme, which has been drastically reduced since 1981. Instead of producing five Pershing II missiles, educational equity for women could be enforced. However, at least five states – California, Texas, Washington, Georgia and Connecticut – have become so dependent on military contractors that their economies would suffer by substantial cuts. Therefore a feminist position which calls for 'conversion' of military to non-military spending must also take into account the paychecks of more than 6 million Americans.[19]

One such effort was made in 1983 and 1984 by the Puget Sound Women's Peace Camp located across the road from the Boeing Aerospace Center in Kent, Washington. The camp near Boeing, a producer of Cruise missiles, completed a chain with one at Seneca, New York (a storage/transshipment site), and the deployment site at Greenham Common, England. The Puget Sound women engaged in an educational campaign of leafleting, vigils, demonstrations and workshops to encourage civilian workers at Boeing to think of conversion to peaceful production. As one of their guidelines for action stated:

> it is not the Boeing workers who have engineered the policies that are leading to world destruction, but rather the government, the Pentagon, and powerful corporations. Our aim is to win allies and to act together to change the current distribution of power, not to alienate Boeing workers by posing ourselves as directly antagonistic to their means of livelihood.[20]

While government officials claim that every 1 billion dollar increase in military spending creates 35,000 new jobs, they neglect to mention that the same amount would result in many more jobs if invested in housing, education or health care. Of all forms of public spending, defence is the least efficient means of generating employment. In fact, military spending actually causes unemployment for women. Since 1980, every time the military budget has gone up 1 billion dollars, 9500 jobs for women have disappeared. This is because women's jobs are heavily concentrated in those economic sectors which are the hardest hit when military spending is high. In the 1970s, almost half of the new jobs gained by women were in services and state and local government. According to one estimate, women now face a net loss of over 1.5 million jobs in these sectors alone each year. Another assessment of women's civilian positions either lost or never created amounted to close to 1,300,000 in 1980. In that year, only 232,000 women, or one-half of 1 per cent of the female labour force, were working directly on military contracts.[21]

Due to the decline of employment opportunities in civilian sectors and the military's recruitment promises of job training and 'equal opportunity', young black women have been enlisting in the armed services, especially the army, in disproportionate numbers. Approximately 11 per cent of all American women in 1982, blacks were 25.7 per cent of the women in the combined armed forces and 42.5 per cent of the enlisted women in the army.[22] Black and poor white women are, in effect, subject to an 'economic draft', even though American women are exempt from the 1980 military registration law.

Once in the military, women are barred from specific jobs, most notably those defined as 'combat'. In 1972, over 90 per cent of American military women were found in three traditional occupational sectors: medical, clerical and communications. Although this had decreased to one-half by 1980, the top three female positions that year remained clerical (25 per cent), nursing (17 per cent) and communications (13 per cent). In August 1982, the US Department of Defense announced that 23 occupational categories, including carpenter, plumber and interior electrician, would be closed to army women. The Department's reasons included such physical factors as women's inability to lift heavy objects and expanded definitions of 'combat' and 'battle area' which incorporated these occupations.[23]

It can be reasonably argued that not only have nuclear weapons made the entire world a 'battle area', but also that within the military itself a clear line no longer exists between 'combat' and 'non-combat'. Four-fifths of the US female military in Vietnam were nurses. All of them saw the worst effects of battle, and those who served with the Mobile Army Surgical Hospital (MASH) Units or on helicopter crews entered 'combat zones'. A woman who is a member of an underground intercontinental missile crew is categorised as 'non-combat', although the weapon she works with will cause far more destruction than any 'combat' infantryman with his rifle. Despite these realities, 'combat' remains a powerful ideological construct because it defines war as a masculine endeavour. As late as 1980, General Robert H. Barrow, Commandant of the US marines, insisted:

> War is man's work. Biological convergence on the battlefield . . . would be an enormous psychological distraction for the male who wants to think that he's fighting for that woman somewhere behind, not up there in the same fox hole with him. It tramples the male ego. When you get right down to it, you've got to protect the manliness of war.[24]

The military establishment appears determined to maintain the traditional gender division of labour. In 1982, the US Army Command cited increased sexual harassment of women as a primary reason for discontinuing its new practice of integrated male-female training units. Although rape is twice as frequent in the military as in civilian life, the US military insists that its female recruits look 'feminine'. Officials also scrutinise women's sexual lives far more closely than men's. According to a 1981 study, women were discharged from the US navy because of homosexual conduct at a rate two and a half times higher than men, and army women were six times more likely than men to be discharged on the grounds of homosexuality.[25]

While a dwindling number of liberal feminists still argue that women's full participation in the military, including conscription and combat, is a precondition for full citizenship and social equality with men, most feminists have become critical of this 'equal opportunity' argument. Instead, they see a direct relationship between militarism and sexism, do not accept the structures and standards of the present, male-dominated society, and question the material and ideological consequences of militarism.

Although women comprise less than 10 per cent of the US armed forces, most female civilians are economically and emotionally militarised by one or more of the following: personal ties to a serviceman or potential serviceman; employment in a defence-related job; the government's rhetoric about 'national security'; advertising and 'educational' campaigns conducted by quasi-private industries; and general patriarchal controls over women's nurturing and care-taking roles.

Many women employed by computer firms, advertising agencies, banks and universities are working directly or indirectly for major military contractors. Electronics companies, in particular, are heavily dependent both on defence contracts and cheap female labour. Cynthia Enloe calls California's Silicon Valley 'a society based on an integrated system of *sexism*, *racism* and *militarism*'. Women comprise 80 per cent of the assembly plant workers, the majority black, Hispanic and Asian, while managerial and technical positions are held overwhelmingly by white men. These companies manufacture communications systems, radar and control mechanisms which are essential for such modern weapons as the Trident II and MX missiles, the B-1B bomber, and the Rapid Deployment Force's Infantry Fight Vehicle. It can be estimated that about 40 per cent of a new navy cruiser is made by women, since it is two-fifths composed of electronics. Women's earnings in defence-related communications and high-tech industries are only 51 per cent of men's, while in civilian industries female workers receive 64 cents of every 'male' dollar. The gender gap in wages is due primarily to occupational segregation. In guided space vehicle plants, for example, women hold 85 per cent of clerical jobs, but only 4 per cent of professional and 7 per cent of managerial positions.[26]

Unlike the government's temporary mobilisation of women during the Second World War, militarised industries conduct ongoing campaigns specifically directed to female employees and consumers. The nuclear power industry, in particular, has made extensive efforts since the mid 1970s to cultivate women's 'nuclear acceptance'. Nuclear Energy Women (NEW), founded in 1975 by fourteen industry professionals, attempts to build 'a more positive relationship' with the female public through education and 'grass-roots' lobbying, as well as a support structure of prominent pro-nuclear women.

NEW is neither an autonomous nor a 'grass-roots' organisation, but rather a courier for the Atomic Industrial Forum (AIF), the largest of the three nuclear trade associations. Other segments of the nuclear complex active in public relations are the US Committee for Energy Awareness (USCEA), which sells nuclear power via a 'Build a Better America' campaign on television and in print, and the Department of Energy (DOE), a government bureau, whose activities include planting pro-nuclear items in the press, distributing industry materials to schools, and financing pro-nuclear research. Through taxes and utility bills, the American public pays to be convinced that nuclear energy is safe, progressive and economical.

A central part of the campaign is economic; women are told that atomic jobs are safe, secure and creative. The nuclear complex ignores studies showing that other energy technologies may provide up to five times more jobs. It also threatens women with economic stagnation, unemployment and deprived living conditions should they oppose technological 'progress'. The nuclear message, Lin Nelson points out, 'taps women's well-founded fears that should there be a substantial revamping of the use of resources, energy, and technology, it may be women who will shoulder the greater burden of sacrifice.'

For example, *Women and Energy: The Vital Link*, a NEW slideshow, emphasises women's dependency on electricity and ridicules alternative energy sources. Without nuclear energy, 'we'll rediscover the solar clothes dryer – a couple of yards of rope and some clothes pins.' If there is an energy shortage, women will lose the labour-saving devices in their homes, which 'have done as much to shape women's destiny as suffragettes or liberationists'.[27]

These industry and government propaganda campaigns are the result of women's resistance to the nuclear world view. Following the Three Mile Island nuclear accident in 1979, scepticism about nuclear power was more widespread among women, especially pregnant women and mothers of pre-school-age children, than among men. Surveys since the mid 1970s indicate that approximately 20 per cent fewer American women than men support the use of nuclear energy. Polls in Sweden, France and Germany show the same gender pattern.

Women in the anti-nuclear movement are twice as likely as men to be local leaders. Dolly Weinhold's fight against the Seabrook plant in New Hampshire, the efforts of the Harrisburg Area Women's Center to prevent the restart of the Three Mile Island plant, and the ongoing struggle of Women of All Red Nations, led by Winona LaDuke, against the nuclear industry's intrusion on Native American land are only a few examples. Numerous groups, such as the National Women's Health Network, Feminist Resources on Energy and Ecology, Solar Sister, Women Against Nuclear Development, and Women for a Nuclear Free Future, monitor the industry's and Nuclear Regulatory Commission's publicity, criticise their poor health and safety record, report on the increasing rates of birth defects and cancer caused by exposure to low levels of radiation, and reveal the unprecedented hazards of nuclear waste transport and storage. These and other organisations also work to promote safer energy options and a more ecologically balanced society, free of sexism, racism and violence.

Women have been coming together across national boundaries to stop the threat of global annihilation. The issue of American dominance within NATO has facilitated these transnational feminist ties, especially since the 1979 decision to deploy Cruise and Pershing II missiles in Western Europe. The women's peace camp at Greenham Common, in existence since 1981, has inspired similar camps throughout the world. In 1983, American and Canadian feminists organised an encampment at the Seneca Army Depot, a storage site and departure point for US nuclear missiles bound for

Europe. Two years later, a web of American women's peace camps extended from Seneca to Minneapolis; Tucson, Arizona, to Puget Sound; and Ann Arbor, Michigan, to Aikens, South Carolina.

Peace camps provide a unique opportunity for women to intervene directly to stop war production, engage in community outreach and education, and create peaceful, non-hierarchical social models. At these camps women work 'at living peacefully and cooperatively while working for a peaceful, cooperative world'.[28] Rituals drawn from women's spirituality and guerrilla theatre contribute to a female-centred culture. These rituals, in which participants express horror at the prospect of nuclear destruction and reaffirm their kinship with our Mother Earth, have also become a regular feature at feminist peace demonstrations.

Women's peace camps are generally linked to local support groups as well as an international network of peace and ecology organisations which shares at least some of their goals. Seneca participants, for example, were able to draw upon the resources of the Women's Pentagon Actions, Women Strike for Peace, the Upstate (New York) Feminist Peace Alliance, and the Finger Lakes Peace Alliance (a local group). In turn, the Seneca encampment inspired protests against the Honeywell Corporation, an arms producer in Minneapolis, and the presidential nuclear sanctuary at Mt Weather near Washington, DC. However, as Donna Warnock has pointed out: 'Despite major theoretical commonalities, feminists are not necessarily nonviolent, and nonviolent activists are not necessarily feminist. This merger is our challenge.'[29]

Two unresolved issues inherited from the Women's Movement are separatism from men and divisions among women. Underlying both is the question of gender differences. Do women bring to the peace movement values, morals and experiences which vary significantly from those of men?

Organisationally, separatism can be traced back to the Woman's Peace Party (WPP), formed in 1915, and its post-1919 successor, the Women's International League for Peace and Freedom (WILPF). A more recent example has been Women Strike for Peace (WSP), created in the early 1960s to stop nuclear testing and end the nuclear arms race. WPP leaders, such as Jane Addams and Lillian Wald, believed that women were less short-sighted than men because they 'viewed all issues and problems from a perspective that gave the preservation of human life preeminence over all other concerns'. The WILPF and WSP have also assumed that the social experiences of women, especially their work as mothers and nurturers, enable them to understand the value of life better than men can.[30]

Today's feminists point out that the purpose of women's peace groups, camps and organisations is not primarily to exclude men, but to include women, especially those with no previous political experience. Many women need to be apart from men in order to overcome their socialised timidity, reclaim power for themselves, and assess their private and public complicity with male-defined values and institutions. Although a few feminists insist that women are innately, even biologically, less violent than men, most are engaged in a more complex analysis of the nature, source and degree of female pacifism.

The work of Nancy Chodorow, Sara Ruddick and Carol Gilligan indicates that important gender differences in moral and ethical development do exist. Although these differences are neither innate nor a direct cause of women's involvement in peace work, they have inspired distinctively feminist perspectives. Chodorow's theory of psychosexual development suggests that early (pre-oedipal) relationships with the mother as primary parent result in different 'relational capacities' for women and men. Girls 'come to experience themselves as less separate than boys' and 'define themselves more in relation to others'. A basis for empathy is therefore 'built into their primary definition of self'. 'Maternal thinking', according to Sara Ruddick, is the result both of women's experiences as daughters and of their social practices as mothers. Among the qualities women develop by caring for children is 'preservative love' balanced by the need to 'foster growth and welcome change'. Since a child 'is itself an "open structure" whose acts are irregular, unpredictable, often mysterious', women tend to develop greater mental flexibility than men, including openness to non-linear and non-rational modes of perception.

Women's thinking has been called 'field-dependent', 'holistic', 'open-ended' and 'contextual'. According to Ruddick, the theory of conflict that 'maternal' or 'holistic' thinkers develop

> bears remarkable similarity to that of pacifists. Both refuse to
> separate means from ends; both wish to treat 'enemies' as

opponents with whom one struggles, to risk trust rather than trusting suspicion, and to seek reconciliation rather than victory.

Women are also 'less apt than men to eroticize combat, more apt to eroticize reconciliation'.[31]

Carol Gilligan also suggests that women's desire to maintain relationships and reconcile competing claims makes them more inclined to pacifism than men. She cites a number of studies which reveal a far greater incidence of violence in men's thoughts and fantasies than those expressed by women. In competitive situations, women 'try to change the rules in order to preserve relationships', while men tend to abide by the rules of the 'game' and 'depict relationships as easily replaced'. Women's sense of morality arises from their 'experience of connection', and they conceive of ethics as 'a problem of inclusion rather than one of balancing claims'. This permits women to perceive life not as a path, but as a web in which there are no clear-cut goals or resolutions, but only numerous contextual choices and connections.[32]

These ethical perceptions and practices based on 'female' qualities of caring, empathy, inclusiveness, connectedness and interdependence appear to be far more conducive to the creation of a peaceful, ecologically-conscious world than a 'masculine' morality which emphasises individual (or national) rights, adherence to rules and strict reciprocity. However, if we insist that 'female' ethics are gender-specific, we reduce the chances of transforming global relations. Not only do far fewer women than men hold positions of power, but, more important, women's traditional values and roles have been manipulated to support war and militarised institutions.

In addition to mothers, wives and nurses, the US military services need prostitutes. In 1982, for example, 92 per cent of the half-million Americans stationed overseas were male. In such Third World countries as Thailand, imported militarism, along with tourism and foreign investments, has contributed to the soaring numbers of displaced rural women who are pressed into commercialised sex in order to support themselves. At home, military and government officials attempt to create loyal 'military wives' out of women married to servicemen. Military wives can help win civilian support by giving the armed forces a more humane, family-like appearance. They also provide cheap or unpaid labour for the military's social agencies and, most important, they reproduce and socialise a new generation of soldiers. Military authorities decide where a family will live, making it difficult for military wives to pursue their own careers. Wives of military men, or of men with previous military service, are more likely to be victims of battering than women whose partners have not served in the armed forces. Asian and Pacific Island women suffer an especially high incidence of physical abuse from their American husbands.[33]

Although women have been traditionally excluded from battle, war is not simply a male institution. New studies based on Chodorow's and Gilligan's theories indicate that women will endorse war when it is consistent with their moral concerns. Ofer Zur has found that

women will support war more enthusiastically than men when an appeal is made based on empathy for oppressed and vulnerable human beings or an emphasis is placed on group cohesion and intensification of interpersonal relationships in the community during war.

In other words, while war does have an appeal to both men and women, 'that appeal is different and is related to the moral concerns which are unique to each gender'.[34] It is obvious that governments have been successful in gaining women's support for war through propaganda which emphasises national unity, protection of home and community and aid to the weak and oppressed. Nevertheless, it also appears that men are more prone to justify war according to legal, rational and abstract criteria, such as treaty violations; they are more likely to dehumanise the enemy and accept an 'us' versus 'them' dichotomy. Men are also more likely than women to condone or justify acts of violence, such as torture and destruction of food supplies, and to endorse the notion of traditional sex roles during wartime: men as aggressive warriors and protectors, women as passive, protected and peaceful beings.

While these gender differences partially support the notion of female compassion, they do not prove that women are innately pacifist or that men are 'naturally' aggressive and violent. Rather, they indicate that feminist visions of a non-oppressive, healthy and peaceful society must be combined with opportunities for men to disassociate masculinity from 'the myth of the warrior' and make the 'rite of passage' into the Nuclear Age.

A network of mental health professionals and peace activists, many of them women, has been consciously applying feminist consciousness-raising processes to mixed groups of women and men. In what has been called 'despair and empowerment work', 'peace circles', 'earth grief', and 'breaking through psychic numbing', people are encouraged to overcome the social taboo against speaking about nuclear weapons and break through the psychological defence mechanisms they have erected to avoid thinking about the Bomb.

Waking Up in the Nuclear Age, founded by psychotherapist Chellis Glendinning, offers 'Despair and Empowerment' workshops in which participants tell their 'nuclear stories', explore feelings and thoughts about nuclear weapons, and become empowered to work for common survival. 'This whole approach of acknowledging our feelings about the planet in danger seems to be distinctly "feminine"', Glendinning told me.[35] Just as she and other women found that sharing their personal histories in consciousness-raising sessions enabled them to overcome sexist conditioning, today's 'Despair and Empowerment' groups may become the basis for personal transformation and political action.

'In the Nuclear Age', Glendinning has written, 'we need, desperately, to remember our connection with one another. . . . We need to subordinate the continuation of the game for the continuation of the relationship.' Peace activist Patricia Ellsberg often speaks of the 'politics of kinship', by which she means our kinship with the earth and all life on it. The only way to ensure peace is a new 'cooperative paradigm' which enlarges our sense of identity to include all the 'others'. 'I've come to see peace work as spiritual practice', she told an audience recently.[36]

Joanna Macy, a Buddhist scholar and social activist, draws from the spiritual traditions of East and West, as well as the disciplines of philosophy and psychology, in order to help people develop the psychological and spiritual resources for social change work. Co-founder of Interhelp, an international network which facilitates Despair and Empowerment work in a variety of ways, Macy is convinced that 'deeper than the fear of nuclear holocaust is the sense that we are destroying the physical basis of life'. Therefore she is engaged in 'deep ecology' as well as peace work, both of which involve theories and practices for moving people beyond identification as a species to an identification with 'the long cosmic story'. Defining herself in part as an 'eco-feminist', Macy sees the need for women as well as men to change, or as she prefers to put it, 'awaken to their real selves, to their own expertise, and to the inter-existence of all beings', for 'we are living in a world in which there is no private salvation'.

Like many eco-feminists and peace workers, Macy argues that issues of peace, ecology, and social justice are 'inextricably intwined'. 'As long as 6 per cent of the world's population consume almost half of the planet's resources, the U.S. will remain committed to a war system.'[37]

Unlike their European counterparts, many American feminists in the peace and ecology movements do not take leftist paradigms for granted. They are, as the above examples indicate, not only more comfortable with a psycho-spiritual approach, but also critical of socialist countries with large defence budgets, patriarchal practices and inadequate environmental policies. Many women are convinced that a materialist ideology is both politically incomplete and psychologically uninspiring.

Nevertheless, I would claim that the visions of American global feminists are similar to those held by non-sectarian socialists: redistribution of the world's resources, a radically different relationship to nature and work, an end to class (as well as race and gender) hierarchy, and a deeply transformed human consciousness. Moreover, both socialist and feminist perspectives are crucial ingredients in pacifist and other social change work.

By connecting personal empowerment with institutional change and planetary healing, feminist processes and visions can provide an essential alternative to personal despair, political powerlessness, economic exploitation and the threat of global destruction. Whether one prefers to call it global feminism, spiritualised socialism, earth-centred spirituality, or some other name, this expanded feminist agenda, incorporating peace, ecology and social justice, revives the hope and possibility that human and other-than-human life will continue to exist and flourish on this planet. As both an inclusive socio-political perspective and salutary spiritual vision, global feminism deserves serious rational and emotional consideration, theoretical and experiential development, and practical, cross-cultural implementation.

Notes

1 POST-WAR CONSERVATISM AND THE FEMININE MYSTIQUE

1. This term is borrowed from the title of Betty Friedan's book, first published in 1963, in order not to confuse the post-Second World War ideology of women's role and place with such nineteenth-century terms as 'woman's sphere'. Although this volume owes to Freidan's book far more than its title, it does not necessarily agree with either its emphasis or its solutions.
2. Quoted in Sandra Dijkstra, 'Simone de Beauvoir and Betty Friedan: The Politics of Omission', *Feminist Studies*, VI, 2 (Summer 1980), 290.
3. Barbara Ehrenreich and Deirdre English, *For Her Own Good: 150 Years of the Experts' Advice to Women* (Garden City, New York: Anchor Press/Doubleday, 1978), pp. 216–17.
4. Richard J. Barnet, *Roots of War* (Baltimore: Penguin Books, 1973), pp 48–9, 118, 109. First published by Atheneum Publishers, New York, 1972.
5. Quoted in William H. Chafe, *The American Woman: Her Changing Social, Economic, and Political Roles, 1920–1970* (New York: Oxford University Press, 1972), p. 187.
6. Mary P. Ryan, *Womanhood in America: From Colonial Times to the Present*, 2nd edn (New York and London: New Viewpoints/A division of Franklin Watts, 1979), p. 173.
7. Ferdinand Lundberg and Marynia F. Farnham, MD, *Modern Woman: The Lost Sex* (New York and London: Harper & Brothers Publishers, 1947), p. 319.
8. Lillian Hellman, *An Unfinished Woman: A Memoir* (Boston: Little, Brown and Company, 1969), pp. 5 6.
9. Barbara Charlesworth Gelpi and Albert Gelpi (eds), *Adrienne Rich's Poetry* (New York: W.W. Norton, 1975), pp. 97, 126–7, 129, 95, 12. Emphasis in the original.
10. Sylvia Plath, *The Bell Jar* (New York: Bantam, 1972), p. 69. Published by arrangement with Harper & Row.
11. Adrienne Rich, *Of Woman Born: Motherhood as Experience and Institution* (New York: W.W. Norton, 1976), pp. 26 and 223. Emphasis in the original.
12. Carol Lopate, 'Daytime Television: You'll Never Want to Leave Home', *Feminist Studies*, III, 3/4 (Spring–Summer 1976), 80.
13. David Sonenschein, 'Love and Sex in the Romance Magazines', in Harry Russel Heubel (ed.), *Things in the Driver's Seat: Readings in Popular Culture* (Chicago: Rand McNally, 1972), pp. 223 and 219. Originally published in *Journal of Popular Culture*, IV, 2 (Fall 1970).
14. As reprinted in Rosalyn Baxandall, Linda Gordon and Susan Reverby (eds), *American's Working Women* (New York: Vintage/Random House, 1976), pp. 302–8.
15. Lundberg and Farnham, *Modern Woman*, pp. 396, 228–9.

16. Mirra Komarovsky, *Women in the Modern World: Their Education and Their Dilemmas* (Boston: Little, Brown, 1953), pp. 77 and 298.

17. Valerie Kincade Oppenheimer, *The Female Labor Force in the United States: Demographic and Economic Factors Governing Its Growth and Changing Composition* (Berkeley: Institute of International Studies, University of California, 1970), pp. 112–13.

18. Nancy Pottishman Weiss, 'Mother, The Invention of Necessity: Dr. Benjamin Spock's *Baby and Child Care*', *American Quarterly*, XXIX, 5 (Winter 1977), 539 and 537.

19. As quoted in Ehrenreich and English, *For Her Own Good*, p. 207. See their section 'Bad Mothers', pp. 203–11. As might be expected, Lundberg and Farnham found that somewhere between 40 to 50 per cent of mothers were rejecting, oversolicitous or overprotective, domineering or overaffectionate.

20. Betty Friedan, *The Feminine Mystique* (New York: Dell, 1974), p. 180. Originally published by W.W. Norton, 1963.

21. Frank S. Caprio, *Female Homosexuality: A Psychodynamic Study of Lesbianism* (New York: Grove Press, 1962) as quoted in Jonathan Katz (ed.), *Gay American History: Lesbians and Gay Men in the U.S.A., A Documentary* (New York: Thomas Y. Crowell, 1976), p. 185. See also Katz's Introduction to 'Treatment 1884–1974', pp. 129–34.

22. Sidney Abbott and Barbara Love, *Sappho Was a Right-On Woman: A Liberated View of Lesbianism* (New York: Stein and Day, 1973), p. 96.

23. Lillian Smith, *Killers of the Dream*, revised edn (New York: W.W. Norton, 1978), pp. 169–70.

24. Maya Angelou, *Singin' and Swingin' and Gettin' Merry Like Christmas* (New York: Bantam, 1977), p. 14. Published by arrangement with Random House.

2   WOMEN AND WORK: 1945–1970

1. Valerie Kincade Oppenheimer, *The Female Labor Force in the United States: Demographic and Economic Factors Governing Its Growth and Changing Composition* (Berkeley: Institute of International Studies, University of California, 1970), pp. 14–15.

2. National Manpower Council, *Womanpower: A Statement by the National Manpower Council with Chapters by the Council Staff* (New York: Columbia University Press, 1957), pp. 328–9.

3. Esther Peterson, 'Working Women', *Daedalus: Journal of The American Academy of Arts and Sciences*, XCIII, 2 (Spring 1964), 683.

4. Black people were about 90 per cent of those labelled 'non-white' in the United States. References are mainly to this group, as government statistics on people of 'Spanish origin' did not begin until 1973. In 1950, only Chinese-American women closely resembled whites in terms of their occupations.

5. Michel Crozier, *The World of the Office Worker*. Translated by David Landau (Chicago: University of Chicago Press, 1971), as quoted in Harry Braverman, *Labour and Monopoly Capital: The Degradation of Work in the Twentieth Century* (New York and London: Monthly Review Press, 1974), pp. 130–1.

6. Oppenheimer, *Female Labor Force*, pp. 181, 171–7, 37.

7. Ibid., pp. 135 and 104.

8. *Womanpower*, pp. 69, 72–3; Oppenheimer, *Female Labor Force*, pp. 130–1; Mirra Komarovsky, *Women in the Modern World: Their Education and Their Dilemmas* (Boston: Little, Brown, 1953), p. 167.

9. Alva Myrdal and Viola Klein, *Women's Two Roles: Home and Work*, 2nd edn (London: Routledge & Kegan Paul, 1968), p. 66.

10. Marion G. Sobol, 'Commitment to Work', in F. Ivan Nye and Lois Wladis Hoffman (eds), *The Employed Mother in America* (Chicago: Rand McNally, 1963), pp. 40–63; Robert Weiss and Nancy Samuelson, 'Social Roles of American Women: Their Contribution to a Sense of Usefulness and Importance', *Journal of Marriage and the Family*, xx (November 1958), 358–66.

11. Nancy Seifer, *Nobody Speaks for Me!: Self Portraits of American Working Class Women* (New York: Simon and Schuster, 1976), p. 262.

12. James E. Conyers, 'Employers' Attitudes toward Working Mothers', in Nye and Hoffman, *The Employed Mother*, pp. 381–3; Margaret O'Brien Steinfels, *Who's Minding the Children?: The History and Politics of Day Care in America* (New York: Simon and Schuster, 1973), p. 72.

13. Margaret Hennig and Anne Jardim, *The Managerial Woman* (New York: Pocket Books, 1978), p. 160. Published by arrangement with Doubleday.

14. Intra-racially, black women have done better in professions than white women. For example, the 1960 Census showed that black female physicians represented 9.7 of all black physicians, while white women were 6.4 per cent of white physicians. However, the percentage of white women in professional occupations was nearly double that of black women.

15. Frieda L. Gehlen, 'Women Members of Congress: A Distinctive Role', and Marcia M. Lee, 'Toward Understanding Why Few Women Hold Public Office: Factors Affecting the Participation of Women in Local Politics', in Marianne Githens and Jewel L. Prestage (eds), *A Portrait of Marginality: The Political Behavior of the American Woman* (New York: David McKay, 1977), pp. 304–19, 127; Kirsten Amundsen, *A New Look at the Silenced Majority: Women and American Democracy* (Englewood Cliffs, New Jersey: Prentice-Hall, 1977), p. 75. Emphasis in the original.

16. Frances Fox Piven and Richard A. Cloward, *Regulating the Poor: The Functions of Public Welfare* (New York: Vintage/Random House, 1972), pp. 138–9, 136. Originally published by Pantheon Books, 1971.

17. Margaret Mead and Frances Balgley Kaplan (eds), *American Women: The Report of the President's Commission on the Status of Women and Other Publications of the Commission* (New York: Charles Scribner's Sons, 1965), pp. 30 and 32.

18. *Womanpower*, p. 255.

19. The effects of maternal employment were drawn from the following articles in Nye and Hoffman, *The Employed Mother*: Alberta Engvall Siegel, Lois Meek Stolz, Ethel Alice Hitchcock and Jean Adamson, 'Dependence and Independence in Children', pp. 67–81; F. Ivan Nye, 'The Adjustment of Adolescent Children', pp. 133–41; Elizabeth Douvan, 'Employment and the Adolescent', pp. 142–64; Lois Wladis Hoffman, 'Effects on Children: Summary and Discussion', pp. 190–212; Robert O. Blood, 'The Husband-Wife Relationship', pp. 282–305.

20. Quoted in *Womanpower*, p. 349.

3 WOMEN AT HOME: CHANGES IN THE PRIVATE SPHERE

1. Mirra Komarovsky, *Blue-Collar Marriage* (New York: Vintage/Random House, 1967), p. 60.

2. Lillian B. Rubin, *Women of a Certain Age: The Midlife Search for Self* (New York: Harper & Row, 1979), p. 55. Emphasis in the original. Helena Z. Lopata, *Occupation: Housewife* (New York: Oxford University Press, 1971), pp. 47–8.

3. Sheila Rowbotham, *Woman's Consciousness, Man's World* (Harmondsworth, Penguin, 1973), p. 76.

4. Chase Manhattan Survey, 'What's a Wife Worth?' in Betsy Warrior and Lisa Leghorn (eds), *Houseworker's Handbook*, 3rd edn (Cambridge, Massachusetts:

Woman's Center, 1975), pp. 17–18. Other estimates are lower, but still a sizable percentage of the gross national product.

5. Gerda Lerner, 'Just a Housewife', in *The Majority Finds Its Past: Placing Women in History* (New York: Oxford University Press, 1979), p. 139.

6. Lillian Breslow Rubin, *Worlds of Pain: Life in the Working-Class Family* (New York: Basic Books, 1976), pp. 60–7; Edwin O. Smigel and Rita Seiden, 'The Decline and Fall of the Double Standard', in Jean E. Friedman and William G. Shade (eds), *Our American Sisters: Women in American Life and Thought* (Boston: Allyn and Bacon, 1973), p. 289.

7. Helen Mayer Hacker, 'Women as a Minority Group', *Social Forces*, xxx, 1 (October 1951), 64.

8. Komarovsky, *Blue-Collar Marriage*, p. 338; Rubin, *Worlds of Pain*, pp. 192–4; Susan Sheehan, *A Welfare Mother* (New York: Mentor/New American Library, 1976), p. 16.

9. Jessie Bernard, *The Future of Marriage* (New York: Bantam, 1973), pp. 29–32 and 52.

10. Mirra Komarovsky, *Women in the Modern World: Their Education and Their Dilemmas* (Boston: Little, Brown, 1953), p. 172. Emphasis in the original.

11. Shere Hite, *The Hite Report: A Nationwide Study of Female Sexuality* (New York: Dell, 1976), p. 229; Ruth Herschberger, *Adam's Rib* (New York: Harper & Row, 1970), pp. 96–8. Originally published by Pellegrini & Cudahy, New York, 1948.

12. Komarovsky, *Blue-Collar Marriage*, p. 85; Rubin, *Worlds of Pain*, pp. 151–2.

13. As quoted in Rosabeth Moss Kanter, *Men and Women of the Corporation* (New York: Basic Books, 1977), p. 110.

14. Rubin, *Worlds of Pain*, p. 125.

15. Adrienne Rich, *Of Woman Born: Motherhood as Experience and Institution* (New York: W.W. Norton, 1976), pp. 277 and 279.

16. Muriel Nellis, *The Female Fix* (New York: Penguin, 1981), p. 2; Mary E. King, Judith Ann Lipshutz and Audrey Moore, 'Health and Fertility Issues and the Dependency of Wives', in Jane Roberts Chapman and Margaret Gates (eds), *Women Into Wives: The Legal and Economic Impact of Marriage* (Beverly Hills, California and London: Sage Publications, 1977), pp. 132–5.

17. Bonnie Thornton Dill, '"The Means to Put My Children Through": Child-Rearing Goals and Strategies Among Black Female Domestic Servants', in La Frances Rodgers-Rose (ed.), *The Black Woman* (Beverly Hills, California and London: Sage Publications, 1980), p. 113. As late as 1975, whites were twice as likely as blacks to be college graduates.

18. Alice S. Rossi, 'Life-Span Theories and Women's Lives', *Signs: Journal of Women in Culture and Society*, vi, 1 (Autumn 1980), 15 and 23.

19. Lopata, *Occupation: Housewife*, pp. 167–72; Joann Vanek, 'Time Spent in Housework', in Nancy F. Cott and Elizabeth H. Pleck (eds), *A Heritage of Her Own: Toward a New Social History of American Women* (New York: Simon and Schuster, 1979), pp. 500–2.

20. Edith M. Stein, 'Women Are Household Slaves', in Aileen S. Kraditor (ed.), *Up From the Pedestal: Selected Writings in the History of American Feminism* (Chicago: Quadrangle, 1970), p. 352. Originally published in *American Mercury*, lxviii (January 1949), 71–6.

21. Rubin, *Worlds of Pain*, p. 104.

22. Doris B. Gold, 'Women and Voluntarism', in Vivian Gornick and Barbara K. Moran (eds), *Women in Sexist Society: Studies in Power and Powerlessness* (New York: New American Library, 1972), pp. 534–5 and 552. Originally published by Basic Books, New York, 1971. G. William Domhoff, *The Higher Circles: The Governing Class in America* (New York: Vintage/Random House, 1971), p. 35.

23. Stephanie Gervis, 'Women Speak Out for Peace', *The Nation*, cxciii, 23 (30 December 1961), 524.

24. Daisy Bates, *The Long Shadow of Little Rock: A Memoir* (New York: David McKay, 1962), as quoted in Gerda Lerner (ed.), *Black Women in White America: A Documentary History* (New York: Vintage/Random House, 1973), p. 422.

4   WOMEN IN THE POLITICAL MOVEMENTS OF THE 1960s

1. Jo Freeman, *The Politics of Women's Liberation: A Case Study of an Emerging Social Movement and Its Relation to the Policy Process* (New York: David McKay, 1975), pp. 15–17 and 29.

2. Sara Evans, *Personal Politics: The Roots of Women's Liberation in the Civil Rights Movement and the New Left* (New York: Alfred A. Knopf, 1979), p. 35.

3. SNCC Founding Statement, in Massimo Teodori (ed.), *The New Left: A Documentary History* (Indianapolis and New York: Bobbs-Merrill, 1969), pp. 99–100; Nash, as quoted in Clayborne Carson, Jr, 'Toward Freedom and Community: The Evolution of Ideas in the Student Nonviolent Coordinating Committee, 1960–1966' (University of California, Los Angeles: unpublished dissertation, 1975), p. 69.

4. Lonnie King, in Howell Raines, *My Soul Is Rested: Movement Days in the Deep South Remembered* (New York: Bantam, 1978), p. 86. Published by arrangement with G. P. Putnam's Sons.

5. Lillian Smith, 'On Women's Autobiography', *Southern Exposure*, iv, 4 (Winter 1977), 49.

6. As quoted in Evans, *Personal Politics*, p. 50.

7. As quoted in Ellen Cantarow and Susan Gushee O'Malley, 'Ella Baker: Organizing for Civil Rights', in Ellen Cantarow, *Moving the Mountain: Women Working for Social Change* (Old Westbury, New York: The Feminist Press, 1980), p. 53.

8. Cynthia Washington, '"We started from different ends of the spectrum"', *Southern Exposure*, iv, 4 (Winter 1977), 14; black woman, as quoted in Evans, *Personal Politics*, p. 81.

9. Evans, *Personal Politics*, p. 88.

10. Quoted in ibid., p. 81.

11. Gloria I. Joseph and Jill Lewis, *Common Differences: Conflicts in Black and White Feminist Perspectives* (Garden City, New York: Anchor/Doubleday, 1981), pp. 109–10.

12. Evans, *Personal Politics*, pp. 234–6 and 87.

13. Stokely Carmichael and Charles V. Hamilton, *Black Power: The Politics of Liberation in America* (New York: Vintage/Random House, 1967), pp. 37, 81, 46–7. Emphasis in the original.

14. Alice Walker, '"The Civil Rights Movement: What Good Was It?"', *The American Scholar*, xxxvi, 4 (Autumn 1967), 551.

15. Ellen Kay Trimberger, 'Women in the Old and New Left: The Evolution of a Politics of Personal Life', *Feminist Studies*, v, 3 (Fall 1979), 442.

16. C. Wright Mills, *The Sociological Imagination* (New York: Grove Press, 1961), p. 188. Originally published by Oxford University Press, 1959.

17. As quoted in Kirkpatrick Sale, *SDS* (New York: Vintage/Random House, 1974), pp. 238–9.

18. SDS: Port Huron Statement, in Teodori, *The New Left*, pp. 165, 167–8.

19. Evans, *Personal Politics*, p. 137.

20. Ibid., p. 157.

21. Ibid., pp. 240–2, 192, 199; Shulamith Firestone, *The Dialectic of Sex: The Case*

for Feminist Revolution (New York: Bantam, 1971), p. 37. Published by arrangement with William Morrow.

22. Ann Popkin, 'The Personal Is Political: The Women's Liberation Movement', in Dick Cluster (ed.), *They Should Have Served That Cup of Coffee: 7 Radicals Remember the 60s* (Boston: South End Press, 1979), pp. 198–200.

23. Marge Piercy, 'The Grand Coolie Dam', in Robin Morgan (ed.), *Sisterhood Is Powerful: An Anthology of Writings from the Women's Liberation Movement* (New York: Vintage/Random House, 1970), pp. 421–38.

24. Robin Morgan, 'Part III: Introductory Note', and 'Goodbye to All That', in *Going Too Far: The Personal Chronicle of a Feminist* (New York: Vintage/Random House, 1978), pp. 118 and 127.

5   WOMEN AND THE 1960s COUNTERCULTURE

1. Dorothy Dinnerstein, *The Mermaid and the Minotaur: Sexual Arrangements and Human Malaise* (New York: Harper & Row, 1976), pp. 267–8. Author's emphasis omitted.

2. Norman O. Brown, *Life Against Death: The Psychoanalytical Meaning of History* (Middletown, Connecticut: Wesleyan University Press, 1970), pp. 307–8. Originally published in 1959.

3. Theodore Roszak, *The Making of a Counter Culture: Reflections on the Technocratic Society and Its Youthful Opposition* (Garden City, New York: Doubleday, 1969), p. 218. See Chapter VII, 'The Myth of Objective Consciousness', pp. 205–38, for full discussion.

4. Philip E. Slater, *The Pursuit of Loneliness: American Culture at the Breaking Point* (Boston: Beacon Press, 1970), p. 90.

5. Ellen Willis, 'The Family: Love It or Leave It', in *Beginning to See the Light: Pieces of a Decade* (Wideview Books/PEI Books, 1982), p. 155. Originally published by Alfred A. Knopf, New York, 1981.

6. Myra Friedman, *Buried Alive: The Biography of Janis Joplin* (New York: Bantam, 1974), p. 155. Originally published by William Morrow, New York.

7. Willis, 'Janis Joplin', in *Beginning to See the Light*, p. 62.

8. Alix Kates Shulman, 'Sex and Power: Sexual Bases of Radical Feminism', *Signs: Journal of Women in Culture and Society*, v, 4 (Summer 1980), 592 and 594.

9. Barbara Ehrenreich and Deirdre English, *For Her Own Good: 150 Years of the Experts' Advice to Women* (Garden City, New York: Anchor/Doubleday, 1978), pp. 259 and 273.

10. Ralph J. Gleason, 'Like a Rolling Stone', *The American Scholar*, XXXVI, 4 (Autumn 1967), 556–7. Emphasis in the original.

11. Katherine Orloff, *Rock 'N Roll Woman* (Los Angeles: Nash Publishing, 1974). Interviews with Grace Slick, Terry Garthwaite and Bonnie Raitt, pp. 160, 73, 65 and 115.

12. Willis, *Beginning to See the Light*, p. 99.

13. Robin Morgan, 'Women Disrupt the Miss America Pageant' and 'Three Articles on WITCH', in *Going Too Far: The Personal Chronicle of a Feminist* (New York: Vintage/Random House, 1978), pp. 64 and 74.

14. Margaret Fuller, 'Woman in the Nineteenth Century', in Perry Miller (ed.), *Margaret Fuller: American Romantic: A Selection from Her Writings and Correspondence* (Ithaca, New York: Cornell University Press, 1963), pp. 137 and 172.

15. Sherry B. Ortner, 'Is Female to Male as Nature Is to Culture?', in Michelle

Zimbalist Rosaldo and Louise Lamphere (eds), *Women, Culture, and Society* (Stanford, California: Stanford University Press, 1974), p. 73.

16. Simone de Beauvoir, *The Second Sex*, translated and edited by H. M. Parshley (New York: Bantam, 1961), pp. 138, 145 and 60.

17. Joseph Epes Brown, *The Sacred Pipe: Black Elk's Account of the Seven Rites of the Oglala Sioux* (Baltimore, Maryland: Penguin, 1971), pp. 5–6.

18. Barbara Starrett, 'I Dream in Female: The Metaphors of Evolution', in Gina Covina and Laurel Galana (eds), *The Lesbian Reader: An Amazon Quarterly Anthology* (Oakland, California: Amazon Press, 1975), p. 112.

19. 'WITCH Documents', in Robin Morgan (ed.), *Sisterhood Is Powerful: An Anthology of Writings from the Women's Liberation Movement* (New York: Vintage/Random House, 1970), pp. 539–40.

20. Jules Henry, *Pathways to Madness* (New York: Vintage/Random House, 1973), p. 374.

21. Rosabeth Moss Kanter, *Commitment and Community: Communes and Utopias in Sociological Perspective* (Cambridge, Massachusetts: Harvard University Press, 1972), p. 174; Kit Leder, 'Women in Communes', *Women: A Journal of Liberation*, I, 1 (Fall 1969), 34.

22. William Hedgepeth and Dennis Stock, *The Alternative: Communal Life in New America* (New York: Macmillan, 1970), p. 74. Emphasis in the original.

23. Kinkade, quoted in Richard Fairfield, *Communes USA: A Personal Tour* (Baltimore, Maryland: Penguin, 1972), p. 98; Kathleen Kinkade, *A Walden Two Experiment: The First Five Years of Twin Oaks Community* (New York: William Morrow, 1973), p. 171.

24. Leder, 'Women in Communes', 34–5.

25. Vivian Estellachild, 'Hippie Communes', *Women: A Journal of Liberation*, II, 2 (Winter, 1971), 40–3; Judith of Lime Saddle, 'Some Views from Women in Communes', *Communities*, 7 (March–April 1974), 13.

6   THE POLITICS OF THE WOMEN'S MOVEMENT

1. Quoted in Judith Hole and Ellen Levine, *Rebirth of Feminism* (New York: Quadrangle, 1971), p. 85. Emphasis in the original.

2. Amy Swerdlow, 'Ladies' Day at the Capitol: Women Strike for Peace Versus HUAC', *Feminist Studies*, VIII, 3 (Fall 1982), 515.

3. Quoted in Hole and Levine, *Rebirth*, pp. 441–2.

4. Kate Millett, *Flying* (New York: Ballantine, 1974), p. 22; NOW, quoted in Sidney Abbott and Barbara Love, *Sappho Was a Right-On Woman: A Liberated View of Lesbianism* (New York: Stein and Day, 1972), p. 134.

5. Jo Freeman, *The Politics of Women's Liberation: A Case Study of an Emerging Social Movement and Its Relation to the Policy Process* (New York: David McKay, 1975), pp. 91–2.

6. Alice S. Rossi, 'Equality Between the Sexes: An Immodest Proposal', *Daedalus*, XCIII, 2 (Spring 1964), 608–9. More recently, however, Rossi has given respectful (and to some feminists, reactionary) consideration to biological differences between men and women. See her 'A Biosocial Perspective on Parenting', *Daedalus*, CVI (Spring 1977), 1–31.

7. Freeman, *Politics*, p. 98.

8. Juliet Mitchell, 'Women: The Longest Revolution', reprinted from *New Left Review* (November–December 1966), distributed by New England Free Press, Somerville, Massachusetts, p. 20. Emphasis in the original.

9. Sheila Rowbotham, *Woman's Consciousness, Man's World* (Harmondsworth: Penguin, 1973), pp. xv and 124; Juliet Mitchell, *Woman's Estate* (Harmondsworth: Penguin, 1971), p. 99.

10. Kirkpatrick Sale, *SDS* (New York: Vintage/Random House, 1974), p. 509.

11. Barbara Burris *et al.*, 'The Fourth World Manifesto', in Anne Koedt, Ellen Levine and Anita Rapone (eds), *Radical Feminism* (New York: Quadrangle, 1973), pp. 335 and 355.

12. Constance M. Carroll, 'Three's a Crowd: The Dilemma of the Black Woman in Higher Education', in Gloria T. Hull *et al.* (eds), *All the Women Are White, All the Blacks Are Men, But Some of Us Are Brave: Black Women's Studies* (Old Westbury, New York: The Feminist Press, 1982), pp. 122–3. Reprinted from Alice S. Rossi and Ann Calderwood (eds), *Academic Women on the Move* (Russell Sage Foundation, 1973).

13. Barbara Ehrenreich and Deirdre English, 'The Manufacture of Housework', in *Capitalism and the Family* (San Francisco: Agenda Publishing Company, 1976), pp. 31–2. Reprinted from *Socialist Revolution*, xxvi (October–December 1975).

14. Heidi Hartmann, 'Capitalism, Patriarchy, and Job Segregation by Sex'; Batya Weinbaum and Amy Bridges, 'The Other Side of the Paycheck: Monopoly Capital and the Structure of Consumption'; Nancy Hartsock, 'Feminist Theory and the Development of Revolutionary Strategy'; and the Combahee River Collective, 'A Black Feminist Statement', in Zillah R. Eisenstein (ed.), *Capitalist Patriarchy and the Case for Socialist Feminism* (New York and London: Monthly Review Press, 1979), pp. 217, 201, 61 and 371.

15. Deirdre English, Barbara Epstein, Barbara Haber and Judy MacLean, 'The Impasse of Socialist-Feminism', *Socialist Review*, xv, 1 (January–February 1985), 103; Adele Clark and Alice Wolfson, 'Socialist-Feminism and Reproductive Rights: Movement Work and Its Contradictions', *Socialist Review*, xiv, 6 (November–December 1984), 114.

16. Joyce Maupin, *Working Women and Their Organizations – 150 Years of Struggle* (Berkeley, California: Union WAGE Educational Committee, 1974), p. 30.

17. Jean Tepperman, *Not Servants, Not Machines: Office Workers Speak Out* (Boston: Beacon Press, 1976), p. 172.

18. Kathie Sarachild, 'Consciousness-Raising: A Radical Weapon' and 'A Program for Feminist Consciousness-Raising', in Redstockings of the Women's Liberation Movement, *Feminist Revolution: An Abridged Edition with Additional Writings* (New York: Random House, 1978), pp. 147 and 202.

19. 'Redstockings Manifesto', in Robin Morgan (ed.), *Sisterhood Is Powerful: An Anthology of Writings from the Women's Liberation Movement* (New York: Vintage/Random House, 1970), p. 533.

20. Pamela Allen, *Free Space: A Perspective on the Small Group in Women's Liberation* (New York: Times Change Press, 1970), pp. 26 and 28.

21. Kate Millett, *Sexual Politics* (New York: Avon/Hearst, 1970), pp. 33 and 58.

22. Shulamith Firestone, *The Dialectic of Sex: The Case for Feminist Revolution* (New York: Bantam, 1971), pp. 37, 11, 130, 72–3 and 206. Emphases in the original. Originally published by William Morrow, New York, 1970.

23. Adrienne Rich, *Of Woman Born: Motherhood as Experience and Institution* (New York: W.W. Norton, 1976), pp. 39 and 284. Emphases in the original.

24. Joreen [Jo Freeman], 'The Tyranny of Structurelessness', in Koedt *et al.*, *Radical Feminism*, p. 293.

25. Gayle Graham Yates, *What Women Want: The Ideas of the Movement* (Cambridge: Massachusetts and London: Harvard University Press, 1975), p. 102.

26. Natalie J. Sokoloff, *Between Money and Love: The Dialectics of Women's Home and Market Work* (New York: Praeger, 1980), pp. 160 and 154.

27. Lisa Leghorn and Katherine Parker, *Woman's Worth: Sexual Economics and the*

World of Women (Boston and London: Routledge & Kegan Paul, 1981), pp. 32 and 80.

28. Robin Morgan, 'Theory and Practice: Pornography and Rape', in *Going Too Far: The Personal Chronicle of a Feminist* (New York: Vintage/Random House, 1978), p. 169.

29. Irene Diamond, 'Pornography and Repression: A Reconsideration of "Who" and "What"', in Laura Lederer (ed.), *Take Back the Night: Women on Pornography* (New York: Bantam, 1982), pp. 189–90, 196–7. Emphasis in the original. Originally published by William Morrow, 1980. Susan Brownmiller, *Against Our Will: Men, Women and Rape* (New York: Bantam, 1976), p. 443. Originally published by Simon and Schuster, 1975.

30. Alice Echols, 'The Taming of the Id: Feminist Sexual Politics, 1968–83' and Gayle Rubin, 'Thinking Sex: Notes for a Radical Theory of the Politics of Sexuality', in Carole S. Vance (ed.), *Pleasure and Danger: Exploring Female Sexuality* (Boston and London: Routledge & Kegan Paul, 1984), pp. 65 and 302.

31. Angela Y. Davis, *Women, Race & Class* (New York: Random House, 1981), p. 204.

32. Rosalind Pollack Petchesky, 'Reproductive Freedom: Beyond "A Woman's Right to Choose"', *Signs: Journal of Women in Culture and Society*, v, 4 (Summer 1980), 670.

33. Carol Gilligan, *In a Different Voice: Psychological Theory and Women's Development* (Cambridge, Massachusetts and London: Harvard University Press, 1982), pp. 19, 100 and 118.

34. Kristin Booth Glen, 'Abortion in the Courts: A Laywoman's Historical Guide to the New Disaster Area', *Feminist Studies*, iv, 1 (February 1978), 9 and 18. Emphasis in the original.

7 SEX, LOVE AND FAMILY RELATIONSHIPS

1. Kate Millett, *Sexual Politics* (New York: Avon/The Hearst Corporation, 1971), p. 6. Originally published by Doubleday, 1970; Linda Phelps, 'Female Sexual Alienation', in Jo Freeman (ed.), *Women: A Feminist Perspective*, 2nd edn (Palo Alto, California: Mayfield Publishing Company, 1979), p. 21.

2. Anne Koedt, 'The Myth of the Vaginal Orgasm', in Anne Koedt, Ellen Levine and Anita Rapone (eds), *Radical Feminism* (New York: Quadrangle/The New York Times Book Co., 1973), p. 206. Emphasis in the original.

3. Margaret Adams, 'The Compassion Trap', in Vivian Gornick and Barbara K. Moran (eds), *Woman in Sexist Society: Studies in Power and Powerlessness* (New York: Signet/New American Library, 1972), p. 556. Originally published by Basic Books, 1971.

4. Shulamith Firestone, *The Dialectic of Sex: The Case for Feminist Revolution* (New York: Bantam, 1971), pp. 138–9. Originally published by William Morrow, 1970.

5. Nancy Chodorow, *The Reproduction of Mothering: Psychoanalysis and the Sociology of Gender* (Berkeley and Los Angeles: University of California Press, 1978), p. 214. Dorothy Dinnerstein's earlier, more impressionistic study, *The Mermaid and the Minotaur: Sexual Arrangements and Human Malaise* (New York: Harper & Row, 1976) also emphasises the need for shared parenting.

6. Ann Barr Snitow, 'The Front Line: Notes on Sex in Novels by Women, 1969–1979', *Signs: Journal of Women in Culture and Society*, v, 4 (Summer 1980), 718.

7. Radicalesbians, 'The Woman Identified Woman', in Koedt *et al.*, *Radical Feminism*, p. 240.

8. Charlotte Bunch, 'Lesbians in Revolt', in Nancy Myron and Charlotte Bunch (eds), *Lesbianism and the Women's Movement* (Baltimore, Maryland: Diana Press, 1975), pp. 30–1; Jill Johnston, *Lesbian Nation: The Feminist Solution* (New York: Simon & Schuster, 1974), p. 90.

9. Lillian Faderman, *Surpassing the Love of Men: Romantic Friendship and Love Between Women from the Renaissance to the Present* (New York: William Morrow, 1981), pp. 17–18.

10. The Combahee River Collective, 'A Black Feminist Statement', in Zillah R. Eisenstein (ed.), *Capitalist Patriarchy and the Case for Socialist Feminism* (New York and London: Monthly Review Press, 1979), pp. 365 and 367.

11. Adrienne Rich, 'Compulsory Heterosexuality and Lesbian Existence', *Signs*, v, 4 (Summer 1980), 648–9; Audre Lorde, 'Uses of the Erotic: The Erotic as Power', in Laura Lederer (ed.), *Take Back the Night: Women on Pornography* (New York: Bantam, 1982), p. 297. Lorde's essay was first published by Out and Out Books, November 1978.

12. Adrienne Rich, 'Women and Honor: Some Notes on Lying (1975)', in *On Lies, Secrets, and Silence: Selected Prose 1966–1978* (New York: W.W. Norton, 1979), p. 190.

13. Gayle Rubin, 'Thinking Sex: Notes for a Radical Theory of the Politics of Sexuality' and Amber Hollibaugh, 'Desire for the Future: Radical Hope in Passion and Pleasure', in Carole S. Vance (ed.), *Pleasure and Danger: Exploring Female Sexuality* (Boston and London: Routledge & Kegan Paul, 1984), pp. 301, 407–8.

14. Betty Friedan, *The Second Stage* (New York: Summit Books/Simon & Schuster, 1981), p. 74.

15. United States Commission on Civil Rights, *A Growing Crisis: Disadvantaged Women and Their Children* (Washington, DC: Clearinghouse Publication 78, May 1983), pp. 12, 7–8; Karin Stallard, Barbara Ehrenreich and Holly Sklar, *Poverty in the American Dream: Women & Children First* (Boston: South End Press, 1983), p. 31.

16. Susan Schechter, *Women and Male Violence: The Visions and Struggles of the Battered Women's Movement* (Boston: South End Press, 1982), p. 12.

17. Ibid., pp. 235, 271–2.

18. Carol Stack, *All Our Kin: Strategies for Survival in a Black Community* (New York: Harper & Row, 1974), pp. 31, 113–14; Rayna Rapp, 'Family and Class in Contemporary America: Notes Toward an Understanding of Ideology', in Barrie Thorne with Marilyn Yalom (eds), *Rethinking the Family: Some Feminist Questions* (New York and London: Longman, 1982), p. 180.

19. Gloria I. Joseph, 'Styling, Profiling, and Pretending: The Games Before the Fall', in Gloria I. Joseph and Jill Lewis, *Common Differences: Conflicts in Black and White Feminist Perspectives* (Garden City, New York: Anchor/Doubleday, 1981), pp. 216 and 192.

20. Gloria I. Joseph, 'Black Mothers and Daughters: Their Roles and Functions in American Society,', in ibid., pp. 123–5.

21. Sara Ruddick, 'Maternal Thinking', *Feminist Studies*, vi, 2 (Summer 1980), 350 and 361.

8 EDUCATION, ART AND SPIRITUALITY

1. Gayle Kimball, 'Defining Women's Culture: Interview with Robin Morgan', in Gayle Kimball (ed.), *Women's Culture: The Women's Renaissance of the Seventies* (Metuchen, New Jersey and London: Scarecrow Press, 1981), p. 31; Adrienne Rich, 'Toward a Woman-Centered University', in Florence Howe (ed.), *Women and the*

Power to Change, A Volume of Essays Sponsored by the Carnegie Commission on Higher Education (New York: McGraw-Hill, 1975), p. 16.

2. Florence Howe, 'Introduction', to Tamar Berkowitz, Jean Mang and Jane Williamson (eds), *Who's Who and Where in Women's Studies* (Old Westbury, New York: The Feminist Press, 1974), p. vii; Florence Howe, *Seven Years Later: Women's Studies Programs in 1976* (Old Westbury, New York: National Advisory Council on Women's Educational Programs, June 1977), p. 15; Marilyn J. Boxer, 'For and About Women: The Theory and Practice of Women's Studies in the United States', *Signs: Journal of Women in Culture and Society*, VII, 3 (Spring 1982), 672.

3. Gloria T. Hull and Barbara Smith, 'Introduction: The Politics of Black Women's Studies', in Gloria T. Hull, Patricia Bell Scott and Barbara Smith (eds), *All the Women Are White, All the Blacks Are Men, But Some of Us Are Brave: Black Women's Studies* (Old Westbury, New York: The Feminist Press, 1982), p. xxvi and course syllabi, pp. 337–78.

4. Florence Howe and Carol Ahlum, 'Women's Studies and Social Change', in Alice S. Rossi and Ann Calderwood (eds), *Academic Women on the Move* (New York: Russell Sage Foundation, 1975), p. 404.

5. United States Commission on Civil Rights, *Characters in Textbooks: A Review of the Literature* (Washington, DC: US Government Printing Office, Clearinghouse Publication 62, May 1980), pp. 10–12, 18–19.

6. Bureau of the Census, US Department of Commerce, *A Statistical Portrait of Women in the United States: 1978* (Washington, DC: US Government Printing Office, Current Population Reports, Special Studies, Series P-23, No. 100, 1980), p. 39; 'Proportion of Degrees Awarded to Women,' *The Chronicle of Higher Education*, XXII (15 June 1981), 8.

7. Betty Willis Brooks and Sharon L. Sievers, 'The New Right Challenges Women's Studies: The Long Beach Women's Studies Program', in Charlotte Bunch and Sandra Pollack (eds), *Learning Our Way: Essays in Feminist Education* (Trumansburg, New York: The Crossing Press, 1983), pp.78–88, and other essays in that volume.

8. David Armstrong, *A Trumpet to Arms: Alternative Media in America* (Los Angeles: J.P. Tarcher, 1981), p. 226.

9. Judy Chicago, *Through the Flower: My Struggle as a Woman Artist* (Garden City, New York: Anchor/Doubleday, 1977), pp. 36 and 55.

10. Alice Walker, 'In Search of Our Mothers' Gardens', in *In Search of Our Mothers' Gardens: Womanist Prose by Alice Walker* (New York: Harcourt Brace Jovanovich, 1983), pp. 233, 240–2.

11. Rita Mae Brown, *Rubyfruit Jungle* (Plainfield, Vermont: Daughters, Inc., 1973), p. 213; June Arnold, *Sister Gin* (Plainfield, Vermont: Daughters, Inc., 1975), p. 189.

12. 'Adrienne Rich and Robin Morgan Talk about Poetry and Women's Culture', in Kirsten Grimstad and Susan Rennie (eds), *The New Woman's Survival Sourcebook* (New York: Alfred A. Knopf, 1975), p. 110.

13. Quoted in Mary Helen Washington, 'Teaching *Black-Eyed Susans*: An Approach to the Study of Black Women Writers', in Hull *et al.*, . . . *But Some of Us Are Brave*, p. 214.

14. Rita M. Gross, 'Female God Language in a Jewish Context', and Rosemary Radford Ruether, 'Motherearth and the Megamachine: A Theology of Liberation in a Feminine, Somatic and Ecological Perspective', in Carol P. Christ and Judith Plaskow (eds), *Womenspirit Rising: A Feminist Reader in Religion* (San Francisco: Harper & Row, 1979), pp. 168 and 48.

15. Mary Daly, *The Church and the Second Sex: With a New Feminist Postchristian Introduction by the Author* (New York: Harper & Row, 1975), pp. 213 and 219; Mary

Daly, *Beyond God the Father: Toward a Philosophy of Women's Liberation* (Boston: Beacon Press, 1973), pp. 6, 33–4, 96–7; Mary Daly, *Gyn/Ecology: The Metaethics of Radical Feminism* (Boston: Beacon Press, 1978).

16. Carol P. Christ, 'Why Women Need the Goddess: Phenomenological, Psychological, and Political Reflections', in Christ and Plaskow, *Womanspirit Rising*, p. 276.

17. Starhawk, *Dreaming the Dark: Magic, Sex & Politics* (Boston: Beacon Press, 1982), pp. 11–12.

18. Starhawk, *The Spiral Dance: A Rebirth of the Ancient Religion of the Great Goddess* (San Francisco: Harper & Row, 1979), pp. 7 and 35.

19. Starhawk, *Dreaming the Dark*, pp. 13 and 28. Emphasis in the original.

20. Ibid., p. 138.

21. Gina Foglia and Dorit Wolffberg, 'Spiritual Dimensions of Feminist Anti-Nuclear Activism', in Charlene Spretnak (ed.), *The Politics of Women's Spirituality: Essays on the Rise of Spiritual Power Within the Feminist Movement* (Garden City, New York: Anchor/Doubleday, 1982), p. 457.

9 RACE AND CLASS IN WOMEN'S LIVES

1. In this chapter, the terms 'racial ethnic women' and 'women of colour' are used to refer to women who are members of groups which are both culturally and racially distinct and, in the US, have shared certain common conditions as oppressed and internally colonised people. 'Third World Women' has international connotations, but it does not fit all Asian-American, especially Japanese-American, women. 'White ethnic' refers to women whose inherited culture has been European and who are usually, but not always, of Catholic or Jewish faith.

2. Bonnie Thornton Dill, 'Race, Class, and Gender: Prospects for an All-inclusive Sisterhood', *Feminist Studies*, IX, 1 (Spring 1983), 134.

3. Frances Beal, 'Double Jeopardy: to be Black & Female' (Detroit, Michigan: Radical Education Project, n.d.) pp. 11 and 4.

4. Michael Wilson, Screenplay, and Deborah Silverton Rosenfelt, Commentary, *Salt of the Earth* (Old Westbury, New York: The Feminist Press, 1978), p. 82. Emphasis in the original. Screenplay copyright 1953.

5. Ellen Cantarow, 'Jessie Lopez De La Cruz: The Battle for Farmworkers' Rights', in *Moving the Mountain: Women Working for Social Change* (Old Westbury, New York: The Feminist Press and New York: McGraw-Hill, 1980), p. 136.

6. Sylvia Gonzales, 'Toward a Feminist Pedagogy for Chicana Self-Actualization', *Frontiers: A Journal of Women Studies*, V, 2 (Summer 1980), 49.

7. Audre Lorde, 'Age, Race, Class, and Sex: Women Redefining Difference', in *Sister Outsider: Essays and Speeches* (Trumansburg, New York: The Crossing Press, 1984), p. 120; Merle Woo, 'Letter to Ma', and Barbara Cameron, '"Gee, You Don't Seem Like An Indian From the Reservation"', in Cherríe Moraga and Gloria Anzaldúa (eds), *This Bridge Called My Back: Writings By Radical Women of Color* (Watertown, Massachusetts: Persephone Press, 1981), pp. 141, 143, 48–50.

8. Donna Redmond, 'I'm proud to Be a Hillbilly', in Kathy Kahn, *Hillbilly Women* (New York: Avon/Hearst, 1973), p. 118.

9. Cherríe Moraga, 'La Güera', in Moraga and Anzaldúa, *This Bridge*, p. 33. Emphasis in the original.

10. Elly Bulkin, 'Hard Ground: Jewish Identity, Racism, and Anti-Semitism', in Elly Bulkin, Minnie Bruce Pratt and Barbara Smith, *Yours in Struggle: Three Feminist Perspectives on Anti-Semitism and Racism* (Brooklyn, New York: Long Haul Press,

1984), p. 149; Alice Walker, 'To the Editors of *Ms.* Magazine', in *In Search of Our Mothers' Gardens: Womanist Prose* (New York: Harcourt Brace Jovanovich, 1983), p. 354.

11. Adrienne Rich, 'Disloyal to Civilization: Feminism, Racism, Gynephobia (1978)', in *On Lies, Secrets, and Silence: Selected Prose 1966–1978* (New York: W.W. Norton, 1979), p. 306; Lorde, 'The Uses of Anger: Women Responding to Racism', and 'Age, Race, Class, and Sex', in *Sister Outsider*, pp. 131 and 119.

12. Barbara Smith and Beverly Smith, 'Across the Kitchen Table: A Sister-to-Sister Dialogue', and Judit Moschkovich, ' " – But I Know You, American Woman"', in Moraga and Anzaldúa, *This Bridge*, pp. 126 and 83. Emphasis in the original. Lorde's letter to Daly is printed in both *Bridge* and *Sister Outsider*.

13. Rich, 'Disloyal to Civilization', p. 308.

14. Lorde, 'Uses of Anger', and 'The Master's Tools Will Never Dismantle the Master's House', in *Sister Outsider*, pp. 132, 111 and 113. Emphases in the original.

15. Walker, p. xi and 'Gifts of Power: The Writings of Rebecca Jackson,' in *Mothers' Gardens*, p. 81. Emphases in the original.

16. Gloria I. Joseph, 'Styling, Profiling, and Pretending: The Games Before the Fall', in Gloria I. Joseph and Jill Lewis, *Common Differences: Conflicts in Black and White Feminist Perspectives* (Garden City, New York: Anchor/Doubleday, 1981), pp. 291 and 189; Oliva M. Espín, 'Cultural and Historical Influences on Sexuality in Hispanic/Latin Women: Implications for Psychotherapy', in Carole S. Vance (ed.), *Pleasure and Danger: Exploring Female Sexuality* (Boston and London: Routledge & Kegan Paul, 1984), p. 158.

17. Bell Hooks, *Ain't I a Woman: Black Women and Feminism* (Boston: South End Press, 1981), pp. 68 and 82.

18. Alfredo Mirandé and Evangelina Enríquez, *La Chicana: The Mexican-American Woman* (Chicago and London: The University of Chicago Press, 1979), p. 183.

19. Espín, 'Cultural and Historical Influences', pp. 155–6; Joseph, 'Styling . . .', p. 214.

20. Joyce A. Ladner, *Tomorrow's Tomorrow: The Black Woman* (Garden City, New York: Anchor/Doubleday, 1971), p. 212; Margarita B. Meville (ed.), *Twice A Minority: Mexican American Women* (St Louis: C.V. Mosby, 1980), p. 11.

21. Robert Coles, MD, *The South Goes North: Volume III of Children of Crisis* (Boston: Little, Brown, 1971), p. 595; Carlos G. Velez-I, 'The Nonconsenting Sterilization of Mexican Women in Los Angeles. Issues of Psychocultural Rupture and Legal Redress in Paternalistic Behavioral Environments', in Melville, *Twice a Minority*, pp. 241–2.

22. Rosalind Pollack Petchesky, *Abortion and Woman's Choice: The State, Sexuality, and Reproductive Freedom* (New York and London: Longman, 1984), pp. 154–5, 149, 152.

23. Velez-I, 'Nonconsenting Sterilization . . .', p. 210, Angela Y. Davis, *Women, Race & Class* (New York: Random House, 1981), pp. 216–19; Peter Layde et al., 'Demographic Trends of Tubal Sterilization in the United States: 1970–75', *Journal of Public Health*, LXX, 8 (1980), 808–12; Dr Helen Rodriguez-Trias, MD, *Women & the Health Care System, Sterilization Abuse: Two Lectures*, 2nd edn (New York: The Women's Center, Barnard College, 1980), pp. 28 and 15; Petchesky, *Abortion and . . . Choice*, pp. 178–80; Thomas M. Shapiro, *Population Control Politics: Women, Sterilization, and Reproductive Choice* (Philadelphia: Temple University Press, 1985), p. 98.

24. Sally J. Andrade, 'Family Planning Practices of Mexican Americans', in Melville, *Twice a Minority*, p. 29.

25. Nan Elsasser, Kyle MacKenzie and Yvonne Tixier y Vigil, *Las Mujeres: Conversations from a Hispanic Community* (Old Westbury, New York: The Feminist Press, 1980), pp. 65 and 55.

26. Redmond, in Kahn, *Hillbilly Women*, pp. 116–17; Sylvia Rabiner, quoted in Louise Kapp Howe, *Pink Collar Workers: Inside the World of Women's Work* (New York: Avon/Hearst, 1978), unnumbered introductory page. Emphasis omitted. Originally published by G. P. Putnam's Sons, 1977.

27. Bettylou Valentine, *Hustling and Other Hard Work: Life Styles in the Ghetto* (New York: Free Press/Macmillan, 1978), pp. 46, 70–1, 132–3; Mary Corcoran, Greg J. Duncan and Martha S. Hill, 'The Economic Fortunes of Women and Children: Lessons from the Panel Study of Income Dynamics', *Signs: Journal of Women in Culture and Society*, x, 2 (Winter 1984), 245–6.

28. Maxine Hong Kingston, *The Woman Warrior: Memoirs of a Girlhood Among Ghosts* (New York: Vintage/Random House, 1976), pp. 214–15.

29. Terry Mason, 'Symbolic Strategies for Change: A Discussion of the Chicana Women's Movement', in Melville, *Twice a Minority*, p. 105.

30. Elliott Curie, Robert Dunn and David Fogarty, 'The New Immiseration: Stagflation, Inequality, and The Working Class', *Socialist Review*, x, 6 (November–December 1980), 12, 19–20. Unless otherwise noted, the statistics presented in the remainder of this chapter were initially compiled by government agencies. Useful summaries and analyses of these government statistics were found in the following publications: *Women's Economic Agenda: a call to action by & for California Women* (Oakland and Los Angeles: Women's Economic Agenda Project, July 1984); United States Commission on Civil Rights, *A Growing Crisis: Disadvantaged Women and Their Children* (Washington, DC: US Government Printing Office, Clearinghouse Publication 78, May 1983); *Growing Numbers, Growing Force: A Report from the White House Mini-Conference on Older Women* (Oakland: Older Women's League Educational Fund, n.d. [1980–81]).

31. Barbara Ehrenreich, *The Hearts of Men: American Dreams and the Flight from Commitment* (Garden City, New York: Anchor/Doubleday, 1983), p. 121.

32. Ibid., p. 86.

33. Corcoran *et al.*, 'Economic Fortunes . . .', p. 245.

34. Barbara J. Nelson, 'Women's Poverty and Women's Citizenship: Some Political Consequences of Economic Marginality', *Signs*, x, 2 (Winter 1984), 217, 221–2.

35. Deborah K. Zinn and Rosemary C. Sarri, 'Turning Back the Clock on Public Welfare', in ibid., pp. 357, 363–4, 367–8.

10 PAID AND UNPAID WORK: THE 1970s AND 1980s

1. Unless otherwise noted, statistics in this chapter are taken from government publications. See Selected Bibliography.

2. Myra Marx Ferree, 'Sacrifice, Satisfaction, and Social Change: Employment and the Family', in Karen Brodkin Sacks and Dorothy Remy (eds), *My Troubles Are Going to Have Trouble With Me: Everyday Trials and Triumphs of Women Workers* (New Brunswick, New Jersey: Rutgers University Press, 1984), p. 74.

3. Phyllis Marynick Palmer, 'White Women/Black Women: The Dualism of Female Identity and Experience in the United States', *Feminist Studies*, IX, 1 (Spring 1983), 162–3. Emphasis in the original.

4. Joan Abramson, *Old Boys, New Women: The Politics of Sex Discrimination* (New York: Praeger, 1979), pp. 64–77, 218–21, 190.

5. Mary Frank Fox, 'Women and Higher Education: Sex Differentials in the Status of Students and Scholars', in Jo Freeman (ed.), *Women: A Feminist Perspective*, 3rd edn (Palo Alto, California: Mayfield, 1984), pp. 240–5.

6. Michael J. Carter and Susan Boslego Carter, 'Women's Recent Progress in the Professions or, Women Get a Ticket To Ride After the Gravy Train Has Left the Station', *Feminist Studies*, VII, 3 (Fall 1981), 500.

7. Sally L. Hacker, 'Sex Stratification, Technology and Organization Change: A Longitudinal Case Study of AT&T', in Rachel Kahn-Hut, Arlene Kaplan Daniels and Richard Colvard (eds), *Women and Work: Problems and Perspectives* (New York and Oxford: Oxford University Press, 1982), pp. 253–5.

8. 'More Women Climbing Corporate Ladder: Study', *California Financial Register*, I, 23 (10–23 November 1982), 3.

9. Naomi B. Lynn, 'Women and Politics: The Real Majority', in Freeman, *Women*, pp. 413–19.

10. Cynthia Fuchs Epstein, *Women in Law* (New York: Anchor/Doubleday, 1983), pp. 212 and 210; Rosabeth Moss Kanter, *Men and Women of the Corporation* (New York: Basic Books, 1977), p. 129.

11. Joanna Brown, 'No Stone Unturned', *In These Times*, VII, 12 (16 February, 1983), 9.

12. William Meyers, 'Child Care Finds a Champion in the Corporation', *New York Times*, Business: Section 3 (4 August 1985), 1 and 6.

13. Evelyn Nakano Glenn and Roslyn L. Feldberg, 'Clerical Work: The Female Occupation', in Freeman, *Women*, p. 317.

14. Kanter, *Men and Women . . .*, pp. 92 and 91. Emphasis in the original.

15. Karen Brodkin Sacks, 'Computers, Ward Secretaries, and a Walkout in a Southern Hospital', in Sacks and Remy, *My Troubles . . .*, pp. 173–90.

16. Naomi Katz and David S. Kemnitzer, 'Women and Work in Silicon Valley: Options and Futures', in ibid., pp. 210–11.

17. Joan Smith, 'The Paradox of Women's Poverty: Wage-Earning Women and Economic Transformation', *Signs: Journal of Women in Culture and Society*, X, 2 (Winter 1984), 294–5, 298, 300, 306, 310.

18. Glenn and Feldberg, in Freeman, *Women*, p. 332.

19. Louise Lamphere, 'On the Shop Floor: Multi-Ethnic Unity against the Conglomerate', in Sacks and Remy, *My Troubles . . .*, pp. 248–9.

20. Barbara M. Wertheimer, ' "Union Is Power": Sketches from Women's Labor History', in Freeman, *Women*, p. 348; Elizabeth Weiner, 'Still Sticking to the Union', *In These Times*, VII, 17 (30 March–5 April 1983), 8.

21. Susan Strasser, *Never Done: A History of American Housework* (New York. Pantheon, 1982), p. 297.

22. Pamela M. Fishman, 'Interaction: The Work Women Do', in Kahn-Hut *et al.*, *Women and Work*, pp. 178–9; Heidi I. Hartmann, 'The Family as the Locus of Gender, Class, and Political Struggle: The Example of Housework', *Signs*, VI, 3 (Spring 1981), 381–3, 385, 389, 392; Dolores Hayden, *The Grand Domestic Revolution: A History of Feminist Designs for American Homes, Neighborhoods, and Cities* (Cambridge, Massachusetts: The MIT Press, 1981), pp. 294–5.

23. Wendy Chavkin, 'Walking a Tightrope: Pregnancy, Parenting, and Work', in Wendy Chavkin, MD (ed.), *Double Exposure: Women's Health Hazards on the Job and at Home* (New York: Monthly Review Press, 1984), p. 202.

24. Catharine A. MacKinnon, *Sexual Harassment of Working Women: A Case of Sex Discrimination* (New Haven and London: Yale University Press, 1979), pp. 217–18.

25. Suzanne C. Carothers and Peggy Crull, 'Contrasting Sexual Harassment in Female- and Male-dominated Occupations', in Sacks and Remy, *My Troubles . . .*, pp. 219–20; Peggy Crull, 'Sexual Harassment and Women's Health', in Chavkin, *Double Exposure*, pp. 106–10.

26. Carothers and Crull, in ibid., p. 224; Crull, in ibid., pp. 103–6.

27. MacKinnon, *Sexual Harassment . . .*, pp. 47–51 and 219.

28. Bernice Lott, Mary Ellen Reilly and Dale R. Howard, 'Sexual Assault and Harassment: A Campus Community Case Study', *Signs*, VIII, 2 (Winter 1982), 312, 315–16. Emphasis in the original.
29. Donald J. Treiman and Heidi I. Hartmann (eds), *Women, Work, and Wages: Equal Pay for Jobs of Equal Worth* (Washington, DC: National Academy Press, 1981), pp. 13–43.
30. Roslyn L. Feldberg, 'Comparable Worth: Toward Theory and Practice in the United States', *Signs*, X, 2 (Winter 1984), 319–20.
31. Bob Arnold, 'Why Can't a Woman's Pay Be More Like a Man's', *Business Week*, No. 2878 (28 January 1985), 83.
32. Clair (Vickery) Brown, 'Home Production for Use in a Market Economy', in Barrie Thorne with Marilyn Yalom (eds), *Rethinking the Family: Some Feminist Questions* (New York and London: Longman, 1982), p. 163.
33. David Beers, '9 to 5 in Barbados', *In These Times*, VIII, 18 (4–10 April 1984), 23; Annette Fuentes and Barbara Ehrenreich, *Women in the Global Factory* (Boston: South End Press, Institute for New Communications, Pamphlet No. 2, 1983), pp. 34–6, 49–50, 54.

11   PROBLEMS, PROSPECTS AND THE FEMINIST FUTURE

1. Carol Virginia Pohli, 'Church Closets and Back Doors: A Feminist View of Moral Majority Women', *Feminist Studies*, IX, 3 (Fall 1983), 549–50.
2. Betty Friedan, *The Second Stage* (New York: Summit/Simon & Schuster, 1981), p. 177.
3. Judith Stacey, 'The New Conservative Feminism', *Feminist Studies*, IX, 3 (Fall 1983), 576–7.
4. Sharon Thompson, 'Search for Tomorrow: On Feminism and the Reconstruction of Teen Romance', in Carole S. Vance (ed.), *Pleasure and Danger: Exploring Female Sexuality* (Boston and London: Routledge & Kegan Paul, 1984), pp. 359, 354–5, 360, 376.
5. Charlotte Bunch, *Bringing the Global Home: Feminism in the '80s – Book III* (Denver, Colorado: Antelope Publications, 1985), p. 15.
6. 'National Plan of Action', adopted at the National Women's Conference, 18–21 November, 1977, Houston, Texas (Washington, DC: US Government Printing Office, 1978), pp. 28, 17–18.
7. Zillah R. Eisenstein, *Feminism and Sexual Equality: Crisis in Liberal America* (New York: Monthly Review Press, 1984), p. 25.
8. Cited in John B. Judis, 'Whose Gender Gap Is It, Anyway?' and Zillah Eisenstein, 'Contradictions Inevitable as Women Become Political Force', *In These Times*, VIII, 27 (13–26 June 1984), 23 and 25.
9. Barbara Ehrenreich, 'When Will American Feminism Catch Up with Its Potential Constituency?' *In These Times*, VIII, 27 (13–26 June 1984), 9–10; Eisenstein, *Feminism and Sexual Equality*, p. 140.
10. Dennis Altman provides this definition of Reaganism in his excellent study *AIDS in the Mind of America* (Garden City, New York: Anchor/Doubleday, 1986), p. 27.
11. Bunch, *Bringing the Global Home*, pp. 31 and 26.
12. See Diana E. H. Russell and Nicole Van de Ven, *Crimes Against Women: Proceedings of the International Tribunal* (Millbrae, California: Les Femmes, 1976).
13. Nicholas Freudenberg and Ellen Zaltzberg, 'From Grassroots Activism to

Political Power: Women Organizing Against Environmental Hazards', in Wendy Chavkin, MD (ed.), *Double Exposure: Women's Health Hazards on the Job and at Home* (New York: Monthly Review Press, 1984), p. 265.

14. Starhawk [Miriam Simos], *Dreaming the Dark: Magic, Sex & Politics* (Boston: Beacon Press, 1982), pp. 216 and 174.

15. Helen I. Safa, 'Runaway Shops and Female Employment: The Search for Cheap Labor', *Signs: Journal of Women in Culture and Society*, VII, 2 (Winter 1981), 432–3 and 425.

16. Lourdes Arizpe and Josefina Aranda, 'The "Comparative Advantages" of Women's Disadvantages: Women Workers in the Strawberry Export Agribusiness in Mexico', *Signs*, VII, 2 (Winter 1981), 470.

17. Aline K. Wong, 'Planned Development, Social Stratification, and the Sexual Division of Labor in Singapore', *Signs*, VII, 2 (Winter 1981), 452.

18. Barbara Ehrenreich and Deirdre English, *For Her Own Good: 150 Years of the Experts' Advice to Women* (Garden City, New York: Anchor/Doubleday, 1978), p. 292. Emphasis in the original.

19. Sheila Tobias, 'Toward a Feminist Analysis of the Defense Budget', *Frontiers: a journal of women studies*, VIII, 2 (1985), 65–8; also, a later version of this article in *Plowshare Press*, X, 3 (Summer 1985), 12.

20. Quoted in Jan Buehler, 'The Puget Sound Women's Peace Camp: Education as an Alternative Strategy', *Frontiers*, VIII, 2 (1985), 44.

21. Marian Anderson, 'Military Spending Creates Few Jobs for Women', *Plowshare Press*, X, 3 (Summer 1985), 1, 10–11.

22. Cynthia Enloe, *Does Khaki Become You?: The Militarization of Women's Lives* (Boston: South End Press, 1983), p. 135. Originally published by Pluto Press, London.

23. Adrienne van Melle-Hermans and Dorothea Woods, 'Statistical Notes', in W. Chapkis (ed.), *Loaded Questions: Women in the Military* (Washington, DC and Amsterdam: Transnational Institute, 1981), p. 90; Enloe, *Does Khaki Become You?* p. 157.

24. Quoted in Enloe, *Does Khaki Become You?* pp. 153–4.

25. Ibid., pp. 147–9, 143.

26. Ibid., pp. 199, 200, 195. Emphases in the original; Katherine DeFoyd, 'Women Face Dead End Jobs in Defense Industry', *Plowshare Press*, X, 3 (Summer 1985), 1.

27. Lin Nelson, 'Promise Her Everything: The Nuclear Power Industry's Agenda for Women', *Feminist Studies*, X, 2 (Summer 1984), 300, 302, 307, 305, 298–9.

28. Buehler, 'Puget Sound . . .', p. 42. Emphases in the original.

29. Cynthia Costello and Amy Dru Stanley, 'Report from Seneca', *Frontiers*, VIII, 2 (1985), 33 and 38; Donna Warnock, 'Patriarchy Is a Killer: What People Concerned About Peace and Justice Should Know', in Pam McAllister (ed.), *Reweaving the Web of Life: Feminism and Nonviolence* (Philadelphia: New Society Publishers, 1982), p. 29.

30. Linda Schott, 'The Woman's Peace Party and The Moral Basis for Women's Pacifism', *Frontiers*, VIII, 2 (1985), 20; Amy Swerdlow, 'Ladies' Day at the Capitol: Women Strike for Peace Versus HUAC', *Feminist Studies*, VII, 3 (Fall 1982), 493–520.

31. Nancy Chodorow, *The Reproduction of Mothering: Psychoanalysis and the Sociology of Gender* (Berkeley and Los Angeles: University of California Press, 1978), pp. 93 and 167; Sara Ruddick, 'Maternal Thinking', *Feminist Studies*, VI, 2 (Summer 1980), 352; Sara Ruddick, 'Pacifying the Forces: Drafting Women in the Interests of Peace', *Signs*, VIII, 3 (Spring 1983), 482 and 484.

32. Carol Gilligan, *In a Different Voice: Psychological Theory and Women's Development*

(Cambridge, Massachusetts and London: Harvard University Press, 1982), pp. 39–43, 44, 160, 148.

33. Enloe, *Does Khaki Become You?* pp. 43, 87, 82.

34. Ofer Zur, PhD, 'Men, Women and War: The Myth of the Warrior and the Beautiful Soul', paper presented at Self, Society and Nuclear Conflict Conference, University of California, San Francisco, 19–20 October 1985, p. 6. Subsequently published as 'Reflections on Gender and War', *Breakthrough*, VII, 3/4 (Spring–Summer 1986); O. Zur, A. Morrison and E. Zaretsky, 'Men, Women and War: Gender Differences in Attitudes Towards War', paper presented at the Western Psychological Association Meetings, San Jose, California, April 1985, p. 7. I wish to thank Ofer Zur for giving me reprints of and permission to quote from these papers.

35. Personal communication from Chellis Glendinning, 22 May 1986. Quoted with permission.

36. Chellis Glendinning, PhD, 'A Systems Approach to Gender and War', paper presented at Self, Society and Nuclear Conflict Conference, University of California, San Francisco, 19–20 October 1985, pp. 6–7. Quoted with permission. Patricia Ellsberg, 'Healing Ourselves, Healing the Planet', speech at the California Institute of Integral Studies Fifth Annual Gala Dinner, San Francisco, 27 June 1986. Quoted with permission.

37. Joanna Macy, notes taken by the author during a meeting at the California Institute of Integral Studies, 24 June 1986, and from her address at the Institute's 18th Annual Commencement ceremonies, San Francisco, California, 28 June 1986. I wish to thank Dr Macy for her generosity and permission to quote.

Selected Bibliography

(Including books not mentioned in the Notes)

Sidney Abbott and Barbara Love, *Sappho Was a Right-On Woman: A Liberated View of Lesbianism* (New York: Stein and Day, 1973).

Joan Abramson, *Old Boys, New Women: The Politics of Sex Discrimination* (New York: Praeger, 1979).

Margot Adler, *Drawing Down the Moon: Witches, Druids, Goddess-Worshippers, and Other Pagans in America Today* (New York: The Viking Press, 1979).

Pamela Allen, *Free Space: A Perspective on the Small Group in Women's Liberation* (New York: Times Change Press, 1970).

Kirsten Amundsen, *A New Look at the Silenced Majority: Women and American Democracy* (Englewood Cliffs, New Jersey: Prentice-Hall, 1977).

Karen Anderson, *Wartime Women: Sex Roles, Family Relations, and the Status of Women During World War II* (Westport, Connecticut and London: Greenwood Press, 1981).

Judith Arcana, *Every Mother's Son: The Role of Mothers in the Making of Men* (Garden City, New York: Anchor/Doubleday, 1983).

——, *Our Mothers' Daughters* (Berkeley, California: Shameless Hussy Press, 1979).

David Armstrong, *A Trumpet to Arms: Alternative Media in America* (Los Angeles: J. P. Tarcher, 1981).

June Arnold, *Sister Gin* (Plainfield, Vermont: Daughters, Inc., 1975).

Rosalyn Baxandall, Linda Gordon and Susan Reverby (eds), *American's Working Women* (New York: Vintage/Random House, 1976).

Frances Beal, 'Double Jeopardy. to be Black & Female' (Detroit: Radical Education Project, n.d.).

Jessie Bernard, *The Future of Marriage* (New York: Bantam, 1973).

——, *The Future of Motherhood* (New York: Penguin, 1974).

Martha Blaxall and Barbara Reagan (eds), *Women and the Workplace: The Implications of Occupational Segregation* (Chicago and London: The University of Chicago Press, 1976).

The Boston Women's Health Book Collective, *The New Our Bodies, Ourselves* (New York: Simon & Schuster, 1984).

Marilyn J. Boxer, 'For and About Women: The Theory and Practice of Women's Studies in the United States', *Signs: Journal of Women in Culture and Society*, VII 3 (Spring 1982) 661–95.

Harry Braverman, *Labor and Monopoly Capital: The Degradation of Work in the Twentieth Century* (New York: Monthly Review Press, 1974).

Norma Broude and Mary D. Garrard (eds), *Feminism and Art History: Questioning the Litany* (New York: Harper & Row, 1982).

Rita Mae Brown, *Rubyfruit Jungle* (Plainfield, Vermont: Daughters, Inc., 1973).

279

Susan Brownmiller, *Against Our Will: Men, Women and Rape* (New York: Bantam, 1976).

Mari Jo Buhle, *Women and American Socialism: 1870–1920* (Urbana, Illinois: University of Illinois Press, 1981).

Elly Bulkin, Minnie Bruce Pratt and Barbara Smith, *Yours in Struggle: Three Feminist Perspectives on Anti-Semitism and Racism* (Brooklyn, New York: Long Haul Press, 1984).

Charlotte Bunch, *Bringing the Global Home: Feminism in the '80s – Book III* (Denver, Colarado: Antelope Publications, 1985).

—— and Nancy Myron (eds), *Class and Feminism: A Collection of Essays from THE FURIES* (Baltimore: Diana Press, 1974).

—— and Sandra Pollack (eds), *Learning Our Way: Essays in Feminist Education* (Trumansburg, New York: The Crossing Press, 1983).

Bureau of the Census, US Department of Commerce, *A Statistical Portrait of Women in the United States* (Washington, DC: US Government Printing Office, Current Population Reports, Special Studies, Series P-23, No. 58, April 1976).

——, ——, *A Statistical Portrait of Women in the United States: 1978* (Washington, DC: US Government Printing Office, Current Population Reports, Special Studies, Series P-23, No. 100, 1980).

Bureau of Labor Statistics, US Department of Labor, *U.S. Working Women: A Databook* (Washington, DC: US Government Printing Office, Bulletin 1977).

Sandra Butler, *Conspiracy of Silence: The Trauma of Incest* (San Francisco: New Glide Publications, 1978).

Ellen Cantarow, *Moving the Mountain: Women Working for Social Change* (Old Westbury, New York: The Feminist Press, 1980).

Clayborne Carson, *In Struggle: SNCC and the Black Awakening of the 1960s* (Cambridge: Harvard University Press, 1981).

Michael J. Carter and Susan Boslego Carter, 'Women's Recent Progress in the Professions or, Women Get a Ticket To Ride After the Gravy Train Has Left the Station', *Feminist Studies*, vii, 3 (Fall 1981), 477–504.

John Case and Rosemary C. R. Taylor (eds), *Co-ops, Communes & Collectives: Experiments in Social Change in the 1960s and 1970s* (New York: Pantheon, 1979).

William H. Chafe, *The American Woman: Her Changing Social, Economic, and Political Roles, 1920–1970* (New York: Oxford University Press, 1972).

——, *Women and Equality: Changing Patterns in American Culture* (New York: Oxford University Press, 1977).

W. Chapkis (ed.), *Loaded Questions: Women in the Military* (Washington, DC and Amsterdam: Transnational Institute, 1981).

Jane Roberts Chapman and Margaret Gates (eds), *Women Into Wives: The Legal and Economic Impact of Marriage* (Beverly Hills and London: Sage Publications, 1977).

Wendy Chavkin, MD (ed.), *Double Exposure: Women's Health Hazards on the Job and at Home* (New York: Monthly Review Press, 1984).

Judy Chicago, *The Dinner Party: A Symbol of Our Heritage* (Garden City, New York: Anchor/Doubleday, 1979).

——, *Through the Flower: My Struggle as a Woman Artist* (Garden City, New York: Anchor/Doubleday, 1977).

'Chicanas en el Ambiente Nacional/Chicanas in the National Landscape', *Frontiers: A Journal of Women Studies*, v, 2 (Summer 1980).

Nancy Chodorow, *The Reproduction of Mothering: Psychoanalysis and the Sociology of Gender* (Berkeley and Los Angeles: University of California Press, 1978).

Carol P. Christ and Judith Plaskow (eds), *Womanspirit Rising: A Feminist Reader in Religion* (San Francisco: Harper & Row, 1979).

Adele Clarke, 'Subtle Forms of Sterilization Abuse: A Reproductive Rights Analysis', in Rita Arditti, Renate Duelli Klein and Shelley Minden (eds), *Test-Tube Women: What Future for Motherhood?* (London and Boston: Pandora Press/Routledge & Kegan Paul, 1984), pp. 188–212.

Nancy F. Cott and Elizabeth H. Pleck (eds), *A Heritage of Her Own: Toward a New Social History of American Women* (New York: Simon & Schuster, 1979).

Gina Covina and Laurel Galana (eds), *The Lesbian Reader: An Amazon Quarterly Anthology* (Oakland, California: Amazon Press 1975).

Ruth Schwartz Cowan, 'The "Industrial Revolution" in the Home: Household Technology and Social Change in the 20th Century', *Technology and Culture*, xvii, 1 (January 1976), 1–23.

Elliott Currie, Robert Dunn and David Fogarty, 'The New Immiseration: Stagflation, Inequality, and the Working Class', *Socialist Review*, x, 6 (November–December 1980), 7–31.

Mariarosa Dalla Costa and Selma James, *The Power of Women and the Subversion of the Community*, 3rd edn (Bristol: Falling Wall Press, 1975).

Mary Daly, *Beyond God the Father: Toward a Philosophy of Women's Liberation* (Boston: Beacon Press, 1973).

——, *The Church and the Second Sex: With a New Feminist Postchristian Introduction by the Author* (New York: Harper & Row, 1975).

——, *Gyn/Ecology: The Metaethics of Radical Feminism* (Boston: Beacon Press, 1978).

Angela Y. Davis, *Women, Race & Class* (New York: Random House, 1981).

Simone de Beauvoir, *The Second Sex*, translated and edited by H. M. Parshley (New York: Bantam, 1961).

Karen DeCrow, *Sexist Justice* (New York: Vintage/Random House, 1974).

Bonnie Thornton Dill, 'Race, Class, and Gender: Prospects for an All-Inclusive Sisterhood', *Feminist Studies*, ix, 1 (Spring 1983), 131–50.

Dorothy Dinnerstein, *The Mermaid and the Minotaur: Sexual Arrangements and Human Malaise* (New York: Harper & Row, 1976).

Ellen DuBois et al., 'Politics and Culture in Women's History: A Symposium', *Feminist Studies*, vi, 1 (Spring 1980), 26–64.

Andrea Dworkin, *Right-Wing Women* (New York: Perigee/G.P. Putnam's Sons, 1983).

Barbara Ehrenreich, *The Hearts of Men: American Dreams and the Flight from Commitment* (Garden City, New York: Anchor/Doubleday, 1983).

—— and Deirdre English, *For Her Own Good: 150 Years of the Experts' Advice to Women* (Garden City, New York: Anchor/Doubleday, 1978).

Diane Ehrensaft, 'When Women and Men Mother', *Socialist Review*, x, 1 (January–February 1980), 37–73.

Zillah R. Eisenstein (ed.), *Capitalist Patriarchy and the Case for Socialist Feminism* (New York: Monthly Review Press, 1979).

——, *Feminism and Sexual Equality: Crisis in Liberal America* (New York: Monthly Review Press, 1984).

——, *The Radical Future of Liberal Feminism* (New York and London: Longman, 1981).

Nan Elsasser, Kyle MacKenzie and Yvonne Tixier y Vigil, *Las Mujeres: Conversations from a Hispanic Community* (Old Westbury, New York: The Feminist Press, 1980).

Cynthia Enloe, *Does Khaki Become You?: The Militarization of Women's Lives* (Boston: South End Press, 1983). Originally published by Pluto Press, London.

Cynthia Fuchs Epstein, *Women in Law* (New York: Anchor/Doubleday, 1983).

Sara Evans, *Personal Politics: The Roots of Women's Liberation in the Civil Rights Movement and the New Left* (New York: Alfred A. Knopf, 1979).

Stuart Ewen, *Captains of Consciousness: Advertising and the Social Roots of the Consumer Culture* (New York: McGraw-Hill, 1976).

282 AMERICAN WOMEN SINCE 1945

Lillian Faderman, *Surpassing the Love of Men: Romantic Friendship and Love Between Women from the Renaissance to the Present* (New York: William Morrow, 1981).

Peter Gabriel Filene, *Him/Her/Self: Sex Roles in Modern America* (New York: New American Library, 1976).

Shulamith Firestone, *The Dialectic of Sex: The Case for Feminist Revolution* (New York: Bantam, 1971).

Jo Freeman, *The Politics of Women's Liberation: A Case Study of an Emerging Social Movement and Its Relation to the Policy Process* (New York: David McKay, 1975).

—— (ed.), *Women: A Feminist Perspective*, 2nd edn (Palo Alto, California: Mayfield Publishing Company, 1979).

—— (ed.), *Women: A Feminist Perspective*, 3rd edn (Palo Alto, California: Mayfield Publishing Company, 1984).

Betty Friedan, *The Feminine Mystique* (New York: W.W. Norton, 1963).

——, *The Second Stage* (New York: Summit Books/Simon & Schuster, 1981).

Myra Friedman, *Buried Alive: The Biography of Janis Joplin* (New York: Bantam, 1974).

Frontiers: A Journal of Women Studies, Special Issue: Women and Peace, VIII, 2 (1985).

Annette Fuentes and Barbara Ehrenreich, *Women in the Global Factory* (Boston: South End Press, 1983).

Carol Gilligan, *In a Different Voice: Psychological Theory and Women's Development* (Cambridge: Harvard University Press, 1982).

Marianne Githens and Jewel L. Prestage (eds), *A Portrait of Marginality: The Political Behavior of the American Woman* (New York: David McKay, 1977).

Todd Gitlin, *The Whole World Is Watching: Mass Media in the Making & Unmaking of the New Left* (Berkeley: University of California Press, 1980).

Nona Glazer-Malbin (ed.), *Old Family/New Family: Interpersonal Relationships* (New York: D. Van Nostrand, 1975).

Kristin Booth Glen, 'Abortion in the Courts: A Laywoman's Historical Guide to the New Disaster Area', *Feminist Studies*, IV, 1 (February 1978), 1–26.

Vivian Gornick and Barbara K. Moran (eds), *Woman in Sexist Society: Studies in Power and Powerlessness* (New York: New American Library, 1972).

Susan Griffin, *Pornography and Silence: Culture's Revenge Against Nature* (New York: Harper & Row, 1981).

——, *Woman and Nature: The Roaring Inside Her* (New York: Harper & Row, 1978).

Kirsten Grimstad and Susan Rennie (eds), *The New Woman's Survival Sourcebook* (New York: Alfred A. Knopf, 1975).

Growing Numbers, Growing Force: A Report from the White House Mini-Conference on Older Women (Oakland, California: Older Women's League Educational Fund, n.d. [1980–81]).

Heidi I. Hartmann, 'The Family as the Locus of Gender, Class, and Political Struggle: The Example of Housework', *Signs: Journal of Women in Culture and Society*, VI, 3 (Spring 1981), 366–94.

Dolores Hayden, *The Grand Domestic Revolution: A History of Feminist Designs for American Homes, Neighborhoods, and Cities* (Cambridge: The MIT Press, 1981).

——, *Redesigning the American Dream: The Future of Housing, Work, and Family Life* (New York: W.W. Norton, 1984).

Margaret Hennig and Anne Jardim, *The Managerial Woman* (New York: Pocket Books, 1978).

Heresies: A Feminist Publication on Art and Politics, The Great Goddess, II, 1 (Spring 1978).

——, *Sex Issue*, III, 4, Issue 12 (1981).

Ruth Herschberger, *Adam's Rib* (New York: Harper & Row, 1970).

Thomas B. Hess and Elizabeth C. Baker (eds), *Art and Sexual Politics: Women's Liberation, Women Artists, and Art History* (New York: Collier/Macmillan, 1973).

Shere Hite, *The Hite Report: A Nationwide Study of Female Sexuality* (New York: Dell, 1976).

Judith Hole and Ellen Levine, *Rebirth of Feminism* (New York: Quadrangle, 1971).

Bell Hooks, *Ain't I a Woman: Black Women and Feminism* (Boston: South End Press, 1981).

Florence Howe and Paul Lauter, *The Impact of Women's Studies on the Campus and the Disciplines* (Washington, DC: The National Institute of Education, February 1980).

Louise Kapp Howe, *Pink Collar Workers: Inside the World of Women's Work* (New York: Avon/Hearst, 1978).

Gloria T. Hull, Patricia Bell Scott and Barbara Smith (eds), *All the Women Are White, All the Blacks Are Men, But Some of Us Are Brave: Black Women's Studies* (Old Westbury, New York: The Feminist Press, 1982).

In These Times, Special Report on the Gender Gap, VIII, 27 (13–26 June 1984), 7–26.

Gloria I. Joseph and Jill Lewis, *Common Differences: Conflicts in Black and White Feminist Perspectives* (Garden City, New York: Anchor/Doubleday, 1981).

Kathy Kahn, *Hillbilly Women* (New York: Avon/Hearst, 1973).

Rachel Kahn-Hut, Arlene Kaplan Daniels and Richard Colvard (eds), *Women and Work: Problems and Perspectives* (New York: Oxford University Press, 1982).

Rosabeth Moss Kanter, *Commitment and Community: Communes and Utopias in Sociological Perspective* (Cambridge: Harvard University Press, 1972).

—— (ed.), *Communes: Creating and Managing the Collective Life* (New York: Harper & Row, 1973).

——, *Men and Women of the Corporation* (New York: Basic Books, 1977).

Jonathan Katz (ed.), *Gay American History: Lesbians and Gay Men in the U.S.A., A Documentary* (New York: Thomas Y. Crowell, 1976).

Nannerl O. Keohane, Michelle Z. Rosaldo and Barbara C. Gelpi (eds), *Feminist Theory: A Critique of Ideology* (Chicago: The University of Chicago Press, 1982).

Gayle Kimball (ed.), *Women's Culture: The Women's Renaissance of the Seventies* (Metuchen, New Jersey and London: Scarecrow Press, 1981).

Maxine Hong Kingston, *The Woman Warrior: Memoirs of a Girlhood Among Ghosts* (New York: Vintage/Random House, 1976).

Anne Koedt, Ellen Levine and Anita Rapone (eds), *Radical Feminism* (New York: Quadrangle, 1973).

Mirra Komarovsky, *Blue-Collar Marriage* (New York: Vintage/Random House, 1967).

——, *Women in the Modern World: Their Education and Their Dilemmas* (Boston: Little, Brown, 1953).

Juanita M. Kreps (ed.), *Women and the American Economy: A Look to the 1980s* (Englewood Cliffs, New Jersey: Prentice-Hall, 1976).

Susan Krieger, *The Mirror Dance: Identity in a Women's Community* (Philadelphia: Temple University Press, 1983).

Annette Kuhn and AnnMarie Wolpe (eds), *Feminism and Materialism: Women and Modes of Production* (London: Routledge & Kegan Paul, 1978).

Joyce A. Ladner, *Tomorrow's Tomorrow: The Black Woman* (Garden City, New York: Anchor/Doubleday, 1972).

Laura Lederer (ed.), *Take Back the Night: Women on Pornography* (New York: Bantam, 1982).

Lisa Leghorn and Katherine Parker, *Woman's Worth: Sexual Economics and the World of Women* (Boston and London: Routledge & Kegan Paul, 1981).

Gerda Lerner (ed.), *Black Women in White America: A Documentary History* (New York: Random House, 1973).

——, *The Majority Finds Its Past: Placing Women in History* (New York: Oxford University Press, 1979).

Helena Z. Lopata, *Occupation: Housewife* (New York: Oxford University Press, 1971).

Audre Lorde, *Sister Outsider: Essays and Speeches* (Trumansburg, New York: The Crossing Press, 1984).

Catharine A. MacKinnon, *Sexual Harassment of Working Women: A Case of Sex Discrimination* (New Haven, Connecticut: Yale University Press, 1979).

Joanna R. Macy, *Despair and Personal Power in the Nuclear Age* (Philadelphia: New Society Publishers, 1983).

Ellen Malos (ed.), *The Politics of Housework* (London: Allison & Busby, 1980).

Del Martin and Phyllis Lyon, *Lesbian/Woman* (New York: Bantam, 1972).

Joyce Maupin, *Working Women and Their Organizations – 150 Years of Struggle* (Berkeley, California: Union WAGE Educational Committee, 1974).

Pam McAllister (ed.), *Reweaving the Web of Life: Feminism and Nonviolence* (Philadelphia: New Society Publishers, 1982).

Margaret Mead and Frances Balgley Kaplan (eds), *American Women: The Report of the President's Commission on the Status of Women and Other Publications of the Commission* (New York: Charles Scribner's Sons, 1965).

Margarita B. Melville (ed.), *Twice A Minority: Mexican American Women* (St Louis: C.V. Mosby, 1980).

Kate Millett, *Sexual Politics* (New York: Avon/Hearst, 1970).

Alfredo Mirandé and Evangelina Enríquez, *La Chicana: The Mexican-American Woman* (Chicago: The University of Chicago Press, 1979).

Juliet Mitchell, *Woman's Estate* (Harmondsworth: Penguin, 1971).

Anne Moody, *Coming of Age in Mississippi* (New York: Dell, 1968).

Cherrié Moraga and Gloria Anzaldúa (eds), *This Bridge Called My Back: Writings by Radical Women of Color* (Watertown, Massachusetts: Persephone Press, 1981).

Robin Morgan, *Going Too Far: The Personal Chronicle of a Feminist* (New York: Vintage/Random House, 1978).

—— (ed.), *Sisterhood Is Global: The International Women's Movement Anthology* (Garden City, New York: Anchor/Doubleday, 1984).

—— (ed.), *Sisterhood Is Powerful: An Anthology of Writings from the Women's Liberation Movement* (New York: Vintage/Random House, 1970).

Alva Myrdal and Viola Klein, *Women's Two Roles: Home and Work*, 2nd edn (London: Routledge & Kegan Paul, 1968).

Nancy Myron and Charlotte Bunch (eds), *Lesbianism and the Women's Movement* (Baltimore: Diana Press, 1975).

National Manpower Council, *Womanpower: A Statement by the National Manpower Council with Chapters by the Council Staff* (New York: Columbia University Press, 1957).

Lin Nelson, 'Promise Her Everything: The Nuclear Power Industry's Agenda for Women', *Feminist Studies*, x, 2 (Summer 1984), 291–314.

F. Ivan Nye and Lois Wladis Hoffman (eds), *The Employed Mother in America* (Chicago: Rand McNally, 1963).

Ann Oakley, *The Sociology of Housework* (New York: Pantheon, 1974).

Tillie Olsen, *Silences* (New York: Delacorte Press/Seymour Lawrence, 1978).

Valerie Kincade Oppenheimer, *The Female Labor Force in the United States: Demographic and Economic Factors Governing Its Growth and Changing Composition* (Berkeley: Institute of International Studies, University of California, 1970).

Katherine Orloff, *Rock 'N Roll Woman* (Los Angeles: Nash Publishing, 1974).

Rosalind Pollack Petchesky, *Abortion and Woman's Choice: The State, Sexuality, and Reproductive Freedom* (New York and London: Longman, 1984).

Esther Peterson, 'Working Women', *Daedalus: Journal of The American Academy of Arts and Sciences*, XCIII, 2 (Spring 1964), 671–99.

Frances Fox Piven and Richard A. Cloward, *Regulating the Poor: The Functions of Public Welfare* (New York: Vintage/Random House, 1972).

Plowshare, Special Issue: Women and Economic Conversion, X, 3 (Summer 1985).

Carol Virginia Pohli, 'Church Closets and Back Doors: A Feminist View of Moral Majority Women', *Feminist Studies*, IX, 3 (Fall 1983), 529–58.

Richard Polenberg, *One Nation Divisible: Class, Race, and Ethnicity in the United States Since 1938* (Harmondsworth: Penguin, 1980).

Population Division, Bureau of the Census, *The Social and Economic Status of the Black Population in the United States: An Historical View, 1790–1978* (Washington, DC: US Government Printing Office, Current Population Reports, Special Studies, Series P-23, No. 80).

Redstockings of the Women's Liberation Movement, *Feminist Revolution: An Abridged Edition with Additional Writings* (New York: Random House, 1978).

Rosetta Reitz, 'Mean Mothers: Independent Women's Blues', *Heresies: A Feminist Publication on Art and Politics*, III, 2 (1980), 57–60.

Adrienne Rich, 'Compulsory Heterosexuality and Lesbian Existence', *Signs: Journal of Women in Culture and Society*, V, 4 (Summer 1980), 631–60.

——, *On Lies, Secrets, and Silence: Selected Prose 1966–1978* (New York: W.W. Norton, 1979).

——, *Of Woman Born: Motherhood as Experience and Institution* (New York: W.W. Norton, 1976).

La Frances Rodgers-Rose (ed.), *The Black Woman* (Beverly Hills and London: Sage Publications, 1980).

Helen Rodriguez-Trias, MD, *Women & the Health Care System, Sterilization Abuse: Two Lectures*, 2nd edn (New York: The Women's Center, Barnard College, 1980).

Alice S. Rossi, 'Life-Span Theories and Women's Lives', *Signs: Journal of Women in Culture and Society*, VI, 1 (Autumn 1980), 4–32.

—— and Ann Calderwood (eds), *Academic Women on the Move* (New York: Russell Sage Foundation, 1975).

Mary Aickin Rothschild, 'White Women Volunteers in the Freedom Summers: Their Life and Work in a Movement for Social Change', *Feminist Studies*, V, 3 (Fall 1979), 466–95.

Sheila Rowbotham, *Woman's Consciousness, Man's World* (Harmondsworth: Penguin, 1973).

Lillian B. Rubin, *Women of a Certain Age: The Midlife Search for Self* (New York: Harper & Row, 1979).

Lillian Breslow Rubin, *Worlds of Pain: Life in the Working-Class Family* (New York: Basic Books, 1976).

Sara Ruddick, 'Maternal Thinking', *Feminist Studies*, VI, 2 (Summer 1980), 342–67.

Mary P. Ryan, *Womanhood in America: From Colonial Times to the Present*, 2nd edn (New York and London: New Viewpoints/Franklin Watts, 1979).

Albie Sachs and Joan Hoff Wilson, *Sexism and the Law: A Study of Male Beliefs and Legal Bias in Britain and the United States* (New York: The Free Press, 1978).

Karen Brodkin Sacks and Dorothy Remy (eds), *My Troubles Are Going to Have Trouble With Me: Everyday Trials and Triumphs of Women Workers* (New Brunswick, New Jersey: Rutgers University Press, 1984).

Kirkpatrick Sale, *SDS* (New York: Vintage/Random House, 1974).

Lydia Sargent (ed.), *Women and Revolution: A Discussion of the Unhappy Marriage of Marxism and Feminism* (Boston: South End Press, 1981).

Susan Schechter, *Women and Male Violence: The Visions and Struggles of the Battered Women's Movement* (Boston: South End Press, 1982).

Hilda Scott, *Working Your Way to the Bottom: The Feminization of Poverty* (London and Boston: Pandora Press, 1984).

Nancy Seifer, *Nobody Speaks for Me!: Self Portraits of American Working Class Women* (New York: Simon and Schuster, 1976).

Susan Sheehan, *A Welfare Mother* (New York: Mentor/New American Library, 1976).

Signs: Journal of Women in Culture and Society, Special Issue: Development and the Sexual Division of Labor, VII, 2 (Winter 1981).

——, *Special Issue: Women and Poverty*, X, 2 (Winter 1984).

——, *Special Issue: Women and Violence*, VIII, 3 (Spring 1983).

Ann Snitow, Christine Stansell and Sharon Thompson (eds), *Powers of Desire: The Politics of Sexuality* (New York: Monthly Review Press, 1983).

Natalie J. Sokoloff, *Between Money and Love: The Dialectics of Women's Home and Market Work* (New York: Praeger, 1980).

Susan Sontag, *Against Interpretation and Other Essays* (New York: Dell, 1966).

Southern Exposure, Generations: Women in the South, IV, 4 (Winter 1977).

Charlene Spretnak (ed.), *The Politics of Women's Spirituality: Essays on the Rise of Spiritual Power Within the Feminist Movement* (Garden City, New York: Anchor/Doubleday, 1982).

Judith Stacey, 'The New Conservative Feminism', *Feminist Studies*, IX, 3 (Fall 1983), 559–83.

Carol B. Stack, *All Our Kin: Strategies for Survival in a Black Community* (New York: Harper & Row, 1974).

Karin Stallard, Barbara Ehrenreich and Holly Sklar, *Poverty in the American Dream: Women & Children First* (Boston: South End Press, 1983).

Starhawk, *Dreaming the Dark: Magic, Sex & Politics* (Boston: Beacon Press, 1982).

——, *The Spiral Dance: A Rebirth of the Ancient Religion of the Great Goddess* (San Francisco: Harper & Row, 1979).

Margaret O'Brien Steinfels, *Who's Minding the Children?: The History and Politics of Day Care in America* (New York: Simon and Schuster, 1973).

Catharine R. Stimpson, Elsa Dixler, Martha J. Nelson and Kathryn B. Yatrakis (eds), *Women and the American City* (Chicago and London: Unversity of Chicago Press, 1980).

Catharine R. Stimpson and Ethel Spector Person (eds), *Special Issue: Women – Sex and Sexuality, Signs: Journal of Women in Culture and Society*, V, 4 (Summer 1980).

Merlin Stone, *When God Was a Woman* (New York: Harcourt Brace Jovanovich, 1976). Originally published as *The Paradise Papers* (Virago Ltd in association with Quartet Books Ltd).

Susan Strasser, *Never Done: A History of American Housework* (New York: Pantheon, 1982).

Amy Swerdlow, 'Ladies' Day at the Capitol: Women Strike for Peace Versus HUAC', *Feminist Studies*, VIII, 3 (Fall 1982), 493–520.

Jean Tepperman, *Not Servants, Not Machines: Office Workers Speak Out* (Boston: Beacon Press, 1976).

Barrie Thorne with Marilyn Yalom (eds), *Rethinking the Family: Some Feminist Questions* (New York and London: Longman, 1982).

Donald J. Treiman and Heidi I. Hartmann (eds), *Women, Work, and Wages: Equal Pay for Jobs of Equal Worth* (Washington, DC: National Academy Press, 1981).

Ellen Kay Trimberger, 'Women in the Old and New Left: The Evolution of a Politics of Personal Life', *Feminist Studies*, V, 3 (Fall 1979), 432–50.

Gaye Tuchman, *Making News: A Study in the Construction of Reality* (New York: Free Press/Macmillan, 1978).

US Commission on Civil Rights, *A Growing Crisis: Disadvantaged Women and Their Children* (Washington, DC: US Government Printing Office, Clearinghouse Publication 78, May 1983).

——, *Characters in Textbooks: A Review of the Literature* (Washington, DC: US Government Printing Office, Clearinghouse Publication 62, May 1980).

Bettylou Valentine, *Hustling and Other Hard Work: Life Styles in the Ghetto* (New York: Free Press/Macmillan, 1978).

Carole S. Vance (ed.), *Pleasure and Danger: Exploring Female Sexuality* (Boston and London: Routledge & Kegan Paul, 1984).

Alice Walker, *The Color Purple* (New York: Harcourt Brace Jovanovich, 1982).

——, *In Love & Trouble: Stories of Black Women* (New York: Harcourt Brace Jovanovich, 1973).

——, *In Search of Our Mothers' Gardens: Womanist Prose* (New York: Harcourt Brace Jovanovich, 1983).

——, *You Can't Keep a Good Woman Down* (New York: Harcourt Brace Jovanovich, 1981).

Mary Lindenstein Walshok, *Blue-Collar Women: Pioneers on the Male Frontier* (Garden City, New York: Anchor/Doubleday, 1981).

Kathryn Weibel, *Mirror Mirror: Images of Women Reflected in Popular Culture* (Garden City, New York: Anchor/Doubleday, 1977).

Nancy Pottishman Weiss, 'Mother, The Invention of Necessity: Dr. Benjamin Spock's *Baby and Child Care*', *American Quarterly*, xxix, 5 (Winter 1977), 519–46.

Ellen Willis, *Beginning to See the Light: Pieces of a Decade* (Wideview Books/PEI Books, 1982). Originally published by Alfred A. Knopf, New York, 1981.

Michael Wilson, Screenplay, and Deborah Silverton Rosenfelt, Commentary, *Salt of the Earth* (Old Westbury, New York: The Feminist Press, 1978).

Women's Bureau, Employment Standards Administration, US Department of Labor, *Mature Women Workers: A Profile* (Washington, DC: US Government Printing Office, 1976).

Women's Economic Agenda: a call to action by & for California Women (Oakland and Los Angeles: Women's Economic Agenda Project, July 1984).

Gayle Graham Yates, *What Women Want: The Ideas of the Movement* (Cambridge: Harvard University Press, 1975).

Index

The words 'female', 'females', 'woman', and 'women' are used throughout the book and are not separately indexed.